Leaving Certificate
Higher Level

Chemistry

Jim McCarthy
Terence White

The Educational Company of Ireland

First published 2014

The Educational Company of Ireland

Ballymount Road

Walkinstown

Dublin 12

www.edco.ie

A member of the Smurfit Kappa Group plc

The paper used in this book comes from Managed Forests in Northern Europe For every tree felled, at least one new tree is planted

ISBN: 978-1-84536-627-8

Book design: Liz White Designs

Cover design: Identikit

Layout: David Houlden

Editor: Life Lines Editorial

Proofreaders: Life Lines Editorial, Antoinette Walker

For permission to reproduce photographs, the author and publisher gratefully acknowledge the following: Shutterstock, iStock, Science Photo Library, Alamy, Wikimedia. Joseph Gay-Lussac © Neveshkin Nikolay/Shutterstock.com.

Web references in this book are intended as a guide for teachers. At the time of going to press, all web addresses were active and contained information relevant to the topics in the book. However the Educational Company of Ireland and the authors do not accept responsibility for the views or information contained on these websites. Content and addresses may change beyond our control and students should be supervised when investigating websites.

CONTENTS

Experiments

Introduction

Layout of chapters

The Leaving Cert Chemistry course is recognised as being a very long course. This book is intended to provide a short, concise account of the entire course. The information provided is based on:

- The syllabus
- Questions from previous Leaving Cert exams.

The language used is straightforward and to the point. Diagrams and photographs have been included where relevant. Key definitions are highlighted and many Remember boxes are provided to help reinforce learning.

Key-definition

A **covalent bond** is formed when two atoms share a pair of electrons.

Remember

The 3d sublevel is of higher energy than the 4s sublevel.

In addition, Key-points are included at the end of every chapter.

All of the prescribed mandatory practical activities are included. They are located in various chapters so that they are integrated with the theory of each activity.

Study Guide

The Study Guide on p.313 will help you to keep track of your revision.

- Work out how much time you have left before the exam and how much time you can devote to each chapter.
- Try to be realistic when setting your targets.
- Tick off the boxes as you meet your goals.
- Re-evaluate your plan if you feel you have been overambitious.
- The night before the exam, check that you have covered all key areas.

Exam Section

How the course is divided

The Leaving Cert Chemistry course is composed of a core and two options. The core is covered in Chapters 1 to 21, while Options 1 and 2 are dealt with in Chapters 22 and 23, respectively.

The exam paper

- There are two sections on the paper.
- Each question carries 50 marks. Eight questions must be attempted.
- There are three questions in Section A, all relating to mandatory experiments.
- There are eight questions in Section B.
- There are no compulsory questions.
- At least two of the questions attempted must be from Section A.
- Question 5 is likely to be based on material from the following chapters in this book: 1, 2, 3, 4, 5, 6 and 7.
- Question 6 is likely to be based on material from the following chapters in this book: 13, 15, 16 and 17.

Timing

- Allow about 10 minutes for reading and selecting questions, 20 minutes for each question, and 10 minutes at the end for checking over and, if necessary, finishing questions.

Topics covered in previous Higher Level exams

The table on p.viii shows a selection of the question numbers asked about each of the mandatory experiments in recent years.

The table below shows a selection of the question numbers asked about each of the mandatory experiments in recent years.

Mandatory experiment	2013	2012	2011	2010	2009	2008	2007	2006	2005	Other
Flame tests					3(a)			5(a)(i)		
Redox reactions of halogens									11(a)(ii)	
Tests for anions	4(g)	7(d)			3	10(a)(iii)			4(f)	4(j) (2004); 10(c) (2003); 4(f) (2002)
Recrystallisation and melting point determination	2(d)		3	10(b)						3 (2004)
Estimation of the relative molecular mass of a volatile liquid		3								3 (2003)
Determination of the concentration of ethanoic acid in vinegar						1				1 (2002)
Determination of the amount of water of crystallisation in sodium carbonate								1		
Estimation of iron in an iron tablet					1					1 (2003)
Iodine-thiosulfate titration							1			
Determination of the percentage of hypochlorite in bleach			1							
Preparation and properties of ethyne					2					2 (2003)
Determination of the heat of reaction of hydrochloric acid with sodium hydroxide	3						3			
Measuring the rate of production of oxygen from hydrogen peroxide						3			3	
Studying the effect on reaction rate of concentration and temperature	7(d)			3	9(a)			7(c)		3 (2002)
Extraction of clove oil from cloves	2(e)		2(b)			2				9(b) (2003)
Preparation of soap				2				2		2 (2002)
Preparation and properties of ethene	2(b)	2		9(c)	2			9(b)	7(c)	2 (2004)
Preparation and properties of ethanal									2	10(a)
Preparation and properties of ethanoic acid	2(a)						2			2(a)
Separation of a mixture of indicators using chromatography	2(c)					2			10(c)	

Mandatory experiment	2013	2012	2011	2010	2009	2008	2007	2006	2005	Other
Equilibrium experiments to illustrate Le Chatelier's Principle	9(b), 9(d)		9(b)					11(b)	9(b)	4(g) (2002)
Determination of free chlorine in swimming pool water or bleach								3		
Determination in water of total suspended solids, total dissolved solids and pH								3		
Estimation of the total hardness of a water sample					1					1 (2004)
Estimation of dissolved oxygen by redox titration	1								1	
Preparation of a standard solution of sodium carbonate		1(b)								
Standardisation of hydrochloride acid using a standard solution of sodium carbonate		1								

The table below shows a selection of the question numbers with parts about particular topics in recent years.

Topic	2013	2012	2011	2010	2009	2008	2007	2006	2005	2004
Elements and the periodic table	5(a)		5(b)	4(b)		4(b)		4(f)	4(d)	
Atomic structure	4(b)	4(c); 11(a)	5(a), 10(c)	5(a); 5(b)	4(a); 10(c)		11(a)	10(a)		4(a)
Radioactivity	10(c)	4(b); 11(a) (i)	4(a), 10(c)	11(b)	4(b)		11(a)		5(a)	11(a)
Electronic structure of atoms	4(a), 5(b), 5(c), 11(a)	4(a); 5(a); 5(b)	5(c); 5(d)	4(a); 5(c); 5(e)	4(c); 5	4(a); 10(c)	5(a)	4(a); 5(a)	5(b); 10(b)	5; 10(b)
Oxidation and reduction	10(b)	4(e); 4(h); 10(c)	4(f)	10(c)(i); 11(a)	10(b)	10(b)	10(c)	10(b)	11(a)	4(g); 4(i)
Ionic and covalent bonding		4(d); 5(c); 5(d); 5(e)	11(b)	4(g); 10(a)		5	5(b)	5(b)	5(c)	5(a)
Shapes of molecules and intermolecular forces	4(d); 10(a)	5(d)	4(c)	10(a); 4(c)	11(b)	4(g); 5	5(c)		4(b)	5(a)
Gas laws and the mole	4(c), 4(h)	4(f)	4(b), 4(d)	4(d)(e) (h)	10(a)	11(b)	10(b)	11(a)	11(b)	10(c)
Calculations based on chemical equations	4(e), 10(b)	10(c)	4(e)					11(a) (v)	4(h); 10(a)	10(a)

Topic	2013	2012	2011	2010	2009	2008	2007	2006	2005	2004
Acids and bases	11(b)	10(b)	7(a), 7(b), 7(c)	8(a)	4(e)		7(a)	4(e)	8(a) (b)	4(e)
Hydrocarbons and thermochemistry	6	4(i); 6	4(i), 6	6	4(d); 6	6	6	6	6	6
Organic chemistry	4(f), 8	8; 10(a)	2(a), 4(j), 8, 10(b)	4(j); 9; 10(b)	4(h); 4(i); 8	9; 11(a)	8; 11(b)	9; 10(c)	7	7
Rates of reaction	4(j), 7	4(g); 9	4(h), 10(a)		9	4(h)	9	7		8
Chemical equilibrium	9	11(b)	9	7	11(a)	7	10(a)	11(b)	9	9
pH	11(b)	10(b)	7(d)	8	4(f)	8(a)	7(b)	8(b)	8(c)	11(b)
Water	4(i)	4(j); 7	4(g), 11(a)	4(i)	4(g); 7	8(b); 10(a)	7(c) (d)	8(a)	8(d) (e)	4(f)
Atmospheric chemistry	4(k)	4(k); 11(c)	4(k), 11(c)	4(k); 11(c)	11(c)	4(k); 11(c)	4(k); 11(c)	4(k)	4(k); 11(c)	4(k); 11(c)
Industrial chemistry	11(c)				4(k)			11(c)		
Crystals			4(k)	11(c)			11(c)			11(c)
Polymers		4(k)	11(c)		4(k)				11(c)	
Metals	4(k), 11(c)	11(c)		4(k)	11(c)	4(k); 11(c)	4(k); 11(c)	4(k); 11(c)	4(k)	4(k)

Exam techniques

- When you receive your exam paper, spend a few minutes examining the content of the various questions. Decide fairly quickly which ones you can do best. Answer those questions first, but do not exceed the recommended 20 minutes per question limit.

- Do not waste too much time trying to think of answers to particular parts of a question. Leave spaces and come back to these later.

- If you are attempting Question 4, it is a good idea to attempt all 11 parts. You will be marked on the best eight.

- Remember to attempt all parts of all the other questions that you choose (except for Questions 10 and 11, and questions on the Options).

- It is very important to show the starting point and the various stages in every calculation, so that the examiner can follow what you are doing.

- If a labelled diagram is specified in the question, this must be included in your answer.

Common mistakes

- Not reading the paper correctly
- Not finishing the paper
- Ignoring the marking scheme – you must take the marking scheme into account when you allocate time to each question or part of a question.
- Missing part of a question: when checking your work at the end of the exam, make sure that you have done all of the parts specified in each question

Past questions and answers

The following question and answer is based on a past Leaving Cert paper and marking scheme. These are provided on the State Examinations Commission website at www.examinations.ie.

Questions

1 (a) The hydrocarbon molecules in petrol typically contain carbon chains with between five and ten carbon atoms. The most widely used petrol in Ireland has an octane number of 95.

    (i) What is meant by the octane number of a fuel? *(5)*

    (ii) The two hydrocarbons used as references when establishing the octane number of a fuel are heptane and 2,2,4-trimethylpentane. Draw the structure of each of these molecules. *(6)*

    (iii) Crude oil is separated into a number of fractions in oil refining. Name the two fractions which contain molecules with the carbon chain lengths needed for petrol. *(6)*

    (iv) Dehydrocyclisation is one of the processes used to increase the octane numbers of hydrocarbons. What two changes to the hydrocarbon molecules occur during this process? *(6)*

    (v) Ethanol is an example of an oxygenate. Give another example of an oxygenate. Give two reasons why oxygenates are added to petrol. *(9)*

  (b) Write a balanced chemical equation for the combustion of ethanol, C_2H_5OH. Given that the heats of formation of ethanol, carbon dioxide and water are –278, –394 and –286 kJ mol^{-1}, respectively, calculate the heat of combustion of ethanol. *(18)*

Answer

(a)

(i) Measure of tendency (likelihood) to auto-ignite (5)

(ii) Heptane: $CH_3CH_2CH_2CH_2CH_2CH_2CH_3$ (3)

2,2,4-trimethylpentane: $(CH_3)_3CCH_2CH(CH_3)_2$ (3)

(iii) Light gasoline (3)

Naphtha (3)

(iv) Removal (loss) of hydrogen (3)

Ring formation (3)

(v) Methyl-t-butyl ether (3)

Raise octane number (3)

Less harmful to the environment (3)

(b)

$C_2H_5OH + 3O_2 \rightarrow 2CO_2 + 3H_2O$ (6)

$\Delta H = \Sigma \Delta H_f(\text{products}) - \Sigma \Delta H_f (\text{reactants})$

$\Delta H = 2 \times -394 / -788$ (3) $+ 3 \times -286 / -858$ (3) $- \{-278$ (3) $+ 0\}$

OR

$2 \times -394 / -788$ (3) $+ 3 \times -286 / -858$ (3) $+ 278$ (3) $- 0$

$\Delta H = -1368$ (3)

Elements and the Periodic Table

1

Learning objectives

In this chapter you will learn about:

1 Elements and their symbols

2 History of the idea of elements

3 The periodic table of the elements

4 History of the periodic table

5 Properties of elements within the main groups

Elements and their symbols

Pure substances are either **compounds** or **elements**. Compounds can be chemically broken down into the elements of which they are made.

Elements cannot be broken down chemically into simpler substances. There are more than 110 different elements known.

Each element is designated by a **symbol** and has its own unique **atomic number**. You are required to know the symbols of all elements with atomic numbers from 1 to 36.

> **Key definition**
>
> An **element** is a substance that cannot be broken down into simpler substances by chemical means.

History of the idea of elements

Ancient Greeks

- In 450 BC, **Empedocles** defined elements as **the basic substances from which all other materials are made**.

- Empedocles stated that there were four elements: earth, air, fire and water.

Robert Boyle

Humphry Davy

Henry Moseley

Robert Boyle

- **Boyle** defined an element as **a substance that cannot be broken down into simpler materials.**

- If a substance could be broken down into simpler materials, then it definitely was not an element.

Humphry Davy

- **Davy** developed powerful new electrochemical techniques for breaking down compounds into elements.

- He isolated the elements potassium, sodium, barium, strontium, calcium and magnesium. *discovered*

Henry Moseley

- In 1913, **Moseley** found using X-rays that the atomic nucleus of each element had a characteristic **positive** charge.

- He called this charge the **atomic number.**

> **Key definition**
>
> An **element** is a substance whose atoms all have the same atomic number.

The periodic table of the elements

In the periodic table of the elements, **elements with similar chemical properties are grouped together.**

In the periodic table, elements are arranged in order of increasing atomic number. Elements that have similar chemical properties are placed in vertical columns called **groups**. For example, chlorine is in Group VII and has chemical properties that are similar to the other Group VII elements, e.g. fluorine, bromine and iodine.

The elements between Groups II and III are known as the **d-block elements**. Each vertical group in this region of the table is known as a **subgroup**: for example, copper, silver and gold make up the copper subgroup.

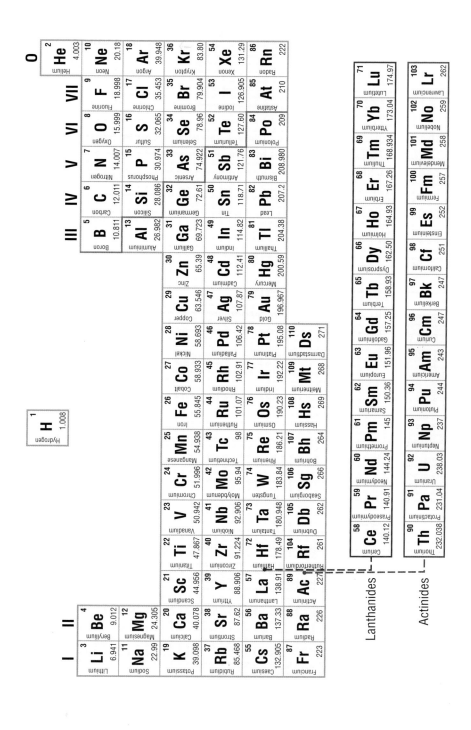

Fig 1.1 *The periodic table*

Directly above the symbol of each element in the periodic table is written its **atomic number**. The **relative atomic mass** is written underneath the symbol. For example, chlorine (Cl) can be seen to have an atomic number of 17 and a relative atomic mass of 35.453.

A horizontal row of elements in the periodic table is called a **period**. The first period contains two elements, hydrogen and helium. There are eight elements in the second period, starting with lithium and ending with neon.

There are also eight elements in the third period, starting with sodium and ending with argon. There are 18 elements in the fourth period, starting with potassium and ending with krypton.

History of the periodic table

Johann Döbereiner

Johann Döbereiner

- In 1817, **Döbereiner** recognised that calcium, strontium and barium had properties that were similar.
- He also noticed that the atomic weight of strontium was almost midway between that of calcium and barium.
- He suggested that elements should fit together in groups of three called **triads**.
- Other examples of triads were chlorine, bromine and iodine, and lithium, sodium and potassium.
- This proposed '**Law of Triads**' was found to be restricted to only a small number of elements.

John Newlands

John Newlands

- In 1863, **Newlands** arranged the elements in order of atomic weight, and found that properties seemed to repeat themselves every eighth element.
- This periodic relationship worked for only the first 17 elements then known.
- Newlands attempted to force all the known elements to fit the pattern, but was unsuccessful.
- Not surprisingly, Newlands' '**Law of Octaves**' was not accepted by other chemists.

Dmitri Mendeleev

- **Mendeleev** found that there was a periodic recurrence of properties when the elements were arranged in order of their atomic weight.

- He placed elements that were similar to one another in groups.

- However, in his **periodic table** published in 1869, he listed separately in subgroups elements such as copper and silver whose properties did not fit in with those of the main groups.

- In Mendeleev's table, the first two horizontal periods contained seven elements, but the next two contained 17 each.

Dmitri Mendeleev

- Mendeleev put the elements iodine and tellurium out of the correct order of their atomic weight, because of their properties. He put tellurium in what we now know as Group VI, and iodine in what we now know as Group VII, even though iodine has the smaller atomic weight.

- He also left gaps in the table in order to make elements fit into proper groups, and predicted the properties that the missing elements ought to have.

- The subsequent discovery of the elements gallium, scandium and germanium showed the accuracy of the predictions.

Group I	Group II	Group III	Group IV	Group V	Group VI	Group VII
H						
Li	Be	B	C	N	O	F
Na	Mg	Al	Si	P	S	Cl
K	Ca	–	–	As	Se	Br

Fig. 1.2 Some of the gaps left for undiscovered elements in Mendeleev's table

Henry Moseley

- One of the apparent anomalies in Mendeleev's table, the placing of tellurium (atomic weight 127.6) before iodine (atomic weight 126.9), was finally explained after **Moseley** discovered in 1914 that each element had a different atomic number.

- In the modern periodic table, elements are arranged in order of atomic number, not atomic weight. Tellurium (atomic number 52) comes before iodine (atomic number 53).

Remember

If the first 36 elements were arranged in order of relative atomic mass, the arrangement would differ from their order in terms of atomic number as follows: potassium would come before argon, and nickel would come before cobalt.

(a) Mendeleev's periodic table (elements mainly in order of atomic weight)

(b) Modern periodic table (elements in order of atomic number)

Fig. 1.3 Iodine and tellurium in the periodic table

Differences between Mendeleev's periodic table and the modern periodic table

Table 1.1

Mendeleev's periodic table	Modern periodic table
Gaps left for undiscovered elements	Gaps have been filled
Group 0 elements missing	Group 0 elements included
Elements discovered since 1869 missing	Elements discovered since 1869 included
d-block elements arranged as subgroups beside each main group	d-block elements arranged as subgroups in a separate block
Elements arranged in order of increasing atomic weight (in almost all cases)	Elements arranged in order of increasing atomic number

Properties of elements within the main groups

Within a group, there are similarities in the physical and chemical properties of the elements. The most reactive elements are the Group I and Group VII elements.

The alkali metals

The Group I elements are called the **alkali metals. They are all very reactive metals, increasing in reactivity down the group.**

Some properties that these elements have in common are as follows:

Physical properties

- They are soft metals.
- They have low densities.

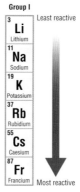

Fig. 1.4 Reactivity trend in Group I

Chemical properties

- When they are freshly cut, they have a metallic shine, but this disappears rapidly due to the reaction of the exposed metal surface with oxygen in the air. The metal oxide is formed.

- They also burn readily in air, forming the metal oxide.

- Sodium reacts as follows:

$$4Na + O_2 \rightarrow 2Na_2O$$

- They react vigorously with water, forming a basic solution and hydrogen. For example, sodium reacts as follows:

$$2Na + 2H_2O \rightarrow 2NaOH + H_2$$

Alkali metals are stored in oil to prevent reactions with water and with atmospheric oxygen.

The alkaline earth elements

The Group II elements are called the **alkaline earth elements. They are all reactive elements, with reactivity increasing down the group.**

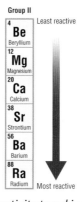

Fig. 1.5 Reactivity trend in Group II

Some properties that magnesium and calcium have in common are as follows:

Physical properties
- They are metals and are harder than the alkali metals.

Chemical properties
- They are less reactive than the corresponding alkali metals. For example, calcium reacts less vigorously with water than the corresponding alkali metal potassium.

Calcium + water → calcium hydroxide + hydrogen

The halogens

The Group VII elements are called **the halogens. They are very reactive non-metals, decreasing in reactivity down the group.**

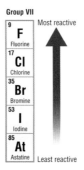

Fig. 1.6 *Reactivity trend in Group VII*

Some properties that these elements have in common are as follows:

Physical properties
- They have low melting and boiling points.

- At room temperature, fluorine and chlorine are yellow-green gases, bromine is a red liquid and iodine is a dark solid.

Chemical properties
- They react with hydrogen to form compounds which dissolve in water to form acidic solutions. For example, in the case of chlorine:

$$H_{2(g)} + Cl_{2(g)} \rightarrow 2HCl_{(g)}$$

Hydrogen chloride gas dissolves in water to form hydrochloric acid solution.

- They react vigorously with sodium (and the other alkali metals), forming white salts. For example:

Sodium + chlorine → sodium chloride

The noble gases

The Group 0 elements are called the **noble gases**. The main properties that these elements have in common are as follows:

Physical properties
- They are all gases at room temperature.
- The boiling point and density increases going down the group.

Chemical properties
- They are the least reactive of all elements.

s-block and p-block elements

The elements in Groups I and II form a block of reactive metals called the **s-block elements**. They have lower densities, lower melting points and lower boiling points than most other metals. They are also more reactive than the d-block metals.

The elements in Groups III, IV, V, VI, VII and 0 are called the **p-block elements**. These are mainly non-metals, but the lower members of some of these groups, for example tin and lead in Group IV, are metals.

Experiment

Specified Demonstration: The reaction of alkali metals with water

The chemical equations for the reactions between alkali metals and water in this demonstration are as follows:

$$2Li_{(s)} + 2H_2O_{(l)} \rightarrow 2LiOH_{(aq)} + H_{2(g)}$$

$$2Na_{(s)} + 2H_2O_{(l)} \rightarrow 2NaOH_{(aq)} + H_{2(g)}$$

$$2K_{(s)} + 2H_2O_{(l)} \rightarrow 2KOH_{(aq)} + H_{2(g)}$$

Procedure
1. Place a small piece of lithium in a trough of water. The lithium slowly moves across the surface of the water as it reacts.

2. Place a small piece of sodium in a trough of water. The sodium rapidly moves across the surface of the water as it reacts.

3. Place a small piece of potassium in a trough of water. The potassium moves very rapidly across the surface of the water as it reacts, catches fire with a lilac flame, and explodes.

Procedure 4 If a piece of red litmus paper is dipped into the trough after any of the alkali metals have been added to water, it turns blue. This indicates that an alkaline solution has been formed (lithium hydroxide, sodium hydroxide and potassium hydroxide are all bases).

Conclusion This demonstration shows clearly that potassium is the most reactive of the three metals, followed by sodium, while lithium is the least reactive of the three.

Key-points!

- An element is a substance that cannot be broken down into simpler substances by chemical means.

- In Mendeleev's periodic table, (1) gaps were left for undiscovered elements, (2) the Group 0 elements were missing, (3) elements discovered since 1869 were missing, (4) d-block elements were arranged as subgroups beside each main group, and (5) elements were arranged in order of increasing atomic weight (in most cases).

- In the modern periodic table, (1) gaps were filled, (2) Group 0 elements were included, (3) elements discovered since 1869 were included, (4) d-block elements were arranged as subgroups in a separate block, and (5) elements were arranged in order of increasing atomic number.

Atomic structure   2

Ideas about atoms

It is generally accepted that matter is composed of minute particles, which may be **atoms**, molecules or ions.

John Dalton's atomic theory

In the early 1800s, **John Dalton** was able to provide indirect evidence for the existence of atoms. Dalton's ideas included the following:

- Atoms are very small indivisible particles.

- The atoms of a given element are identical to each other, and have the same mass and chemical properties.

- Atoms of different elements vary in mass.

John Dalton

- A compound contains atoms of two or more elements combined together in fixed proportions.

Using his theory, Dalton was able to account for experimentally based laws of chemistry, such as the **law of conservation of mass**.

William Crookes

William Crookes

A discharge tube is a long glass tube fitted with a metal electrode at each end. When the gas inside is at a very low pressure, passing electricity through the tube results in invisible rays travelling in straight lines from the cathode – the negative electrode – to the anode – the positive electrode.

William Crookes showed that these rays, which were called cathode rays, travelled in straight lines, and that small objects placed in the path of the rays cast a sharp shadow in the fluorescence at the end of the tube. This convinced him that cathode rays consisted of particles.

Thomson and the electron

In 1897, **J.J. Thomson**, at the Cavendish Laboratory in Cambridge, showed that cathode rays were attracted by the positive plate in an electric field. This meant that they had a negative charge. Thomson measured the ratio of charge to mass (e/m) for the particles. He found that these negatively charged particles were about 2000 times lighter than hydrogen atoms and were to be found in all matter.

J.J. Thomson

Johnstone Stoney

The Irish scientist **George Johnstone Stoney** anticipated the existence of negative particles. His suggested name for them, electrons, was then adopted for the particles found by Thomson.

George Johnstone Stoney

Robert Millikan

In 1911, the American scientist **Robert Millikan** devised and conducted his famous oil drop experiment, which allowed the charge on the electron to be measured accurately.

Thomson's plum pudding model

Thomson suggested that atoms were positively charged spheres in which negatively charged electrons were embedded, similar to a plum pudding. However, this model was soon shown to be inadequate.

Robert Millikan

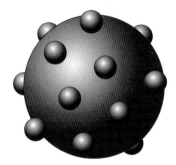

Fig. 2.1 *Thomson's plum pudding model of the atom*

The nucleus

Ernest Rutherford directed his assistants Geiger and Marsden to fire alpha particles at very thin gold foil. They used a zinc sulfide screen to detect scattered alpha particles.

- Most of the alpha particles were not deflected at all, showing that they had passed through basically empty space.

- Some particles were deflected at small angles.

- A small number of particles were deflected at angles greater than 90°, and a very small number actually bounced back towards their source.

Ernest Rutherford

Rutherford explained that:

- The deflection of the alpha particles was due to their going close to and being repelled strongly by a dense concentration of positive charge.

- The alpha particles that bounced back did so because they collided with a small dense mass.

- Nearly all of the mass of the atom is densely concentrated in a tiny **positively charged** central region called the **nucleus**.

- The rest of the atom is mostly empty space.

- The electrons move around in the rest of the atom's volume, balancing the positive charge of the nucleus and keeping the atom neutral.

James Chadwick

Protons and neutrons

Rutherford found that **protons** made up the positive part of all atoms.

Rutherford could explain the charge on the nucleus (but not all of its mass) in terms of the number of its protons. He suggested that the nucleus also contained other particles of equal mass to protons, but with no charge. In 1932, **James Chadwick** produced the evidence for these particles, which were called **neutrons**.

Properties of electrons, protons and neutrons

The masses, charges and locations of electrons, protons and neutrons are summarised in Table 2.1.

Table 2.1

Particle	Relative mass	Relative charge	Location in atom
Electron	1/1836	−1	Outside the nucleus
Proton	1	+1	In the nucleus
Neutron	1	0	In the nucleus

Atomic number (Z)

All atoms of the same element contain the same number of protons. This number of protons identifies what element it is. The English physicist **Henry Moseley** called the number of protons in the nucleus the **atomic number**. It is given the symbol **Z**.

The atomic number gives three pieces of information about an element:

1 The number of protons in the nucleus of an atom of the element.

2 The number of electrons in an atom of the element.

3 The position of the element in the modern periodic table.

Key definition

The **atomic number** of an element is the number of protons in the nucleus of an atom of the element.

Mass number (A)

The **mass number** of an atom is the sum of the numbers of protons and neutrons in the nucleus of the atom. It is given the symbol **A**. The number of neutrons can be calculated by subtracting Z from A, i.e. number of neutrons = A – Z.

Information about an atom can now be written more fully by including the atomic number and the mass number. For example:

$$^{19}_{9}\text{F}$$

The subscript 9 is the atomic number, Z, and the superscript 19 is the mass number, A. The number of neutrons = A – Z = 19 – 9 = 10.

Key definition

The **mass number** of an atom is the sum of the numbers of protons and neutrons in the nucleus of the atom.

Question

2.1 State the number of protons and neutrons for the calcium atom, $^{40}_{20}\text{Ca}$.

Answer

The atomic number Z = 20, so there are 20 protons. The mass number A = 40.
Number of neutrons = A – Z = 40 – 20 = 20.

Question

2.2 An atom of argon has 18 protons and 22 neutrons. Indicate the mass number and atomic number for the atom.

Answer

Since the number of protons is 18, the atomic number Z = 18.

The mass number A = the sum of the numbers of protons and neutrons

= 18 + 22 = 40

Isotopes

Atoms with the same number of protons but different numbers of neutrons are called **isotopes**. In other words, isotopes have the same atomic number (Z) but different mass numbers (A).

Naturally occurring hydrogen consists of three isotopes: ^1H (1 proton and no neutron); ^2H (1 proton and 1 neutron); and ^3H (1 proton and 2 neutrons). The ^1H isotope is by far the most abundant isotope of hydrogen.

Naturally occurring carbon consists of three isotopes: carbon-12 (i.e. ^{12}C, with 6 protons and 6 neutrons); carbon-13 (i.e. ^{13}C, with 6 protons and 7 neutrons); and carbon-14 (i.e. ^{14}C, with 6 protons and 8 neutrons).

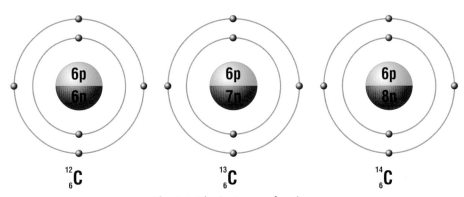

Fig. 2.2 The isotopes of carbon

Key definition

Isotopes are atoms with the same number of protons but different numbers of neutrons.

Relative atomic mass (A_r)

Key definition

The **relative atomic mass** of an element is the average mass of an atom of the element relative to one-twelfth the mass of an atom of carbon-12.

2.3 In a sample of silicon, 92.2% of the atoms are silicon-28, 4.7% are silicon-29 and 3.1% are silicon-30. Calculate the relative atomic mass, A_r, of silicon.

Answer

The abundance of each isotope is multiplied by its mass, the sum of these products is calculated and the result divided by 100.

$$A_r(Si) = [(92.2 \times 28) + (4.7 \times 29) + (3.1 \times 30)] / 100$$

$$= [2581.6 + 136.3 + 93] / 100$$

$$= 2810.9 / 100$$

$$= 28.11$$

Key-points!

- The atomic number of an element is the number of protons in the nucleus of an atom of the element.

- The mass number of an atom is the sum of the numbers of protons and neutrons in the nucleus of the atom.

- Isotopes are atoms with the same number of protons but different numbers of neutrons.

- The relative atomic mass (A_r) of an element is the average mass of an atom of the element relative to one-twelfth the mass of an atom of carbon-12.

3 Radioactivity

Learning objectives

In this chapter you will learn about:

1 The discovery of radioactivity

2 Marie and Pierre Curie

3 What is meant by radioactivity?

4 Types of radiation

5 Distinction between nuclear and chemical reactions

6 Radioisotopes and half-life

7 Background radiation

8 Uses of radioisotopes

Henri Becquerel

The discovery of radioactivity

- **Henri Becquerel** wrapped a photographic plate in black paper, put crystals of a uranium compound on it, and placed it in a dark place.

- A few days later, he developed the plate and found an image of the crystals.

- He concluded that the crystals themselves had emitted the radiation that had caused the image on the photographic plate.

Marie and Pierre Curie

Marie and Pierre Curie

- The Polish chemist **Marie Curie** and her husband **Pierre** carried out further research on uranium compounds and other substances that emitted the radiation discovered by Becquerel.

- Marie Curie called this newly discovered radiation **radioactivity**.

- The Curies isolated two new elements from the radioactive pitchblende ore within a few years. These elements – polonium and radium – are much more radioactive than uranium.

What is meant by radioactivity?

Types of radiation

There are three types of radiation emitted by radioactive isotopes:

- α particles, which have a positive charge
- β particles, which have a negative charge
- γ rays, which are neutral.

α particles (alpha particles)

These particles consist of two protons and two neutrons, i.e. they are helium nuclei. They move relatively slowly and are stopped quite easily, for example by human skin or by a few sheets of paper.

An example of an α emitter is americium-241, which is used in many smoke detectors. It decays according to the following equation:

$$^{241}_{95}\text{Am} \rightarrow \ ^{237}_{93}\text{Np} + \ ^{4}_{2}\text{He} + \text{energy}$$

The new element formed is neptunium.

β particles (beta particles)

In some radioactive elements, neutrons disintegrate into protons and electrons. The electrons – β particles – are emitted from the atom in a fast-moving stream. They are more penetrative than α particles but can be stopped by a 5 mm thickness of aluminium.

Carbon-14, which is used to determine the age of things, is an example of a β emitter. It decays according to the following equation:

$$^{14}_{6}\text{C} \rightarrow {}^{14}_{7}\text{N} + {}^{0}_{-1}\text{e} + \text{energy}$$

The atomic number increases by one, which means that a new element, nitrogen, is formed.

γ rays (gamma rays)

The third type of radioactivity emitted by radioactive isotopes is a form of energy called γ rays. These rays have no mass or charge. They move very quickly and have much greater penetration than α or β radiation. Thick shields of concrete or lead can stop them.

Key definition

Gamma rays are high-energy electromagnetic radiation, with greater penetrating ability than beta particles.

An example of a γ emitter is cobalt-60, which is used for cancer treatment and for food irradiation.

$$^{60}_{27}\text{Co} \rightarrow {}^{60}_{27}\text{Co} + \text{hf} \longrightarrow \text{energy emitted.}$$

The equation shows that no new element is formed, but energy is emitted.

Distinction between nuclear and chemical reactions

Table 3.1 Differences between nuclear and chemical reactions

Nuclear reactions	Chemical reactions
New element may be formed	New element not formed
Changes occur in nucleus	No change in nucleus
No chemical bonds broken or formed	Chemical bond-breaking and forming occurs

When an isotope undergoes beta decay, its atomic number increases by 1, while its mass number remains unchanged.

3.1 Write an equation for the beta decay of the radioactive isotope $^{32}_{15}P$.

Answer

When the ^{32}P isotope undergoes beta decay, its atomic number increases by 1, while its mass number remains unchanged.

$$^{32}_{15}P \rightarrow \, ^{32}_{16}S + \, ^{0}_{-1}e$$

(handwritten annotations: "+1" under the 15→16, "16" circled)

When an isotope undergoes alpha decay, its **atomic number decreases by 2**, while its **mass number decreases by 4**.

Question

3.2 Write an equation for the alpha decay of the radioactive isotope $^{222}_{86}Rn$.

Answer

When the ^{222}Rn isotope undergoes alpha decay, its atomic number decreases by 2, while its mass number decreases by 4.

$$^{222}_{86}Rn \rightarrow \, ^{218}_{84}Po + \, ^{4}_{2}He$$

(handwritten annotations: "-4" and "-2" showing the changes)

Radioisotopes and half-life

Unstable, radioactive isotopes are called **radioisotopes**. Carbon-12, for example, is stable, whereas carbon-14 is a radioisotope.

Radioactive atoms decay in such a way that the number of them present is halved after a fixed interval of time passes. This interval of time is called the **half-life** of the sample. Some radioisotopes decay very quickly and have short half-lives.

Key definition

The **half-life** of a radioactive isotope is the time taken for half of the atoms in a sample of the isotope to decay.

Background radiation

A low level of ionising radiation surrounds us at all times.

- More than half of the background radiation is caused by radon gas. This is formed by the decay of radioisotopes found in rocks in the ground. Radon barriers are incorporated into new buildings to prevent the gas seeping into the buildings.

- The artificial sources of background radiation are mostly medical. They include cobalt-60, which is used in cancer treatment, and medical X-rays.

Uses of radioisotopes

Radioisotopes have many uses and are particularly important in archaeology, in medicine and in food preservation.

Table 3.2

Radiation type	Isotope	Use
α particles	Am-241	Smoke detectors
β particles	C-14	Archaeology: estimating the age of objects by carbon dating
γ rays	Co-60	Medicine: the treatment of cancer by radiotherapy
γ rays	Co-60	Food preservation: irradiation of food

 Experiment

Specified Demonstration: Properties of α, β and γ radiation

Chemicals needed : α, β and γ sources.

Range of absorbers: sheets of paper, 5 mm sheet of aluminium, 4 cm block of lead.

Procedure : 1 Assemble the apparatus as shown in Fig. 3.1 (but without any radioactive source present).

2 Measure the average background count per minute.

Procedure

3 Place an α source 4 cm from the Geiger-Müller tube window and take a count for one minute. Subtract the average background count and record your results.

4 Repeat for the β and γ sources. Subtract the average background count from each reading and record your results.

5 For each of the sources, place the paper, aluminium and lead in turn between the source and the Geiger-Müller tube window. Subtract the average background count from each reading, and record your results.

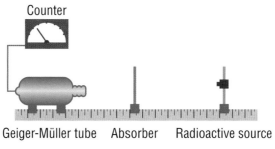

Counter

Geiger-Müller tube   Absorber   Radioactive source

Fig. 3.1 Geiger-Müller tube

Remember

The paper is sufficient to block the alpha radiation, while the aluminium blocks the beta radiation, and the thick block of lead is needed to block the gamma radiation.

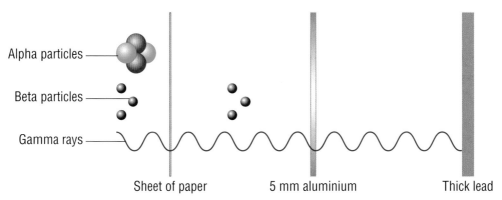

Alpha particles

Beta particles

Gamma rays

Sheet of paper   5 mm aluminium   Thick lead

Fig. 3.2 The relative penetrating powers of alpha, beta and gamma radiation

Conclusion : This demonstration shows clearly that gamma radiation is the most penetrating of the three types of radiation, followed by beta particles, while alpha particles are the least penetrating of the three.

Key-points!

- Radioactivity is defined as the spontaneous breaking up of certain unstable nuclei, accompanied by the emission of radiation.
- Alpha particles are helium nuclei, with a positive charge and little penetrating ability.
- Beta particles are electrons, with a negative charge and greater penetrating ability than alpha particles.
- Gamma rays are high-energy electromagnetic radiation, with greater penetrating ability than beta particles.
- In a nuclear reaction, (1) a new element may be formed, (2) changes occur in the nucleus, and (3) no chemical bonds are broken or formed.
- In a chemical reaction, (1) a new element is not formed, (2) there is no change in the nucleus, and (3) chemical bond-breaking and forming occurs.
- The half-life of a radioactive isotope is the time taken for half of the atoms in a sample of the isotope to decay.

Electronic Structure of Atoms

4

Learning objectives

In this chapter you will learn about:

1 Bohr's model of the atom
2 Energy levels in atoms
3 Emission and absorption of light by elements
4 Spectral series
5 Absorption spectra
6 Line spectra as evidence for energy levels
7 Atomic orbitals
8 Electronic configurations of atoms
9 Electronic configurations of ions
10 Limitations of the Bohr theory
11 Atomic radii
12 Ionisation energies
13 The periodic table and electronic structure

Bohr's model of the atom

In 1913, Danish physicist **Niels Bohr** put forward a theory of the hydrogen atom. He stated that:

- The hydrogen electron is restricted to those regions of the atom that have certain energy values (**energy levels**).
- When an electron moves from a higher level of energy (E_2) to a lower level of energy (E_1), a definite amount of energy equal to the energy difference between the two levels is emitted: $E_2 - E_1 = hf$, where h = Planck's constant and f = frequency of the light emitted.

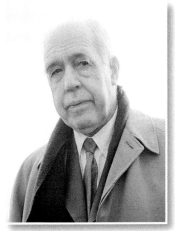

Niels Bohr

- If an atom absorbs an amount of energy equal to the energy difference between the energy level (E_1) the electron is in and a higher energy level (E_2), the electron will move to the higher level. Again, $E_2 - E_1 = hf$.

- Associated with each energy level is an integer, n, called the principal quantum number.

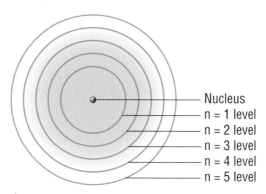

Fig. 4.1 Energy levels in atoms

Bohr's model worked well for hydrogen but less well for other atoms.

Energy levels in atoms

Electrons in atoms occupy energy levels that are outside the nucleus. Different energy levels in atoms have different energy values, and have different capacities for electrons.

Key definition

An **energy level** is a region of definite energy within the atom that electrons can occupy.

Table 4.1 Energy levels and electron capacities

Energy level	Capacity
n = 1	2
n = 2	8
n = 3	18
n = 4	32

Table 4.2 Electrons in atoms of first 20 elements in periodic table

Element	Atomic number	Electron arrangement			
		n = 1	n = 2	n = 3	n = 4
Hydrogen	1	1			
Helium	2	2			
Lithium	3	2	1		
Beryllium	4	2	2		
Boron	5	2	3		
Carbon	6	2	4		
Nitrogen	7	2	5		
Oxygen	8	2	6		
Fluorine	9	2	7		
Neon	10	2	8		
Sodium	11	2	8	1	
Magnesium	12	2	8	2	
Aluminium	13	2	8	3	
Silicon	14	2	8	4	
Phosphorus	15	2	8	5	
Sulfur	16	2	8	6	
Chlorine	17	2	8	7	
Argon	18	2	8	8	
Potassium	19	2	8	8	1
Calcium	20	2	8	8	2

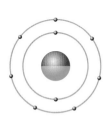

Fluorine (2,7)

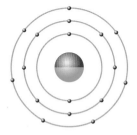

Chlorine (2,8,7)

Fig. 4.2 Arrangement of electrons in atoms of the Group VII elements

In general, elements in the same group of the periodic table have the same number of electrons in the outermost energy level of their atoms. The only exception to this is helium in Group 0. It has just two electrons in the outermost energy level of its atoms, unlike neon and argon, which each have eight.

Emission and absorption of light by elements

Many elements and their salts, when vaporised in a flame, emit light. The light emitted has a colour characteristic of the particular element.

Mandatory Experiment 4.1: Flame tests (Li, Na, K, Ba, Sr and Cu)

Procedure

1 In the fume cupboard, clean the platinum wire using concentrated hydrochloric acid.

2 Crush the salt to be tested with a pestle and mortar.

3 Dip the platinum wire in concentrated hydrochloric acid and then in the salt to be tested.

4 Place the platinum wire in the flame of the Bunsen burner (Fig. 4.3) and note the colour given off.

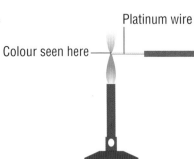

Fig. 4.3

5 Repeat the experiment for each of the other salts. Again, note the colour in each case.

6 The expected results are shown in Table 4.3.

(A wooden splint, soaked overnight in water, may be used instead of a platinum wire in this experiment.)

Table 4.3

Element	Flame colour
Barium	Yellow-green
Copper	Blue-green
Lithium	Deep red
Potassium	Lilac
Sodium	Yellow
Strontium	Red

The colours that particular elements, such as strontium and barium, emit in a flame are often seen in firework displays. For example, strontium nitrate is used to give a red colour in fireworks, while barium nitrate gives a green colour.

If an element is a gas, like neon, or is easily vaporised, like mercury or sodium, it will emit light of a characteristic colour when placed in a discharge tube at low pressure and subjected to a high voltage (Fig. 4.4).

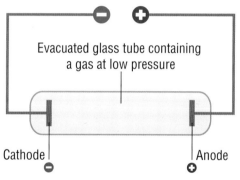

Fig. 4.4 Discharge tube

For example, a sodium discharge tube emits yellow light when subjected to a high voltage. Yellow streetlights are a type of discharge tube containing sodium vapour.

A spectroscope can be used to analyse the light emitted by elements. When the light emitted from a discharge tube containing hydrogen is analysed using a spectroscope, a series of coloured lines of definite wavelength against a dark background is observed. This type of spectrum is called a **line spectrum**.

The emission spectra of other elements are also line spectra. The emission spectrum of an element is characteristic of that element, and is different from that of any other element.

Key definition

A **line spectrum** is a series of coloured lines against a dark background.

 ## Experiment

Specified Demonstration: Observation of line spectra of elements using a spectroscope

Procedure   1 View the light from the discharge tube containing hydrogen using the direct vision spectroscope.

2 A number of coloured lines against a dark background should be seen.

Spectral series

Late in the nineteenth century, it was discovered that the wavelengths present in the hydrogen spectrum fall into definite sets, called spectral series. The Swiss physicist **Johann Balmer** discovered the first of these series in 1885, when studying the visible region of the hydrogen spectrum. The **Balmer series** contains all of the lines in the visible region of the hydrogen spectrum.

Absorption spectra

An absorption spectrum of an element consists of a series of dark lines against a coloured background. These dark lines are at exactly the same wavelengths as the coloured lines in the emission spectrum of the element.

Line spectra as evidence for energy levels

The fact that only definite frequencies of light are emitted by hydrogen atoms gives strong experimental evidence that the electron in the hydrogen atom is restricted to definite energy levels. The Bohr theory accounts for the line spectrum of the hydrogen atom as follows:

Under normal circumstances, the hydrogen electron is in the n = 1 energy level, the **ground state** for the hydrogen atom. If the electron receives enough energy it moves to the n = 2 energy level, which is an **excited state** for the hydrogen atom. An electron in this state, being relatively unstable, will eventually drop back to the ground state, emitting energy equal to the difference between the energies of the n = 2 and n = 1 energy levels. As a result, a line is obtained in the spectrum in the ultraviolet region.

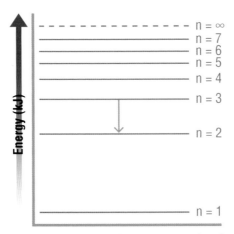

Fig. 4.5 Electrons dropping into the n = 2 energy level emit visible light

The ground state electron may receive enough energy to be excited to the n = 3 level. This electron in the n = 3 energy level need not necessarily drop back directly to the ground state. Instead, it can drop to the n = 2 energy level (Fig. 4.5), emitting light of a particular wavelength in the visible region. This line is one of the Balmer series. All of the lines in the Balmer series are due to electrons dropping from higher levels to the n = 2 energy level.

Other elements and energy levels

For elements other than hydrogen, according to the Bohr theory, the number of electrons that could be accommodated in an energy level could not exceed $2n^2$.

Table 4.4 Number of electrons in energy levels

Energy level	Maximum no. of electrons
n = 1	2
n = 2	8
n = 3	18
n = 4	32

The line spectra of elements other than hydrogen may be explained in terms of energy levels as follows:

- Electrons in an atom are restricted to particular energy levels.
- Electrons receive sufficient energy in a flame or in a discharge tube to move to higher energy levels.
- They are now unstable, and rapidly fall to lower levels.
- Each time they do this, they emit light of a definite wavelength, whose energy is equal to the energy difference between the two levels.
- This light appears as one of the lines in the line spectrum of the element.

The line spectrum of each element is unique to that element because atoms of each element have a different arrangement of energy levels, and this gives rise to different electronic transitions.

Atomic orbitals

In 1923, the French physicist Louis de Broglie stated that electrons, like light, have the properties of waves as well as of particles.

There is considerable uncertainty about the location of an electron in an atom at any given time. In 1927, **Werner Heisenberg** stated his **Uncertainty Principle**.

Key definition

The **Heisenberg Uncertainty Principle** states that it is not possible to determine at the same time the exact position and velocity of an electron.

Because of the uncertainty about the exact location of an electron in an atom, at any particular time, it is more meaningful to refer to the probability of finding the electron in a particular position within the atom. In calculating this probability, use is made of the fact that the electron has a wave nature.

Key definition

An **atomic orbital** is defined as a region in space where the probability of finding an electron is relatively high.

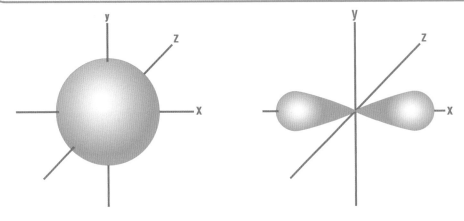

Fig. 4.6 s orbital   Fig. 4.7 p orbital

Types of orbital

There are a number of different types of orbital: s orbitals are spherical (Fig. 4.6); p orbitals have a dumb-bell shape (Fig. 4.7); d orbitals and f orbitals have more complex shapes. All orbitals can hold a maximum of two electrons.

Table 4.5 Shape and orientation of orbitals

Energy level	Orbital	Shape	Orientation
n = 1	1s	Spherical	
n = 2	2s $2p_x$, $2p_y$ and $2p_z$	Spherical Dumb-bell	At right angles to each other
n = 3	3s $3p_x$, $3p_y$ and $3p_z$ Five 3d orbitals	Spherical Dumb-bell	At right angles to each other
n = 4	4s $4p_x$, $4p_y$ and $4p_z$ Five 4d orbitals Seven 4f orbitals	Spherical Dumb-bell	At right angles to each other

Electronic configurations of atoms

A group of orbitals that all have the same energy is called an **energy sublevel**. For example, the $2p_x$, $2p_y$ and $2p_z$ orbitals make up the 2p sublevel, while the five 3d orbitals make up the 3d sublevel. Different types of sublevels have different capacities, as shown in Table 4.6.

Table 4.6 Sublevels and their capacities

Sublevel	Capacity
1s	2
2s	2
2p	6
3s	2
3p	6
3d	10
4s	2
4p	6

To find out how electrons are arranged in different kinds of atoms, a diagram such as Fig. 4.8 may be used. Electrons are assigned to the various sublevels, using the **Aufbau Principle.**

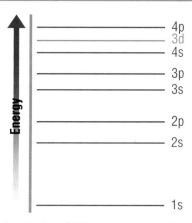

Fig. 4.8 *Order of filling in energy sublevels*

In working out the electronic configuration of an atom, electrons are allocated to the sublevel of lowest energy until this is full. Then electrons are placed in the sublevel of next lowest energy, and the process is repeated until all of the electrons are accounted for.

Key definition

The **Aufbau Principle** states that electrons will occupy the lowest energy sublevel available.

Question

4.1 What is the electronic configuration of sodium?

Answer

Sodium has 11 electrons. Using the order of filling energy sublevels shown in Fig. 4.8, the electronic configuration of sodium is $1s^2 2s^2 2p^6 3s^1$.

All elements in Groups I and II of the periodic table have the outermost electrons in their atoms occupying an s sublevel. Hence this region of the periodic table is referred to as the s-block.

Question

4.2 What is the electronic configuration of chlorine?

Answer

Chlorine has 17 electrons. Using the order of filling energy sublevels shown in Fig. 4.8, the electronic configuration of chlorine is $1s^2 2s^2 2p^6 3s^2 3p^5$.

Chlorine can be referred to as a p-block element. This is because, like all elements that are members of one of Groups III, IV, V, VI, VII and 0 in the periodic table, it has the outermost electrons in its atoms occupying a p sublevel.

Question

4.3 What is the electronic configuration of nickel?

Answer

Nickel has 28 electrons. Using the order of filling energy sublevels shown in Fig. 4.8, the electronic configuration of nickel is $1s^2 2s^2 2p^6 3s^2 3p^6 4s^2 3d^8$.

This approach to working out electronic configurations works for all but two of the first 36 elements. The electronic configurations of two of the d-block elements are exceptional, as indicated in Table 4.7.

Table 4.7 Electronic configurations of d-block elements

Element	Actual electron configuration
Copper	$1s^22s^22p^63s^23p^64s^13d^{10}$
Chromium	$1s^22s^22p^63s^23p^64s^13d^5$

These unexpected configurations are due to the extra stability, in the case of chromium of a structure with half-filled 3d and 4s sublevels, and in the case of copper of a structure with a full 3d and a half-filled 4s sublevel.

Electronic configurations of ions

The electronic configurations of ions of s-block and p-block elements are worked out in a similar way to that used for the electronic configuration of atoms.

Question

4.4 What is the electronic configuration of Ca^{2+}?

Answer

A calcium atom has 20 electrons. This means that a calcium ion (Ca^{2+}) has 18 electrons. The electronic configuration of Ca^{2+} is $1s^22s^22p^63s^23p^6$.

Question

4.5 What is the electronic configuration of F^-?

Answer

A fluorine atom has 9 electrons. This means that a fluoride ion (F^-) has 10 electrons. The electronic configuration of F^- is $1s^22s^22p^6$.

Arrangement of electrons in individual orbitals

Electrons tend to occupy orbitals of equal energy singly where possible, as in the cases of carbon and nitrogen. In an atom such as the oxygen atom, pairing is necessary in the $2p_x$ orbital, but the other 2p electrons occupy the $2p_y$ and $2p_z$ orbitals singly, instead of occupying the same orbital.

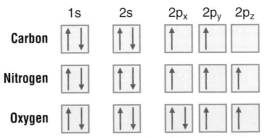

Fig. 4.9 *The arrangement of electrons in orbitals in carbon, nitrogen and oxygen*

4.6 What is the arrangement of electrons in individual orbitals in a silicon atom?

Answer

Silicon has 14 electrons. Using the order of filling energy sublevels shown in Fig. 4.8, the electronic configuration of silicon is $1s^2 2s^2 2p^6 3s^2 3p^2$.

Each 2p orbital is full, and so the 2p electrons are arranged as follows:

$2p_x^2 2p_y^2 2p_z^2$. In the 3p sublevel, there are two electrons available. These occupy the $3p_x$ and the $3p_y$ respectively: $3p_x^1 3p_y^1$.

Thus, the expanded electronic configuration of silicon is:

$1s^2 2s^2 2p_x^2 2p_y^2 2p_z^2 3s^2 3p_x^1 3p_y^1$.

Limitations of the Bohr theory

- Only worked well for hydrogen
- Did not take into account the fact that electrons have the properties of waves as well as of particles
- Did not allow for the Heisenberg Uncertainty Principle
- Did not explain the discovery of sublevels
- Did not account for the existence of orbitals

Atomic radii

Key definition

The **atomic radius** of an element is defined as half the distance between the nuclei of two atoms of the element that are joined together by a single covalent bond.

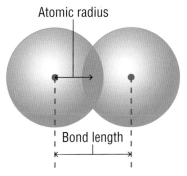

Atomic radius

Bond length

Fig. 4.10 The atomic radius is equal to half the distance between the nuclei of the two atoms

The size of the atomic radius of an element depends on nuclear charge, number of energy levels used, and the screening effect of inner electrons.

The atomic radius increases on going down a group, because of the addition of extra **filled** energy levels, and the resultant extra screening by inner levels.

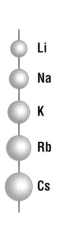

Li

Na

K

Rb

Cs

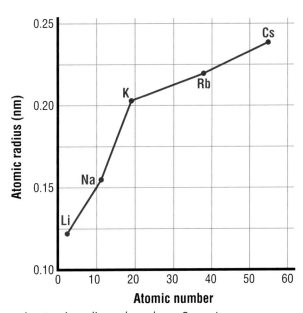

Fig. 4.11 The increase in atomic radius values down Group I

The atomic radius decreases on going from left to right across a period, because of the increasing nuclear charge.

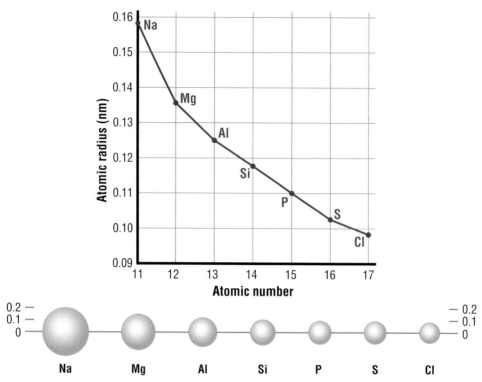

Fig. 4.12 *The downward trend in atomic radius values across the third period*

This screening results in the **effective nuclear charge** experienced by the outermost electron being much less than the full nuclear charge.

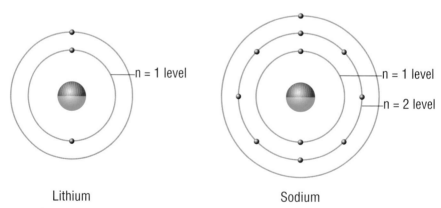

Lithium   Sodium

Fig. 4.13 *The outer electron in a lithium atom is screened by electrons in the n = 1 energy level only. The outer electron in the sodium atom is screened by electrons in both the n = 1 and n = 2 energy levels*

Ionisation energies

$$X_{(g)} \rightarrow X^+_{(g)} + e^-$$

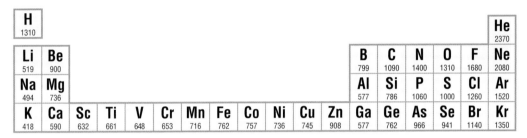

Fig. 4.14 Table of first ionisation energy values for the first 36 elements

The first ionisation energy of an element is measured in kilojoules per mole.

The first ionisation energy values **generally increase** on going from left to right **across a period**. This is due to:

- The increase in nuclear charge
- The decrease in atomic radius.

On going **down a group**, the values of the first ionisation energies **decrease**. This is due to:

- The increase in atomic radius, which makes it easier to remove an electron from an atom despite the increased nuclear charge
- The screening effect of inner energy levels.

Exceptions to the trend across a period

On going across the second period from left to right, first ionisation energy values generally increase.

- However, beryllium (electronic configuration $1s^2 2s^2$) has a higher first ionisation energy value than the next element, boron ($1s^2 2s^2 2p_x^1$).
- The beryllium atom, having a **full outer sublevel**, is particularly stable.

Another exception in the second period to the general trend occurs between nitrogen and oxygen.

- The first ionisation energy of nitrogen (electronic configuration $1s^2 2s^2 2p_x^1 2p_y^1 2p_z^1$) is greater than that of oxygen (electronic configuration $1s^2 2s^2 2p_x^2 2p_y^1 2p_z^1$).

- The nitrogen atom, having **a half-full outer sublevel**, is particularly stable.

Similar exceptions to the general trend occur between Groups II and III and between Groups V and VI in other periods, for similar reasons.

Ionisation energies and energy levels

> **Key definition**
>
> The **second ionisation energy** is the energy required to remove the most loosely bound electron from each singly charged positive ion in a mole of these ions.

$$X^+_{(g)} \rightarrow X^{2+}_{(g)} + e^-$$

When all of the successive ionisation energy values for an element, for example magnesium, are measured, it is found that the first ionisation energy is less than the second ionisation energy, which in turn is less than the third ionisation energy, and so on. **This trend is due to the increasing positive charge and decreasing radius of the species losing the electron.**

The values do not increase in a regular manner, however, and this gives evidence for the existence of energy levels in the magnesium atom.

Magnesium

The magnesium atom has 12 electrons, with 2 in the $n = 3$ level, 8 in the $n = 2$ level, and 2 in the $n = 1$ level. There is a very large difference between the second ionisation energy, when the second electron is removed from the outer ($n = 3$) level, and the third ionisation energy, when the third electron is removed from an inner level ($n = 2$). A similar 'jump' occurs between the 10th ionisation energy, where the electron is in the $n = 2$ level, and the 11th ionisation energy, where the electron removed is in the $n = 1$ level.

The periodic table and electronic structure
The alkali metals

The Group I elements in the periodic table – the alkali metals – all have similar chemical properties because they have similar outer electronic configurations. The radii of the atoms of these elements increase, with the addition of extra energy levels, and consequent extra screening, on going down the group. As a result, the outermost electron is more loosely held and more easily removed, leading to increased reactivity. This is why potassium is more reactive than sodium, which in turn is more reactive than lithium.

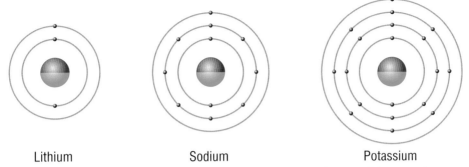

| Lithium | Sodium | Potassium |

Fig. 4.15 The reactivity of an alkali metal atom increases as the size of the atom increases

The halogens

The Group VII elements, the halogens, very often gain electrons in their reactions. The halogens have similar chemical properties because of their similar outer electronic configurations. Halogen atoms increase in radius on going down the group, with an increase in the number of energy levels and resulting extra screening. Their ability to gain electrons diminishes accordingly. This is why bromine is less reactive than chlorine, which in turn is less reactive than fluorine.

In general, elements in the same group of the periodic table have similar chemical properties because they have similar outer electronic configurations.

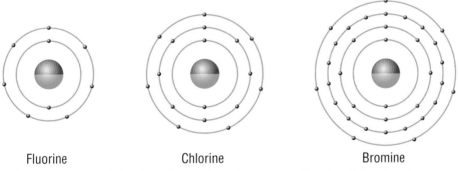

| Fluorine | Chlorine | Bromine |

Fig. 4.16 The reactivity of a halogen atom decreases as the size of the atom increases

Key-points!

- An energy level is a region of definite energy within the atom that electrons can occupy.

- A line spectrum is a series of coloured lines against a dark background.

- The absorption spectrum of an element is the spectrum that is observed after white light has been passed through the element.

- The Heisenberg Uncertainty Principle states that it is not possible to determine at the same time the exact position and velocity of an electron.

- An atomic orbital is a region in space where the probability of finding an electron is relatively high.

- An energy sublevel is a group of atomic orbitals that all have the same energy.

- The Aufbau Principle states that electrons will occupy the lowest energy sublevel available.

- The atomic radius of an element is defined as half the distance between the nuclei of two atoms of the element that are joined together by a single covalent bond.

- The first ionisation energy of an element is defined as the minimum energy in kilojoules required to remove the most loosely bound electron from each isolated atom in a mole of the element in its ground state.

- The second ionisation energy is the energy required to remove the most loosely bound electron from each singly charged positive ion in a mole of these ions.

Oxidation and Reduction 5

Learning objectives

In this chapter you will learn about:

1. Oxidation and reduction in terms of loss and gain of electrons
2. Oxidising agents
3. Reducing agents
4. Redox reactions in Group VII elements
5. The electrochemical series
6. Electrolysis
7. Electrolysis demonstrations
8. Electroplating

Oxidation and reduction

In an **oxidation–reduction** reaction (redox reaction) there is a transfer of electrons from one chemical species to another. In redox reactions, both **oxidation**, or loss of electrons, and **reduction**, or gain of electrons, occur. A chemical species is said to be oxidised if it loses electrons, for example Zn in the reaction

$$Zn_{(s)} + Cu^{2+}_{(aq)} \rightarrow Zn^{2+}_{(aq)} + Cu_{(s)}$$

while it is reduced if it gains electrons, for example Cu^{2+} in the above reaction.

Burning, rusting and the browning of apples are everyday examples of redox reactions.

Key definition

Oxidation is the loss of electrons.

Key definition

Reduction is the gain of electrons.

Rusting of iron

In the rusting of iron, iron reacts with oxygen and water, forming first Fe^{2+} ions and eventually Fe^{3+} ions. In this reaction, the iron atoms lose electrons and are oxidised. Oxygen atoms gain electrons and are reduced.

In reactions such as

$$2Na_{(s)} + Cl_{2(g)} \rightarrow 2NaCl_{(s)}$$

metals are oxidised when forming compounds, since they form positive ions and therefore lose electrons. In the above example, the metal sodium loses electrons and is oxidised. The non-metal chlorine gains electrons and is reduced.

Question

5.1 What is oxidised and what is reduced in the following reaction?

$$2Ca_{(s)} + O_{2(g)} \rightarrow 2CaO_{(s)}$$

Answer

Calcium on reacting with oxygen forms positive ions by losing electrons, and is oxidised. Oxygen gains electrons from calcium and is reduced.

In a reaction such as

$$2NaCl_{(s)} \rightarrow 2Na_{(s)} + Cl_{2(g)}$$

sodium ions in sodium chloride gain electrons to form sodium atoms, and are therefore reduced. Chloride ions lose electrons to form chlorine molecules and are oxidised.

Question

5.2 What is oxidised and what is reduced in the following reaction?

$$ZnSO_{4(aq)} + Mg_{(s)} \rightarrow Zn_{(s)} + MgSO_{4(aq)}$$

Answer

Magnesium on reacting with zinc sulfate forms positive ions by losing electrons, and is oxidised. Zinc gains electrons from magnesium and is reduced.

Oxidising agents

Key definition

An **oxidising agent** is a substance that allows oxidation to happen by gaining electrons itself.

In a redox reaction, the oxidising agent is itself reduced. For example, in the reaction

$$Cu^{2+}_{(aq)} + Mg_{(s)} \rightarrow Cu_{(s)} + Mg^{2+}_{(aq)}$$

the copper ion, which is itself reduced, is the oxidising agent.

Table 5.1 Common oxidising agents

Oxidising agent	Use
Oxygen	Combustion, respiration
Hydrogen peroxide	Stain removal

Point to note

Swimming pool water treatment

Water in swimming pools is kept in good condition by the addition of oxidising agents that kill microorganisms by oxidising them. Chlorine or compounds of chlorine such as sodium hypochlorite are used. When either of these substances is added to water, the oxidising agent HOCl is formed. When this acts as an oxidising agent, it is reduced to the chloride ion (Cl^-).

Reducing agents

In a redox reaction, the reducing agent is itself oxidised. For example, in the reaction

$$Cu^{2+}_{(aq)} + Mg_{(s)} \rightarrow Cu_{(s)} + Mg^{2+}_{(aq)}$$

magnesium, which is itself oxidised, is the reducing agent.

Key definition

A **reducing agent** is a substance that allows reduction to happen by losing electrons itself.

Table 5.2 Common reducing agents

Reducing agent	Use
Sulfur dioxide	Bleaching agent
Hydrogen	Reduction of organic compounds

Question

5.3 What is (i) the oxidising agent and (ii) the reducing agent in the following reaction?

$$Zn^{2+}_{(aq)} + Ca_{(s)} \rightarrow Zn_{(s)} + Ca^{2+}_{(aq)}$$

Answer

(i) Since zinc gains electrons in the reaction, it is reduced and therefore is the oxidising agent.

(ii) Since calcium loses electrons in the reaction, it is oxidised and therefore is the reducing agent.

Redox reactions in Group VII elements

The Group VII elements can all act as oxidising agents, oxidising, for example, solutions containing sulfite ions or iron(II) ions. Chlorine is a more powerful oxidising agent than bromine, which in turn is more powerful than iodine.

 **Experiment**

Mandatory Experiment 5.1: Redox reactions of the halogens

(i) Reactions with halides

Chlorine oxidises bromide and iodide to bromine and iodine, respectively.

$$Cl_{2(aq)} + 2Br^-_{(aq)} \rightarrow 2Cl^-_{(aq)} + Br_{2(aq)}$$

$$Cl_{2(aq)} + 2I^-_{(aq)} \rightarrow 2Cl^-_{(aq)} + I_{2(aq)}$$

Bromine can release iodine from a solution of its salts:

$$Br_{2(aq)} + 2I^-_{(aq)} \rightarrow 2Br^-_{(aq)} + I_{2(aq)}$$

Procedure   1 Add 2 cm³ of a chlorine solution and a sodium bromide solution, respectively, to separate test tubes and mix. An orange colour should appear, indicating that bromine has been formed.

2 Add 2 cm³ of a chlorine solution and a potassium iodide solution, respectively, to separate test tubes and mix. A reddish-brown colour should appear, indicating that iodine has been formed.

3 Add 2 cm³ of a bromine solution and a potassium iodide solution, respectively, to separate test tubes and mix. A reddish-brown colour should appear, indicating that iodine has been formed.

(ii) Reactions with iron(II) salts and with sulfites

Solutions of chlorine, bromine and iodine are all able to oxidise iron(II) ions to iron(III) ions, and to oxidise sulfite ions to sulfate ions in aqueous solution. They react with iron(II) ions as follows:

$$Cl_{2(aq)} + 2Fe^{2+}_{(aq)} \rightarrow 2Cl^{-}_{(aq)} + 2Fe^{3+}_{(aq)}$$

$$Br_{2(aq)} + 2Fe^{2+}_{(aq)} \rightarrow 2Br^{-}_{(aq)} + 2Fe^{3+}_{(aq)}$$

$$I_{2(aq)} + 2Fe^{2+}_{(aq)} \rightarrow 2I^{-}_{(aq)} + 2Fe^{3+}_{(aq)}$$

They react with sulfite ions as follows:

$$Cl_{2(aq)} + SO_3^{2-}_{(aq)} + H_2O_{(l)} \rightarrow 2Cl^{-}_{(aq)} + SO_4^{2-}_{(aq)} + 2H^{+}_{(aq)}$$

$$Br_{2(aq)} + SO_3^{2-}_{(aq)} + H_2O_{(l)} \rightarrow 2Br^{-}_{(aq)} + SO_4^{2-}_{(aq)} + 2H^{+}_{(aq)}$$

$$I_{2(aq)} + SO_3^{2-}_{(aq)} + H_2O_{(l)} \rightarrow 2I^{-}_{(aq)} + SO_4^{2-}_{(aq)} + 2H^{+}_{(aq)}$$

1 Add 2 cm³ of a chlorine solution and an iron(II) sulfate solution, respectively, to separate test tubes and mix. Then add 10 drops of sodium hydroxide solution to the mixture. A greenish-brown precipitate should form – this indicates the presence of Fe^{3+} ions.

2 Repeat using a bromine solution instead of a chlorine solution. A greenish-brown precipitate should form – this indicates the presence of Fe^{3+} ions.

3 Repeat using an iodine solution instead of a chlorine solution. A greenish-brown precipitate should form – this indicates the presence of Fe^{3+} ions.

4 Add 2 cm³ of the chlorine solution and a sodium sulfite solution, respectively, to separate test tubes and mix. Using a dropping pipette, add a few drops of barium chloride solution. Now add 2 cm³ of dilute hydrochloric acid. A white precipitate insoluble in the hydrochloric acid should be observed – this indicates the presence of sulfate ions.

5 Repeat using a bromine solution instead of a chlorine solution. A white precipitate insoluble in the hydrochloric acid should be observed – this indicates the presence of sulfate ions.

6 Repeat using an iodine solution instead of a chlorine solution. A white precipitate insoluble in the hydrochloric acid should be observed – this indicates the presence of sulfate ions.

The trend in oxidising power of the halogens on going down the group is due to:

- The increase in atomic radius, which makes it more difficult for the atom to gain electrons

- The extra screening caused by the addition of extra energy levels, which has the same effect.

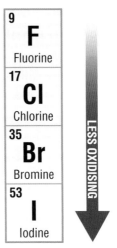

Fig. 5.1 The trend in oxidising ability of the halogens

The electrochemical series

In the **electrochemical series** the metals are arranged in order of tendency to lose electrons. The higher a metal is in the electrochemical series, the more reactive it is.

Displacement of metals

A metal will displace a less reactive metal, that is, one which is below it in the electrochemical series, from a solution of its salts. The more reactive metal is oxidised, and the less reactive metal is reduced. For example, if magnesium ribbon is dipped in copper sulfate solution, it becomes coated with copper, as the following reaction occurs:

Potassium	K
Calcium	Ca
Sodium	Na
Magnesium	Mg
Aluminium	Al
Zinc	Zn
Iron	Fe
Tin	Sn
Lead	Pb
Hydrogen	H
Copper	Cu
Silver	Ag
Gold	Au

INCREASING TENDENCY TO LOSE ELECTRONS

Fig. 5.2 The electrochemical series

$$Mg_{(s)} + CuSO_{4(aq)} \rightarrow MgSO_{4(aq)} + Cu_{(s)}$$

The magnesium is oxidised and the copper is reduced. The further apart metals are in the electrochemical series, the more readily this type of displacement reaction will occur.

Point to note

Applications of displacement reactions

An application of this type of reaction is the use of a less valuable metal – scrap iron – to displace a more valuable and less reactive metal, copper, from a solution of its salts:

$$Fe_{(s)} + CuSO_{4(aq)} \rightarrow FeSO_{4(aq)} + Cu_{(s)}$$

 **Experiment**

Mandatory Experiment 5.2: Displacement reactions of metals

In this experiment, zinc and magnesium, respectively, are reacted with a solution of copper(II) sulfate.

$$Zn_{(s)} + CuSO_{4(aq)} \rightarrow ZnSO_{4(aq)} + Cu_{(s)}$$

$$Mg_{(s)} + CuSO_{4(aq)} \rightarrow MgSO_{4(aq)} + Cu_{(s)}$$

Procedure

1 Half fill two boiling tubes with acidified copper(II) sulfate solution.

2 Add the magnesium ribbon to the solution in one boiling tube. The blue colour of the copper(II) sulfate solution should fade and a brownish precipitate of copper metal should be seen.

3 Add the zinc powder to the solution in the other boiling tube. The blue colour of the copper(II) sulfate solution should fade and a brownish precipitate of copper metal should be seen.

Electrolysis

Electrolytes are substances that conduct electricity when dissolved in water or when melted. Acids like hydrochloric acid, bases like sodium hydroxide, and salts like sodium chloride are all electrolytes. Electrolytes are chemically changed when an electric current is passed through them. This process is called **electrolysis (Fig. 5.3)**.

Key definition

Electrolysis is the use of electric current to cause a chemical reaction.

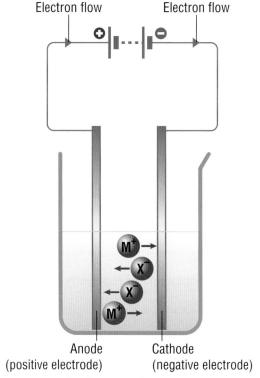

Fig. 5.3 *What happens during electrolysis*

Points to note

Oxidation occurs at the anode.

Reduction occurs at the cathode.

Experiment

Specified Demonstration (to be observed using an animation or video clip): Demonstration of ionic movement

During electrolysis of a solution, positive ions (cations) are attracted to the negative electrode (cathode) and negative ions (anions) are attracted to the positive electrode (anode). The coloured ions in this demonstration are:

$$copper(II) \ [Cu^{2+}_{(aq)}] - blue$$

$$chromate(VI) \ [CrO_4^{2-}_{(aq)}] - yellow$$

Procedure

1 Add urea to a solution of copper(II) chromate in 2 M hydrochloric acid. This is done to increase the density of the solution.

2 Add the resulting solution to a U-tube until it is about half full.

3 Add 2 M hydrochloric acid to each arm of the U-tube, taking care to avoid mixing the layers.

4 Complete setting up the apparatus as shown in the diagram.

5 The blue copper(II) ions should be observed moving towards the cathode, and at the same time the yellow chromate(VI) ions move towards the anode.

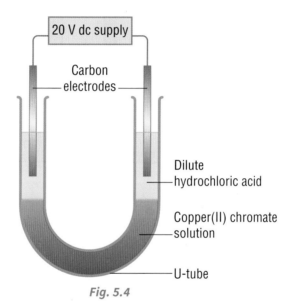

Fig. 5.4

Electrolysis demonstrations
Electrolysis of aqueous solutions

In the electrolysis of copper(II) sulfate solution using copper electrodes, copper at the anode is oxidised and dissolves, and copper is formed at the cathode.

Points to note

Electrolysis of aqueous copper(II) sulfate solution using copper electrodes

At the anode, copper is oxidised:

$$Cu_{(s)} \rightarrow Cu^{2+}_{(aq)} + 2e^-$$

At the cathode, copper ions are reduced:

$$Cu^{2+}_{(aq)} + 2e^- \rightarrow Cu_{(s)}$$

In the electrolysis of acidified water using inert electrodes, oxygen gas is formed at the anode and hydrogen gas is formed at the cathode (Fig. 5.5).

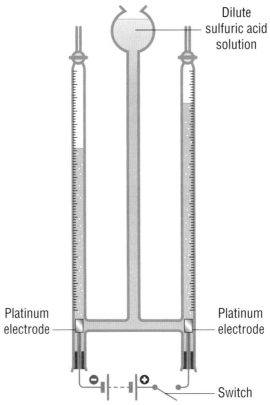

Dilute sulfuric acid solution

Platinum electrode

Platinum electrode

Switch

Fig. 5.5 Electrolysis of acidified water using a voltameter

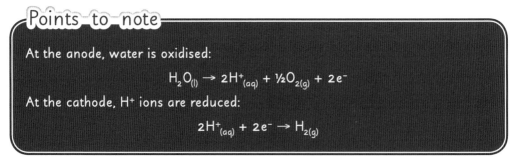

Points to note

At the anode, water is oxidised:

$$H_2O_{(l)} \rightarrow 2H^+_{(aq)} + \tfrac{1}{2}O_{2(g)} + 2e^-$$

At the cathode, H$^+$ ions are reduced:

$$2H^+_{(aq)} + 2e^- \rightarrow H_{2(g)}$$

Experiment

Specified Demonstration: Electrolysis of aqueous sodium sulfate solution using universal indicator

In the electrolysis of sodium sulfate solution using inert electrodes, oxygen gas is formed at the anode, and hydrogen gas is formed at the cathode. At the cathode, molecules of water are reduced, according to the equation:

$$2H_2O_{(l)} + 2e^- \rightarrow H_{2(g)} + 2OH^-_{(aq)}$$

At the anode, molecules of water are oxidised, according to the equation:

$$H_2O_{(l)} \rightarrow 2H^+_{(aq)} + \frac{1}{2}O_{2(g)} + 2e^-$$

Procedure

1 Add about 2 cm³ of universal indicator solution to 250 cm³ sodium sulfate solution. Stir well and fill the voltameter with this solution.

2 Switch on the power supply and increase the voltage to 10 V.

3 The green colour of the indicator should turn blue at the cathode because of the alkaline solution formed there, and red at the anode because of the acidic solution formed there.

Experiment

Specified Demonstration: Electrolysis of aqueous potassium iodide using phenolphthalein indicator

In the electrolysis of potassium iodide solution using inert electrodes, iodine is formed at the anode, and hydrogen gas is formed at the cathode.

At the cathode, molecules of water are reduced, according to the equation:

$$2H_2O_{(l)} + 2e^- \rightarrow H_{2(g)} + 2OH^-_{(aq)}$$

At the anode, the I⁻ ions are oxidised, according to the equation:

$$2I^-_{(aq)} \rightarrow I_{2(s)} + 2e^-$$

Procedure

1 Add about 10 drops of phenolphthalein indicator to 250 cm³ potassium iodide solution. Stir well and fill the voltameter with this solution.

2 Switch on the power supply and increase the voltage to 10 V.

3 A pink colour should be observed at the cathode because of the alkaline solution formed there. A brown colour at the anode shows that iodine is formed there.

Electroplating

In electroplating, a layer of a metal is put onto the surface of another metal. Cutlery made of nickel can be coated with silver by electroplating. This increases the value of the cutlery and improves its appearance.

Another example of electroplating is the coating of steel with chromium to improve its appearance and resistance to corrosion.

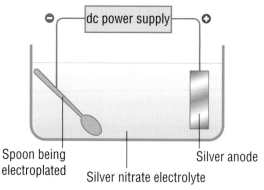

Spoon being electroplated

Silver nitrate electrolyte

Silver anode

Fig. 5.6 *Arrangement for plating a spoon with silver*

Copper is purified using impure copper as an anode and pure copper as a cathode, with acidified copper(II) sulfate used as the electrolyte.

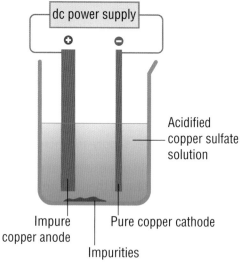

Acidified copper sulfate solution

Impure copper anode

Pure copper cathode

Impurities

Fig. 5.7 *Arrangement for purifying copper*

Table 5.3

Practical applications of electroplating
Chromium-plating of steel
Silver-plating of nickel (cutlery)
Purification of copper

Key-points!

- Oxidation is the loss of electrons.

- Reduction is the gain of electrons.

- An oxidising agent is a substance that allows oxidation to happen by gaining electrons itself.

- A reducing agent is a substance that allows reduction to happen by losing electrons itself.

- Electrolysis is the use of electric current to cause a chemical reaction.

- Electroplating is the coating of a metal onto the surface of another metal using electrolysis.

6 Ionic and Covalent Bonding

Chemical compounds

A **compound** is formed when two or more elements combine in a chemical reaction. For example, if hydrogen gas is burned in oxygen gas, the compound water is formed.

$$2H_{2(g)} + O_{2(g)} \rightarrow 2H_2O_{(l)}$$

Unlike elements, compounds can be broken down chemically into simpler substances, and ultimately to their elements.

Each compound has a fixed composition and it can be represented by a chemical formula, e.g. H_2O.

Hydrated substances contain molecules of water in definite proportions, usually locked into a crystal structure. Washing soda (hydrated sodium carbonate) is one example. It contains 10 parts of water to one part of sodium carbonate, so its formula is $Na_2CO_3.10H_2O$.

Water bound in this way is described as **water of crystallisation**. It can be driven off by heating to give the corresponding **anhydrous** compound.

$$Na_2CO_3.10H_2O_{(s)} \rightarrow Na_2CO_{3(s)} + 10H_2O_{(l)}$$

Key definition

Water of crystallisation is water chemically combined in definite proportions in a crystalline compound.

Noble gas electron configuration

The elements of Group 0 of the periodic table, the noble gases, are found to be very stable and unreactive compared with most other elements. This is due to the stability of their outer electronic configurations.

The uses of helium and argon are related to their chemical unreactivity.

- Helium is used in weather balloons and blimps, because it has a very low density, but unlike hydrogen it is not flammable.

- Electric light bulbs are filled with argon to prevent the tungsten filament from evaporating or reacting.

Table 6.1 shows the distribution of electrons in the main energy levels of noble gas atoms.

Table 6.1

Atom	Electron arrangement
Helium (He)	2
Neon (Ne)	2, 8
Argon (Ar)	2, 8, 8
Krypton (Kr)	2, 8, 18, 8

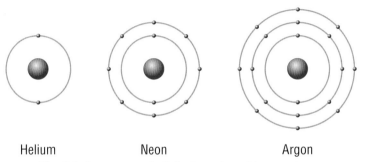

Helium   Neon   Argon
Fig. 6.1 Arrangement of electrons in noble gas atoms

Apart from helium, whose outer level (and only occupied level) needs just two electrons to be filled, each of the other noble gases has eight electrons – an octet – in its outer level.

Given the relative unreactivity of the noble gases, it is clear that having eight electrons in the outer level, or having a filled outer level, is a stable arrangement of electrons.

Octet rule and exceptions

The octet rule states that atoms on reaction tend to reach an electron arrangement with eight electrons in the outermost energy level. Elements achieve these stable noble gas configurations by losing, gaining or sharing electrons when they react to form compounds.

For example, in the formation of sodium chloride from sodium, the sodium atom – whose electron arrangement is 2, 8, 1 – loses an electron to chlorine, ending up as the sodium ion Na^+ with an arrangement of 2, 8.

On the other hand, chlorine gains an electron from sodium and its electron arrangement goes from 2, 8, 7 in the neutral atom to 2, 8, 8 in the chloride ion. In other words, both elements obey the octet rule and end up with eight electrons in the outer level.

Question

6.1 Use the octet rule and the electron structures of magnesium and bromine to predict the formula of magnesium bromide.

Answer

The electronic structure of magnesium is: Mg 2, 8, 2

The electronic structure of bromine is: Br 2, 8, 18, 7

To obey the octet rule and end up with eight electrons in the outer level, magnesium loses two electrons to form the magnesium ion Mg^{++}, and bromine gains one electron to form the bromide ion, Br^-. So that the total charge is zero, two bromine atoms are required, gaining one electron each. Consequently, the formula of magnesium bromide is $MgBr_2$.

A similar method is used to predict the formulas of compounds of complex ions. It is not possible to use the octet rule to work out the charges on such ions. The information required is shown in Table 6.2.

Table 6.2 Formulas of complex ions

Anion	Formula
Hydroxide	OH^-
Carbonate	CO_3^{2-}
Nitrate	NO_3^-
Hydrogencarbonate	HCO_3^-
Sulfite	SO_3^{2-}
Sulfate	SO_4^{2-}
Phosphate	PO_4^{3-}
Dichromate(VI)	$Cr_2O_7^{2-}$
Ethanoate	CH_3COO^-
Ammonium	NH_4^+
Manganate(VII)	MnO_4^-

Question

6.2 What is the formula of sodium carbonate?

Answer

The electronic structure of sodium is: Na 2, 8, 1

The sodium ion is Na^+ and the carbonate ion is CO_3^{2-}. Two sodium ions and one carbonate ion are required so that the total charge is zero. Thus, the formula is Na_2CO_3.

Exceptions to the octet rule

There are several exceptions to the octet rule:

1 Hydrogen, lithium, beryllium and boron tend to reach the electronic structure of helium.

2 The d-block elements do not usually obey the octet rule.

3 The rule works in some cases for sulfur and phosphorus, but not in others.

Valency

Valency gives a measure of the combining power of an atom. For example, a carbon atom forms four bonds when it reacts, so it has a valency of 4.

> **Key definition**
>
> The **valency** of an element is the number of bonds each atom of the element forms when it reacts.

The valency of an element can usually be worked out by calculating the number of electrons that its atoms would need to lose or gain to attain a stable electronic structure such as that of the nearest noble gas in the periodic table.

Table 6.3 Valencies of s-block and p-block elements

Group number	Valency	Group number	Valency
I	1	V	3
II	2	VI	2
III	3	VII	1
IV	4	0	0

Transition elements have variable valencies, some of which are shown in Table 6.4.

Table 6.4 Valencies of transition elements

Element	Valency
Chromium	2, 3, 6
Manganese	2, 3, 4, 6, 7
Iron	2, 3, 6
Copper	1, 2

Question

6.3 What is the formula of water, a compound containing oxygen and hydrogen only?

Answer

Oxygen has a valency of 2, while hydrogen has a valency of 1. An oxygen atom will therefore form two bonds, and hydrogen will form one bond. Two hydrogen atoms are therefore required to bond with one atom of oxygen.

Fig. 6.2

Thus, the formula of water is H_2O.

Ionic bonding

When atoms combine together to form compounds, there is a change in the arrangement of the electrons in the outermost energy level of each atom. Some of these electrons form links called chemical bonds between the atoms. Usually the new arrangement is more stable than the original situation.

Ionic bonds are usually found in compounds that contain metals combined with non-metals. The word **ion** is used to describe any species that has unequal numbers of protons and electrons, and so carries an electric charge. Like atoms, ions are extremely small.

Metal atoms lose one or more electrons and become positively charged ions or **cations**. A sodium ion (Na^+) is formed when a sodium atom loses one electron. The ion has an overall charge of +1 because it has 11 protons but only 10 electrons. In terms of electron structure, the change is:

$$Na\ 2, 8, 1 - 1e^- \rightarrow Na^+\ 2, 8$$

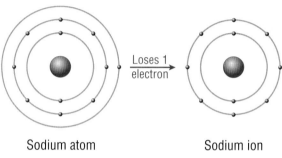

Sodium atom   Loses 1 electron   Sodium ion

Fig. 6.3

Non-metal atoms gain one or more electrons and become negatively charged ions or **anions**. A chloride ion (Cl^-) is formed when a chlorine atom gains one electron. The ion has an overall charge of –1 because it has 17 protons and 18 electrons. In terms of electron structure, the change is:

$$Cl\ 2, 8, 7 + 1e^- \rightarrow Cl^-\ 2, 8, 8$$

In order that an ionic bond can be formed, as between sodium and chlorine, electrons are **transferred** from the metal atoms to the non-metal atoms during the chemical reaction, forming ions.

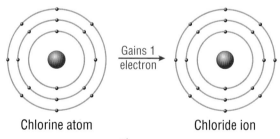

Chlorine atom   Gains 1 electron   Chloride ion

Fig. 6.4

Key definition

An **ionic bond** is the electrostatic force of attraction between oppositely charged ions.

6.4 Draw a dot and cross diagram to show the formation of an ionic bond between potassium and fluorine.

Answer

$$K^{\bullet} \quad + \quad {}^{x}_{xx}\overset{xx}{F}{}^{x}_{x} \longrightarrow [K]^{+} \quad + \quad \left[{}^{x}_{xx}\overset{xx}{\bullet}{F}{}^{x}_{x} \right]^{-}$$

(2, 8, 8, 1)	(2, 7)	(2, 8, 8)	(2, 8)
Potassium atom	Fluorine atom	Potassium ion	Fluoride ion

Fig. 6.5

The charges on the potassium and fluoride ions are equal but opposite. They balance each other and the resulting formula of potassium fluoride is KF.

Ionic crystal structure

In ionic bonding, the oppositely charged ions attract each other to form a rigid three-dimensional lattice. Each ion in the lattice is surrounded by others of opposite charge.

Fig. 6.6 shows the structure of a small part of a single sodium chloride crystal. Many millions of sodium and chloride ions are arranged in this way in a single crystal of sodium chloride to make up a giant ionic structure. It may be deduced that ions are extremely small in size.

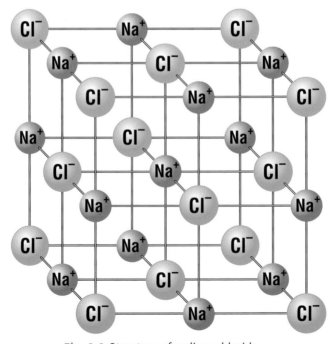

Fig. 6.6 Structure of sodium chloride

In a NaCl crystal, each sodium ion in the lattice is surrounded by six chloride ions, and each chloride ion is surrounded by six sodium ions. However, not all ionic substances have the same crystalline structure as sodium chloride.

Characteristics of ionic substances

- Ionic substances have high melting points and high boiling points, and are hard solids at room temperature.

- They cannot conduct electricity in the solid state because the ions are held tightly in the crystal and are not free to move.

- Most ionic substances dissolve in water to some extent.

- Ionic substances conduct electricity when molten or in aqueous solution – they are electrolytes.

Ionic materials in everyday life

- Salt tablets are taken to replace salt lost from the body by sweating.

- Brine, a solution of sodium chloride, has long been used for curing bacon. This effectively is a preservation process.

- Fluoridation of water supplies to prevent tooth decay is carried out by adding a salt of fluorine such as sodium fluoride (NaF) or sodium fluorosilicate (Na_2SiF_6).

Tests for anions

 **Experiment**

Mandatory Experiment 6.1: Tests for anions in aqueous solutions: chloride (Cl^-), carbonate (CO_3^{2-}), nitrate (NO_3^-), sulfate (SO_4^{2-}), phosphate (PO_4^{3-}), sulfite (SO_3^{2-}), hydrogencarbonate (HCO_3^-)

(a) To test for the carbonate (CO_3^{2-}) and hydrogencarbonate (HCO_3^-) anions

Carbonate and hydrogencarbonate ions both react with dilute hydrochloric acid to produce carbon dioxide gas.

$$\text{(i) } NaHCO_{3(aq)} + HCl_{(aq)} \rightarrow NaCl_{(aq)} + H_2O_{(l)} + CO_{2(g)}$$

$$\text{(ii) } Na_2CO_{3(aq)} + 2HCl_{(aq)} \rightarrow 2NaCl_{(aq)} + H_2O_{(l)} + CO_{2(g)}$$

To distinguish between carbonate and hydrogencarbonate ions, a solution of magnesium sulfate is added. Since magnesium carbonate is insoluble in water, a white precipitate indicates that the salt is a carbonate (Fig.6.7).

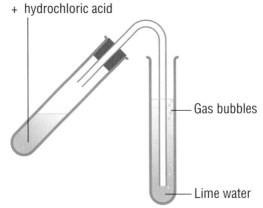

Hydrogencarbonate (or carbonate) solution + hydrochloric acid

Gas bubbles

Lime water

Fig. 6.7

$$Na_2CO_{3(aq)} + MgSO_{4(aq)} \rightarrow Na_2SO_{4(aq)} + MgCO_{3(s)}$$

The absence of a precipitate indicates a hydrogencarbonate because magnesium hydrogencarbonate is soluble in water:

$$2NaHCO_{3(aq)} + MgSO_{4(aq)} \rightarrow Na_2SO_{4(aq)} + Mg(HCO_3)_{2(aq)}$$

However, on heating this solution, a white precipitate is formed because hydrogencarbonates decompose into carbonates on heating:

$$Mg(HCO_3)_{2(aq)} \rightarrow MgCO_{3(s)} + H_2O_{(l)} + CO_{2(g)}$$

(b) To test for the sulfite (SO_3^{2-}) and sulfate (SO_4^{2-}) anions

Both sulfite and sulfate ions react with barium chloride solution, producing white precipitates of barium sulfite and barium sulfate, respectively.

$$(i)\ Na_2SO_{3(aq)} + BaCl_{2(aq)} \rightarrow 2NaCl_{(aq)} + BaSO_{3(s)}$$

$$(ii)\ Na_2SO_{4(aq)} + BaCl_{2(aq)} \rightarrow 2NaCl_{(aq)} + BaSO_{4(s)}$$

Barium sulfite reacts and dissolves in hydrochloric acid but barium sulfate does not.

$$BaSO_{3(s)} + 2HCl_{(aq)} \rightarrow BaCl_{2(aq)} + H_2O_{(l)} + SO_{2(g)}$$

This reaction is used to distinguish between sulfite and sulfate ions.

(c) To test for the chloride (Cl^-) anion

Solutions containing chloride ions react with silver nitrate solution, producing a white precipitate of silver chloride.

$$NaCl_{(aq)} + AgNO_{3(aq)} \rightarrow NaNO_{3(aq)} + AgCl_{(s)}$$

This precipitate dissolves when dilute ammonia solution is added.

(d) To test for the nitrate (NO$_3^-$) anion

Solutions containing nitrate ions react with a mixture of iron(II) sulfate solution and concentrated sulfuric acid. When concentrated sulfuric acid is added to a mixture of nitrate and iron(II) sulfate solutions, a brown ring develops slowly where the sulfuric acid layer and the layer containing the mixture meet (Fig. 6.8).

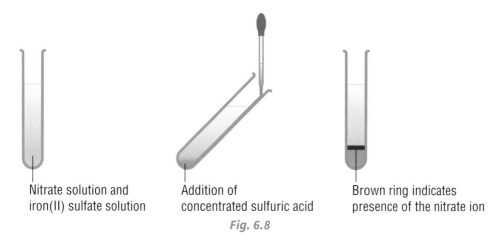

Nitrate solution and iron(II) sulfate solution

Addition of concentrated sulfuric acid

Brown ring indicates presence of the nitrate ion

Fig. 6.8

(e) To test for the phosphate (PO$_4^{3-}$) anion

Solutions containing phosphate ions react on heating with an ammonium molybdate reagent, in the presence of concentrated nitric acid, forming a yellow precipitate. This precipitate dissolves when ammonia solution is added.

Table 6.5 Tests and results for anions in aqueous solutions

Anion	Test	Result
Carbonate and hydrogencarbonate	Add dilute HCl to carbonate or hydrogencarbonate solution	Gas produced that turns limewater milky
Carbonate	Add MgSO$_{4(aq)}$ to carbonate solution	White precipitate
Hydrogencarbonate	Add MgSO$_{4(aq)}$ to hydrogencarbonate solution	White precipitate **on heating**
Sulfate	Add BaCl$_{2(aq)}$ to sulfate solution	White precipitate that is **insoluble** in dilute HCl solution
Sulfite	Add BaCl$_{2(aq)}$ to sulfite solution	White precipitate that is **soluble** in dilute HCl solution

Chloride	Add $AgNO_{3(aq)}$ to chloride solution	White precipitate that is **soluble** in dilute NH_3 solution
Nitrate	Mix nitrate solution with cold $FeSO_{4(aq)}$. Pour concentrated H_2SO_4 down inside of test tube	Brown ring forms
Phosphate	Add ammonium molybdate reagent and a few drops of concentrated HNO_3, and heat gently	Yellow precipitate, which is **soluble** in ammonia solution

Covalent bonding

When atoms combine chemically other than by ionic bonding, **molecules** are formed. These may consist of atoms of the same element, such as the hydrogen molecule (H_2), or of atoms of different elements, such as the sulfuric acid molecule (H_2SO_4). Molecules, like atoms, are minute.

Atoms can gain the stability of the noble gas configuration by **sharing** electron pairs in their outer levels. Each shared pair of electrons is regarded as one **covalent bond**. Shared electrons count as part of the outer level of both atoms of the bond.

The simplest example of this type of bonding is the hydrogen molecule (H_2). A hydrogen atom has one electron. In order to obtain a full outer level and gain the electron structure of the nearest noble gas, each of two hydrogen atoms share a pair of electrons, and a covalent bond is formed. Since there is just one shared pair of electrons, this is a **single bond**.

$$H^{\times} \ + \ \cdot H \ \longrightarrow \ H \overset{\times}{\cdot} H$$

Fig. 6.9

Key definition

A **covalent bond** is formed when two atoms share a pair of electrons.

Question

6.5 Draw a dot and cross diagram of the fluorine molecule (F_2).

Answer

The fluorine molecule (F_2) is another example of a single covalent bond between two atoms of the same element.

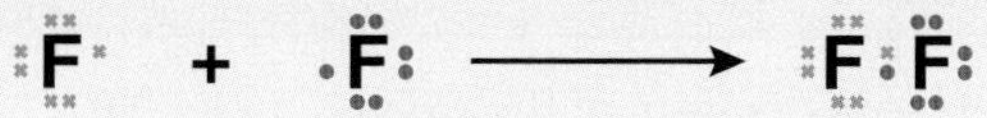

$$\overset{\times\times}{\underset{\times\times}{\times}}\!F\!\overset{\cdot}{\cdot} \quad + \quad \cdot\overset{\cdot\cdot}{\underset{\cdot\cdot}{F}}\!\!\cdot \quad \longrightarrow \quad \overset{\times\times}{\underset{\times\times}{\times}}\!F\!\overset{\cdot}{\cdot}\!F\!\overset{\cdot\cdot}{\underset{\cdot\cdot}{}}$$

Fig. 6.10

Since fluorine atoms have seven electrons in their outer levels, this time the octet rule is obeyed and each atom gains the electron structure of neon.

Question

6.6 Draw a dot and cross diagram of the hydrogen sulfide molecule (H_2S).

Answer

Hydrogen sulfide is an example of a molecule with three atoms, where both hydrogens are bonded to the sulfur.

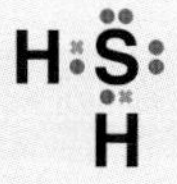

Fig. 6.11

Since the sulfur atom has six electrons in its outer level, it needs to gain two electrons to reach the electronic structure of argon. It does this by sharing electrons with each of two hydrogen atoms. The hydrogen atoms reach the configuration of helium in the process. The resultant hydrogen sulfide molecule has **two single covalent bonds**.

Shared electron pairs that form covalent bonds are called **bond pairs**. Pairs of electrons not involved in bonding are called **lone pairs** or non-bonding pairs. A hydrogen sulfide molecule has two bond pairs of electrons and two lone pairs of electrons.

Fig. 6.12

Double and triple covalent bonds

Some atoms form covalent bonds by sharing two or three pairs of electrons. An example of a molecule with two shared pairs is the oxygen molecule (O_2). Since an oxygen atom has six electrons in the outer level, it needs to gain two electrons, or a share of two electrons, to reach the electron structure of neon. Two oxygen atoms share two pairs of electrons to reach the octet.

Question

6.7 Draw a dot and cross diagram of the oxygen molecule (O_2).

Answer

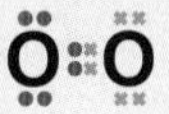

Fig. 6.13

A **double covalent bond** is formed in which two pairs of electrons are shared.

The double bond in the oxygen molecule can also be represented as $O = O$.

When three electron pairs are shared to form a bond, a triple covalent bond is formed. The nitrogen molecule is an example in which this type of bonding is found. Since a nitrogen atom has five electrons in the outer level, it needs to gain a share of three more electrons to reach the electron structure of neon. Two nitrogen atoms share three electrons each to reach the octet.

Question

6.8 Draw a dot and cross diagram of the nitrogen molecule (N_2).

Answer

:N⦂⦂⦂N:

Fig. 6.14

A **triple covalent bond** is formed in which three pairs of electron are shared.

The triple bond in the nitrogen molecule can also be represented as $N \equiv N$.

A single covalent bond between two atoms is called a σ (sigma) bond. A σ bond is always formed between two atoms in a molecule if they are covalently bonded.

Overlapping p orbitals   Molecular orbital

Fig. 6.15 *Sigma bonding by end-on overlap of p orbitals*

In double or triple bonds, sideways overlap is possible between two p atomic orbitals, each containing one electron. In this case, a π (pi) bond is formed.

An example of a π bond is found in the oxygen molecule (O_2). The $O = O$ double bond, like all double bonds, consists of one δ bond and one π bond. Triple bonds, such as that in the nitrogen molecule ($N \equiv N$), consist of one δ bond and two π bonds. Of the two types of covalent bond, δ bonds are stronger.

> ## Key definition
>
> A **sigma bond** is a covalent bond between two atoms formed by end-on overlap of orbitals.

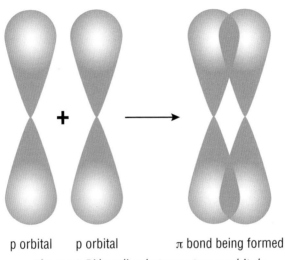

p orbital   p orbital π bond being formed

Fig. 6.16 Pi bonding between two p orbitals

> ## Key definition
>
> A **pi bond** is a covalent bond between two atoms formed by sideways overlap of orbitals.

Polar and non-polar covalent bonding

Molecules such as hydrogen (H_2), oxygen (O_2), nitrogen (N_2), chlorine (Cl_2) and bromine (Br_2) each contain only one type of atom. Consequently, the nuclei of the atoms attract the shared electrons in the covalent bond equally. The bond is a pure covalent bond and is said to be **non-polar**.

However, most covalent bonds are formed between atoms that are quite different from each other.

Usually, different types of atoms will attract the electrons unequally in a covalent bond. The atom with the lesser share of electrons will become slightly positively charged, indicated by δ^+, and the other atom will become slightly negatively charged, indicated by δ^-. In the hydrogen chloride molecule (HCl), for example, the chlorine atom has a greater attraction for the shared pair of electrons than the hydrogen atom.

Consequently, the molecule is represented as follows:

$$H^{\delta+} - Cl^{\delta-}$$

Key definition

A **polar covalent bond** is a covalent bond in which there is unequal sharing of electrons.

Experiment

Specified Demonstration: Polarity test for liquids using a charged plastic rod

If a liquid contains polar molecules, a flow of that liquid from a burette will be attracted to a charged polythene rod, resulting in the flow bending.

Procedure
1 Add 25 cm³ of the liquid under investigation to a clamped dry burette.

2 Place a beaker under the jet.

3 Charge the polythene rod with the cloth by rubbing it.

4 Open the burette tap and allow the liquid to run into the beaker.

5 Bring the charged rod close to the liquid stream.

6 If the liquid is polar, the liquid stream bends towards the rod.

Characteristics of covalent substances

- Most covalent substances are liquids or gases at room temperature. Those that are solids have low melting and boiling points.

- In general, they do not conduct electricity when molten or in solution. However, some molecules such as HCl react with water to form ions and the solution formed can then conduct electricity.

- Most covalent substances do not dissolve readily in water. However, polar covalent compounds have some ionic character and are more likely to form aqueous solutions.

Polar and non-polar materials in everyday life

Table 6.6

Polar	Non-polar
Water (for washing clothes)	Cooking oil
Glucose (in Lucozade)	Petrol

 Experiment

Mandatory Experiment 6.2: Recrystallisation of benzoic acid and determination of its melting point

(a) Recrystallisation

An impure solid may be purified by recrystallisation.

Procedure

1 Flute a filter paper, place it in a funnel, and keep it warm and moist by standing it over a source of steam.

2 Place about 1 g of the impure benzoic acid sample in a small beaker and dissolve it in the minimum amount of boiling water.

3 Pour the boiling solution through the filter paper in small portions, collecting the filtrate in a warm conical flask. If any crystals form in the filter paper, add a little boiling water to dissolve them.

4 Transfer the filtrate to a warm beaker, and evaporate off the water until traces of crystal begin to appear on the sides of the beaker. Allow the filtrate to cool to room temperature.

5 Carefully filter the recrystallised mixture, by vacuum filtration if possible.

6 Wash the crystals with small portions of ice-cold deionised water and allow to dry.

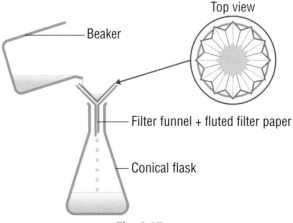

Top view

Beaker

Filter funnel + fluted filter paper

Conical flask

Fig. 6.17

(b) Melting point determination

The melting point range of a substance is the narrow band of temperatures between the temperature at which melting begins and the temperature at which the entire solid has liquefied.

The melting point range of an impure substance is lower and wider than that of a pure sample of the same substance.

Using an aluminium block

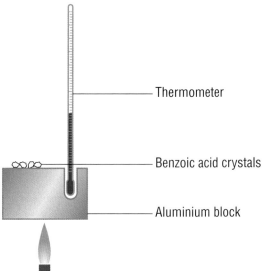

Thermometer

Benzoic acid crystals

Aluminium block

Bunsen burner

Fig. 6.18

Procedure
1 Place a few crystals of the substance to be melted on the surface of a clean aluminium block into which a thermometer has been placed.

2 Use a Bunsen burner or hot plate to heat the block slowly.

3 Record the melting point range, that is, the temperature at which melting begins and the temperature at which it ends.

Question

6.9 2.4 g of impure benzoic acid was recrystallised and, after drying, 2.1 g of the purified acid was obtained. What was the percentage yield of purified benzoic acid?

Answer

Percentage yield = 2.1 × 100% / 2.4 = 87.5%

Experiment

Specified Demonstration: Testing solubility of ionic and covalent substances in different solvents

In general, ionic or polar covalent substances dissolve in polar solvents such as water. Non-polar substances dissolve in non-polar solvents such as cyclohexane.

1 Measure 3 cm³ of water into each of a number of test tubes.

2 Place a spatula tipfull of one of the solid substances into one of the test tubes.

3 Stopper and shake. Note whether the substance has dissolved or not.

4 Repeat this procedure for the other solid substances.

5 Repeat this procedure for all of the solid substances using cyclohexane as a solvent.

6 Repeat this procedure for the liquids being tested using water and cyclohexane, respectively, as solvents.

7 Record your results, indicating whether the solute and solvent are polar or non-polar in each case.

Electronegativity

The ability of an atom in a covalent bond to attract the shared electrons to itself is given by the atom's **electronegativity** value.

On the Pauling scale of electronegativity, which runs from 0 to 4, the higher the electronegativity value an atom has, the better it is at attracting the shared electrons towards itself. As can be seen in the periodic table (Fig. 6.19), electronegativities increase from left to right across a period, and decrease from the top to the bottom of a group.

Key definition

Electronegativity is the relative attraction of an atom for shared pairs of electrons in a covalent bond.

1 Down a group

On going down a group, adding an extra level of electrons shields the outer electrons from the nucleus, so that even though the nuclear charge is increasing, the electrons are not attracted as strongly. This, along with an increase in atomic radius, results in a decrease in electronegativity.

2 Across a period

Electronegativity increases across a period as the atomic number – the number of protons in the nucleus – increases and atomic radius decreases. The larger the nuclear charge and the smaller the atomic radius, the greater the attraction for the electron pair in a covalent bond.

Fig. 6.19 Electronegativities of the elements

1 H 2.1																	2 He --
3 Li 1.0	4 Be 1.5											5 B 2.0	6 C 2.5	7 N 3.0	8 O 3.5	9 F 4.0	10 Ne --
11 Na 0.9	12 Mg 1.2											13 Al 1.5	14 Si 1.8	15 P 2.1	16 S 2.5	17 Cl 3.0	18 Ar --
19 K 0.8	20 Ca 1.0	21 Sc 1.3	22 Ti 1.5	23 V 1.6	24 Cr 1.6	25 Mn 1.5	26 Fe 1.8	27 Co 1.8	28 Ni 1.8	29 Cu 1.9	30 Zn 1.6	31 Ga 1.6	32 Ge 1.8	33 As 2.0	34 Se 2.4	35 Br 2.8	36 Kr --

Predicting the nature of bonds

Electronegativity differences can be used to predict the type of bond between two atoms.

1 If the electronegativity difference is zero or very small, the bond can be regarded as being non-polar covalent. For example, the H–H bond in the hydrogen molecule (H_2) and the C–S bond in carbon disulfide (CS_2) are both non-polar.

2 In cases where the electronegativity difference is greater than 1.7, the degree of ionic character is greater than the degree of covalent character, so the bond is predicted to be ionic. For example, the bond in sodium chloride (NaCl), where the electronegativity difference is 3.0 – 0.9 = 2.1, is ionic.

3 The bond is predicted to be polar covalent if the electronegativity difference is less than 1.7. For example, the bond in hydrogen chloride (HCl) is predicted to be polar covalent because the electronegativity difference is 3.0 – 2.1 = 0.9.

Question

6.10 Use electronegativity values to predict the type of bond in (i) NaF, (ii) CO_2, (iii) PH_3 and (iv) H_2S.

Answer

(i) The electronegativity difference between sodium and fluorine is 4.0 – 0.9 = 3.1, which is >1.7. The bonding in NaF is predicted to be ionic.

(ii) The electronegativity difference between carbon and oxygen is 3.5 – 2.5 = 1.0, which is <1.7 but >0. The bonding in CO_2 is predicted to be polar covalent.

(iii) The electronegativity difference between phosphorus and hydrogen is 2.1 – 2.1 = 0. The bonding in PH_3 is predicted to be non-polar covalent.

(iv) The electronegativity difference between hydrogen and sulfur is 2.5 – 2.1 = 0.4, which is <1.7 but not much greater than 0. The bonding in H_2S is predicted to be weakly polar covalent.

Key-points!

- Water of crystallisation is water chemically combined in definite proportions in a crystalline compound.

- The valency of an element is the number of bonds each atom of the element forms when it reacts.

- An ionic bond is the electrostatic force of attraction between oppositely charged ions.

- A covalent bond is formed when two atoms share a pair of electrons.

- A sigma bond is a covalent bond between two atoms formed by end-on overlap of orbitals.

- A pi bond is a covalent bond between two atoms formed by sideways overlap of orbitals.

- A polar covalent bond is a covalent bond in which there is unequal sharing of electrons.

- Electronegativity is the relative attraction of an atom for shared pairs of electrons in a covalent bond.

Shapes of Molecules and Intermolecular Forces   7

Learning objectives

In this chapter you will learn about:

1 Shapes of molecules

2 Electron pair repulsion theory

3 Relationship between symmetry and polarity

4 Intramolecular bonding and intermolecular forces

Shapes of molecules

Molecules are formed when atoms are joined together by covalent bonds. The arrangement in space of the atoms dictates the shape of the molecule.

Fig. 7.1 Beryllium chloride molecules are linear

Diatomic molecules consist of just two atoms, which can be connected by a straight line, so the shape is said to be **linear**: for example, oxygen (O_2), hydrogen (H_2) and hydrogen chloride (HCl). It is possible for molecules with more than two atoms to be linear also, e.g. beryllium chloride ($BeCl_2$).

If a molecule with three atoms is not linear like beryllium chloride, each atom must be out of line with the other two. Such molecules are angular or **V-shaped**, e.g. water (H_2O).

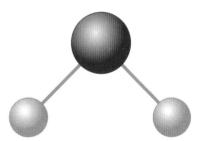

Fig. 7.2 Water molecules are V-shaped

Two possibilities arise in molecules with four atoms, where one is the central atom to which the other three are bonded. If the four atoms lie in the same plane with the three outlying atoms pointing towards the vertices of an equilateral triangle, the shape is **trigonal planar**, e.g. boron trifluoride (BF_3).

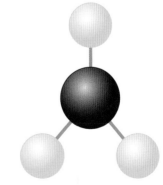

Fig. 7.3 Boron trifluoride molecules are trigonal planar

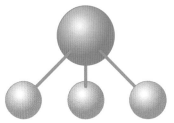

If the central atom is above the plane of the other three, but the arrangement is otherwise similar, the shape is **pyramidal**, e.g. ammonia (NH_3).

Fig 7.4 Ammonia molecules are pyramidal

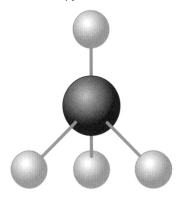

In molecules with four atoms joined to a central atom, with the four outlying atoms arranged as far from each other as possible, they are directed towards the corners of a regular tetrahedron. This shape is **tetrahedral**, e.g. methane (CH_4).

Fig. 7.5 Methane molecules are tetrahedral

Electron pair repulsion theory

Molecules with bonding pairs only

The beryllium hydride molecule (BeH_2) has two hydrogen atoms bonded to the central beryllium atom. There are two bonding pairs of electrons in the valence shell of beryllium. These electron pairs repel each other so as to get as far apart as possible.

The result is a linear arrangement of electron pairs, so the molecule has a **linear** shape.

$$H : Be : H$$

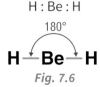

Fig. 7.6

The bond angle – $\angle HBeH$ – is 180°.

The electronic structure for the boron trifluoride molecule is shown in Fig. 7.7.

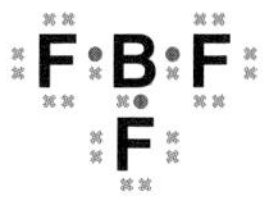

Fig. 7.7

There are three bonding pairs in the valence shell of boron. The furthest apart that three electron pairs can be arranged is when they are directed towards the vertices of an equilateral triangle.

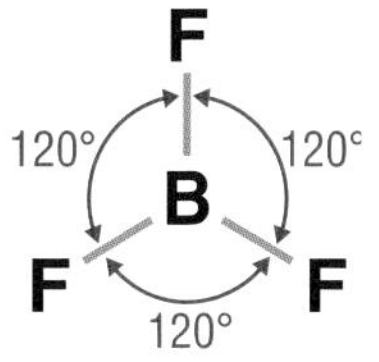

The result is a trigonal arrangement of electron pairs, so the molecule has a **trigonal planar** shape.

Each bond angle (∠FBF) is 120°.

Fig. 7.8

A methane molecule (CH_4) has four bonding pairs (shown in Fig. 7.9):

The mutual repulsion causes them to have a tetrahedral arrangement. Thus, the methane molecule has a **tetrahedral** shape.

Each bond angle (∠HCH) is 109.5°.

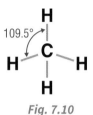

Fig. 7.9

In all molecules containing two, three or four bonding pairs only, the arrangement of the electron pairs can be predicted or explained by counting the number of these pairs.

Fig. 7.10

Table 7.1

Number of electron pairs	Arrangement of electron pairs	Bond angle	Shape of molecule	Example
2	Linear	180°	Linear	BeH_2
3	Trigonal planar	120°	Trigonal planar	BF_3
4	Tetrahedral	109.5°	Tetrahedral	CH_4

Molecules with both lone pairs and bonding pairs

The order of strength of repulsions between electron pairs is as follows:

lone pair: lone pair > lone pair: bonding pair > bonding pair: bonding pair

In ammonia (NH_3), the valence shell of nitrogen contains four electron pairs – three bonding pairs and one lone pair. The presence of four electron pairs indicates a tetrahedral arrangement. However, the presence of the lone pair causes the bond angle to be about 107° rather than the expected 109.5°.

Fig. 7.11 Water

Fig. 7.12 Ammonia

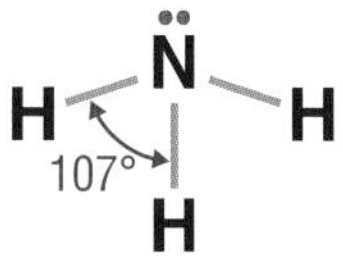

Fig. 7.13

Since a lone pair rather than an atom occupies one of the corners of the tetrahedron, the shape of the molecule is **pyramidal**.

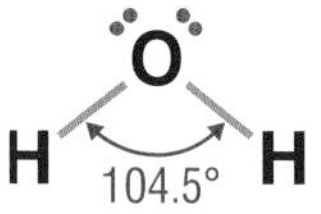

Fig. 7.14

In the water molecule, there are two bonding pairs and two lone pairs in the valence shell of the central oxygen atom. The distortion is thus greater than in the case of ammonia, so the expected tetrahedral angle in the arrangement of electron pairs is reduced to 104.5°. Since lone pairs rather than atoms occupy two of the corners of the tetrahedron, the shape of the molecule is **V-shaped**.

Table 7.2

Molecule	Number of electron pairs	Number of lone pairs	Arrangement of electron pairs	Bond angle	Shape of molecule
NH_3	4	1	Distorted tetrahedral	107°	Pyramidal
H_2O	4	2	Distorted tetrahedral	104.5°	V-shaped

Table 7.3 summarises the relationship between the shape of a molecule and the number and types of electron pairs around the central atom.

Table 7.3

Number of electron pairs around the central atom	Shape of molecule	Example
2 bonding pairs	Linear	BeH_2
3 bonding pairs	Trigonal planar	BF_3
4 bonding pairs	Tetrahedral	CH_4
3 bonding pairs and 1 lone pair	Pyramidal	NH_3
2 bonding pairs and 2 lone pairs	V-shaped	H_2O

Relationship between symmetry and polarity

Coinciding centres of positive and negative charge

Sometimes a molecule can be non-polar overall, even though the individual bonds are polar. This occurs when the centre of positive charge coincides with the centre of negative charge.

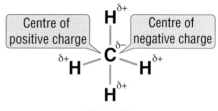

Fig. 7.15

Each C–H bond in methane is slightly polar, with the carbon atom having a partial negative charge and each hydrogen atom a partial positive charge. The central carbon atom is the centre of negative charge, and since the molecule has a perfect tetrahedral shape, it is also the centre of positive charge. That is, the centre of positive charge coincides with the centre of negative charge and the molecule is non-polar.

Separated centres of positive and negative charge

In the case of the ammonia molecule, which has a pyramidal shape, the nitrogen atom at the apex of the pyramid is the centre of negative charge. The centre of positive charge is at the geometrical centre of the three hydrogen atoms that form an equilateral triangle at the base of the pyramid. Thus, the centres of positive and negative charge are separated, resulting in a polar molecule.

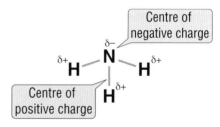

Fig. 7.16

Intramolecular bonding and intermolecular forces

Intramolecular bonding means the bonding **within** the molecule that holds the atoms together. An example is the pure covalent bond holding the two atoms of hydrogen together in a molecule of hydrogen gas.

Intermolecular forces mean forces **between** molecules. Table 7.4 shows the types of intermolecular force and the kind of substance in which these forces are found.

Table 7.4 Intermolecular forces and substances

Intermolecular forces	Type of substance
van der Waals forces	Non-polar and polar
Hydrogen bonding	Containing N–H, O–H or H–F bonds
Dipole–dipole interactions	Polar

Van der Waals forces

Van der Waals forces are weak attractive forces caused by the movement of electrons within a molecule. In the non-polar hydrogen molecule (H_2), for example, the only pair of electrons present is shared equally between the two hydrogen atoms. Electron movement within the bond may result in them both being nearer to one atom than the other at a particular point in time. This creates a temporary polarity – called a **temporary dipole** – in the molecule.

$$H^{\delta+} - H^{\delta-}$$

If two molecules with similar temporary dipoles happen to be orientated with opposite charges directed at each other, an attractive force will exist between the two molecules.

$$H^{\delta+} - H^{\delta-} \text{ ------ } H^{\delta+} - H^{\delta-}$$

Another possibility is that a temporary dipole in one molecule will induce a similar dipole in a neighbouring molecule, with a result similar to the above. The combined effect of these temporary and induced dipoles is to produce weak attractive forces – van der Waals forces – between neighbouring molecules, resulting in increased boiling points.

The greater the number of electrons in a molecule, the greater the number of possible temporary dipoles, and the greater the intermolecular attraction. This explains why oxygen gas (with 16 electrons per molecule) has a higher boiling point than hydrogen (with only 2 electrons per molecule).

Dipole–dipole interactions between polar molecules

Dipole–dipole interactions between polar molecules are another example of intermolecular forces, with similar effects such as higher than expected boiling points. They differ from van der Waals forces in that the dipoles are permanent due to the polarity in the molecule. Because they are permanent, they are stronger than van der Waals forces.

Ethene (C_2H_4) ($M_r = 28$) and methanal (HCHO) ($M_r = 30$) would be expected to have similar boiling points due to the similar size of their relative molecular masses. However, HCHO is polar and the consequent dipole–dipole attractions cause a much higher boiling point than that of C_2H_4.

These dipole–dipole attractions must be overcome when liquid methanal boils.

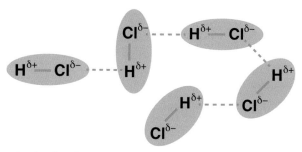

Fig. 7.17 *Dipole–dipole interactions between hydrogen chloride molecules*

Hydrogen bonding

In water molecules, the O–H bond is highly polar due to the large electronegativity difference between oxygen and hydrogen. Oxygen carries a partial negative charge and hydrogen carries a partial positive charge. Consequently, an oxygen atom will have a strong attraction for hydrogen atoms on neighbouring molecules, and vice versa.

These strong intermolecular forces cause a much higher than expected boiling point in water, 373 K. Hydrogen bonding is also the main intermolecular force that holds molecules of water together in ice crystals.

Hydrogen bonding is also evident in ammonia and in hydrogen fluoride, but not in hydrogen chloride. It is only atoms which are both small and electronegative, such as F, O and N, that can form hydrogen bonds. In larger atoms, such as Cl, the charge is too diffuse or scattered to be effective. Hydrogen bonds are usually many times weaker than covalent bonds, but many times stronger than other dipole–dipole attractions.

Table 7.5 Intermolecular forces and substances

Type of substance	Intermolecular forces
Non-polar	van der Waals forces
Containing N–H, O–H or H–F bonds	Hydrogen bonding and van der Waals forces
Polar (but not containing N–H, O–H or H–F bonds)	Dipole–dipole interactions and van der Waals forces

Key-points!

- Molecules with two bonding pairs around the central atom are linear.
- Molecules with three bonding pairs around the central atom are trigonal planar.
- Molecules with four bonding pairs around the central atom are tetrahedral.
- Molecules with three bonding pairs and one lone pair around the central atom are pyramidal.
- Molecules with two bonding pairs and two lone pairs around the central atom are V-shaped.
- Electron pair repulsion theory: The electron pairs in the valence (outer) shell of the central atom repel each other and end up as far apart as is geometrically possible. Lone pairs have a greater repelling effect than bonding pairs.
- A molecule with polar bonds is non-polar when the centres of positive and negative charge coincide.
- Hydrogen bonding is a special type of dipole–dipole interaction, which occurs when hydrogen is bonded to small, highly electronegative atoms such as O, N or F.
- A molecule with polar bonds is polar when the centres of positive and negative charge are separated.
- Intermolecular forces and substances: (1) van der Waals forces are found in non-polar and polar substances, (2) hydrogen bonding is found in substances containing N–H, O–H or H–F bonds, (3) dipole–dipole interactions are found in polar substances.
- Substances and intermolecular forces: (1) non-polar substances contain van der Waals forces, (2) substances containing N–H, O–H or H–F bonds have hydrogen bonding and van der Waals forces, (3) polar substances (but not those containing N–H, O–H or H–F bonds) have dipole–dipole interactions and van der Waals forces.

Gas Laws and the Mole   8

Particles in solids, liquids and gases

It is now generally accepted that all solids, liquids and gases are composed of particles, which may be atoms or molecules or ions. These particles are very small.

The differences between solids, liquids and gases are due to differences in the arrangement and freedom of movement of their particles. The particles of a solid constantly vibrate. The particles in a liquid are still close together, but they can slip by one another easily. Gas particles are relatively far apart and move very rapidly.

Diffusion

Key definition

Diffusion is the spontaneous spreading out of a substance due to the natural movement of its particles.

Diffusion experiments provide experimental evidence for the existence of particles.

Specified Demonstration: Diffusion of ammonia and hydrogen chloride gases

Procedure   In this demonstration, ammonia and hydrogen chloride gases are allowed to diffuse from opposite ends of the glass tube. When ammonia and hydrogen chloride come in contact with each other, a white cloud of ammonium chloride is formed. The cloud forms at first nearer the hydrochloric acid end because the less dense ammonia gas diffuses more quickly.

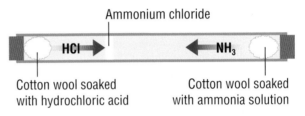

Ammonium chloride

HCl →   ← NH$_3$

Cotton wool soaked   Cotton wool soaked
with hydrochloric acid   with ammonia solution

Fig. 8.1

Specified Demonstration: Diffusion of smoke in air

Procedure   1   Get a smouldering piece of brown paper.

2   Observe the movement of the smoke through the surrounding air.

Diffusion in liquids is much slower than diffusion in gases.

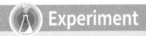 Experiment

Specified Demonstration: Diffusion of ink in water

Procedure   1   Three-quarters fill a beaker with water.

2   Using a pipette, carefully place some blue ink under the water at the bottom of the beaker.

3   Allow to stand overnight.

4   Using a background of white paper, the blue colour of the ink will be seen to have spread out.

Gas laws: Boyle's law and Charles's law

Gases have a number of laws in common governing their physical properties.

Boyle's law

In 1662, the Irish physicist **Robert Boyle** discovered the way in which the volume of air varied with changing pressure. He found that at a constant temperature:

Point to note

$$P \times V = \text{constant}$$

where P = pressure of the air, and V = volume of the air.

Key definition

Boyle's law: At a constant temperature, the volume of a given mass of any gas is inversely proportional to the pressure of the gas.

Charles's law

In 1787, the French physicist **Jacques Charles** discovered that equal volumes of different gases at constant pressure all expanded by the same amount for a given rise in temperature.

Jacques Charles

Key definition

Charles's law

At a constant pressure, the volume of a given mass of any gas is directly proportional to the Kelvin temperature.

In mathematical form:

Point to note

$$V / T = \text{constant}$$

Gas laws: the laws of Gay-Lussac and Avogadro

Joseph Gay-Lussac

Gay-Lussac's law of combining volumes

By 1808, the French chemist **Joseph Gay-Lussac** was able to state his **law of combining volumes.**

> ### Key definition
>
> **Gay-Lussac's law of combining volumes:** When gases react, the volumes consumed in the reaction bear a simple whole number ratio to each other and to the volumes of any gaseous product of the reaction, if all volumes are measured under the same conditions of temperature and pressure.

Avogadro's law

In 1811, the Italian chemist **Amedeo Avogadro** stated what is now known as **Avogadro's law.**

> ### Key definition
>
> **Avogadro's law:** Equal volumes of gases, under the same conditions of temperature and pressure, contain equal numbers of molecules.

Amedeo Avogadro

The mole

The mole is the SI unit of amount of substance.

> ### Key definition
>
> A **mole** of any substance is defined as the amount of substance that contains as many particles (atoms or molecules or ions) as there are atoms of ^{12}C in 12 g of ^{12}C.

The number of atoms of the ^{12}C isotope in 12 g of ^{12}C can be measured. It is found to be approximately 6×10^{23}. This is the number of particles per mole for all substances, and is called the **Avogadro constant (L)**:

Point to note

$L = 6 \times 10^{23}$ mol^{-1}.

Question

8.1 How many atoms are there in 3 moles of helium gas? (Helium gas is composed of helium atoms.)

Answer

1 mole $= 6 \times 10^{23}$ atoms

3 moles $= 3 \times 6 \times 10^{23}$ atoms

$= 18 \times 10^{23}$ atoms

$= 1.8 \times 10^{24}$ atoms

Question

8.2 How many molecules are there in 0.1 moles of nitrogen gas? (Nitrogen gas is composed of molecules.)

Answer

1 mole $= 6 \times 10^{23}$ molecules

0.1 moles $= 0.1 \times 6 \times 10^{23}$ molecules

$= 0.6 \times 10^{23}$ molecules

$= 6 \times 10^{22}$ molecules

Question

8.3 How many atoms are there in 0.25 moles of carbon dioxide gas? (Carbon dioxide gas is composed of CO_2 molecules.)

Answer

1 mole $= 6 \times 10^{23}$ molecules

0.25 moles $= 0.25 \times 6 \times 10^{23}$ molecules

$= 1.5 \times 10^{23}$ molecules

In every CO_2 molecule, there are 3 atoms.

Number of atoms in 0.25 moles of carbon dioxide $= 3 \times 1.5 \times 10^{23}$

$= 4.5 \times 10^{23}$

Question

8.4 A sample of hydrogen gas contains 1.5×10^{22} molecules. How many moles is this?

Answer

6×10^{23} molecules $= 1$ mole

1.5×10^{22} molecules $= 1.5 \times 10^{22} / 6 \times 10^{23}$ moles

$= 0.025$ moles

Molar volume of gases

One mole of any gas should occupy the same volume as one mole of any other gas under the same conditions of temperature and pressure. It is usual for volumes of gases to be compared at a standard temperature and pressure.

Point to note

Standard temperature and pressure (STP)

Pressure $= 101,325$ Nm^{-2} $= 101,325$ Pa Temperature $= 273$ K

The volume occupied by one mole of a gas at STP is called **the molar volume at STP** of the gas. It can be taken to be the same for all gases.

Point to note

Molar volume at STP $= 22.4$ l $= 22,400$ cm^3 $= 2.24 \times 10^{-2}$ m^3

Question

8.5 What is the volume in litres at STP of 0.05 moles of fluorine gas?

Answer

1 mole $= 22.4$ l at STP

0.5 moles $= 0.05 \times 22.4$ l at STP

$= 1.12$ l

Question

8.6 How many moles are there in 560 cm^3 of hydrogen gas at STP?

Answer

22,400 cm^3 at STP $= 1$ mole

560 cm^3 at STP $= 560 / 22,400$ moles

$= 0.025$ moles

Relative molecular mass

> **Key definition**
>
> The **relative molecular mass (M_r)** of a substance is the average mass of a molecule of the substance relative to one-twelfth of the mass of an atom of ^{12}C.

Question

8.7 Calculate the relative molecular mass of (i) sulfur dioxide (SO_2), (ii) nitric acid (HNO_3).

Answer

(i) $M_r(SO_2)$ $= 1 \times 32 + 2 \times 16 = 32 + 32 = 64$

(ii) $M_r(HNO_3)$ $= 1 \times 1 + 1 \times 14 + 3 \times 16$

$= 1 + 14 + 48$

$= 63$

Molar mass

The molar mass of a substance has the same numerical value as its relative molecular mass. Relative molecular mass is measured on the ^{12}C scale, while molar mass is measured in g mol^{-1}.

> **Key definition**
>
> The **molar mass** of a substance is the mass in grams of one mole of the substance.

Question

8.8 What is the mass of 5.5 moles of carbon dioxide?

Answer

$M_r(CO_2)$	$= 44$
Mass of 1 mole of carbon dioxide	$= 44$ g
Mass of 5.5 moles of carbon dioxide	$= 5.5 \times 44$ g
	$= 242$ g

8.9 How many moles in 14 g of nitrogen?

Answer

$M_r(N_2)$ = 28

28 g   = mass of 1 mole of nitrogen

14 g   = mass of 14/28 moles

     = 0.5 moles

More calculations involving the mole

In solving more complicated problems that involve moles, the following diagram, showing the relationship between a mole of a substance, its mass, its volume at STP and the number of its particles, may be useful.

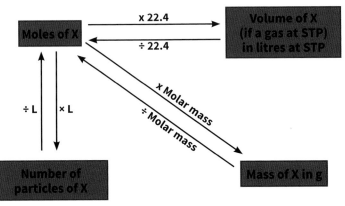

Fig. 8.2

8.10 How many molecules are there in 560 cm^3 of chlorine gas at STP?

Answer

22,400 cm^3 at STP = 1 mole

560 cm^3 at STP   = 560 / 22,400 moles

                  = 0.025 moles

1 mole   = 6 × 10^{23} molecules

0.025 moles   = 0.025 × 6 × 10^{23} molecules

                  = 0.15 × 10^{23} molecules

                  = 1.5 × 10^{22} molecules

Question

8.11 How many atoms are there in 840 cm^3 of butane gas at STP, given that the chemical formula for butane is C_4H_{10}?

Answer

22,400 cm^3 at STP	= 1 mole
840 cm^3 at STP	= 840 / 22,400 moles
	= 0.0375 moles
1 mole	= 6 × 10^{23} molecules
0.0375 moles	= 0.0375 × 6 × 10^{23} molecules
	= 0.225 × 10^{23} molecules
	= 14 × 0.225 × 10^{23} atoms (since there are 14 atoms in each butane molecule)
	= 3.15 × 10^{23} atoms

Question

8.12 What is (i) the volume at STP and (ii) the number of molecules in 24 g of sulfur dioxide?

Answer

(i)
$M_r(SO_2)$	= 64
64 g SO_2	= 1 mole
24 g SO_2	= 24 / 64 moles
	= 0.375 moles
1 mole	= 22.4 l at STP
0.375 moles	= 0.375 × 22.4 l
	= 8.4 l

(ii)
1 mole	= 6 × 10^{23} molecules
0.375 moles	= 0.375 × 6 × 10^{23} molecules
	= 2.25 × 10^{23} molecules

8.13 What is the mass in g of 140 cm^3 of oxygen gas at STP?

Answer

22,400 cm^3 of oxygen gas at STP	= 1 mole
140 cm^3 of oxygen gas at STP	= 140 / 22,400 moles
	= 0.00625 moles
$M_r(O_2)$	= 32
1 mole O_2	= 32 g
0.00625 moles O_2	= 0.00625 × 32 g
	= 0.2 g

Combined gas law

Boyle's law, Charles's law and Avogadro's law can be grouped together to give the **combined gas law**:

$$\frac{P_1V_1}{T_1} = \frac{P_2V_2}{T_2}$$

where P_1, V_1 and T_1 are the initial pressure, volume and Kelvin temperature, respectively, and P_2, V_2 and T_2 are the final pressure, volume and Kelvin temperature, respectively.

8.14 If a definite mass of gas occupies 500 cm^3 at a pressure of 101,000 Pa and a temperature of 27°C, what is its volume in cm^3 at STP?

Answer

$$\frac{P_1V_1}{T_1} = \frac{P_2V_2}{T_2}$$

P_1 = 101,000 Pa P_2 = 101,325 Pa

V_1 = 500 cm^3 V_2 = ? cm^3

T_1 = 27°C T_2 = 273 K

    = 27 + 273 K

    = 300 K

$$\frac{101,000 \times 500}{300} = \frac{101,325 \times V_2}{273}$$

$$V_2 = \frac{101,000 \times 500 \times 273}{300 \times 101,325}$$

$$= 453.5 \text{ cm}^3$$

Kinetic theory of gases

The **kinetic theory of gases** was developed by **James Clerk Maxwell** and **Ludwig Boltzmann** towards the end of the nineteenth century. In this theory, it is assumed that:

1 Gases are made up of particles whose diameters are negligible compared to the distances between them.

2 There are no attractive or repulsive forces between these particles.

3 The particles are in constant rapid random motion, colliding with each other and with the walls of the container.

4 The average kinetic energy of the particles is proportional to the Kelvin temperature.

5 All collisions are perfectly elastic (for example, if a particle travelling at 450 ms^{-1} collides with a wall of its container, it rebounds with the same speed).

The kinetic theory is only completely valid for ideal gases.

Key definition

An **ideal gas** is a gas that obeys all of the assumptions of the kinetic theory under all conditions of temperature and pressure.

Reasons why gases deviate from ideal gas behaviour

The behaviour of real gases deviates from that of an ideal gas to the greatest extent at **low temperatures** and at **high pressures**.

- One of the assumptions of the kinetic theory is that the diameters of gas particles are negligible compared to the distances between them. At low temperatures and at high pressures, the diameters are not negligible compared to the distances between them.

- Another assumption of the kinetic theory is that there are no attractive or repulsive forces between these particles. At low temperatures and at high pressures, this assumption is not valid, because the gas particles are in close proximity to each other. The stronger the intermolecular forces, the less like an ideal gas will a real gas behave under these conditions.

Real gases behave most like an ideal gas at high temperatures and at low pressures. Under these conditions:

- The particles of a real gas are relatively far away from each other.

- The assumptions of the kinetic theory are reasonably valid.

- However, the assumption that collisions between molecules are perfectly elastic is never true for a real gas.

8.15 State which of the following gases you would expect to come closest to ideal behaviour, and which you would expect to deviate most from ideal behaviour: H_2, HF, F_2. Explain your answers.

Answer

Hydrogen molecules and fluorine molecules are both non-polar, with only van der Waals forces between their molecules. Hydrogen fluoride molecules are polar, with hydrogen bonding and van der Waals forces between their molecules.

Hydrogen fluoride will deviate most from ideal behaviour because it has the strongest intermolecular forces. The van der Waals forces between hydrogen molecules are weaker than those between fluorine molecules because there are fewer electrons in a hydrogen molecule. Therefore, hydrogen will come closest to ideal behaviour because it has the weakest intermolecular forces.

Equation of state for an ideal gas

Point to note

The equation of state for an ideal gas is usually written as follows:

PV = nRT

where P = pressure, V = volume, n = number of moles, R is a constant known as the **universal gas constant**, and T = Kelvin temperature.

The value of R is 8.31 J $K^{-1}mol^{-1}$.

The relationship PV = nRT is referred to as the equation of state for an **ideal** gas because it is obeyed only approximately by real gases.

Calculations involving the ideal gas law

It is important to use units that are consistent with those of the universal gas constant (R) when doing calculations involving the ideal gas law. The units of R are J $K^{-1}mol^{-1}$. The units for V, P, T and n that are consistent with this are shown in Table 8.1.

Table 8.1

Measure	Unit
Volume	m^3
Pressure	Pa
Temperature	K
Number of moles	mol

8.16 2.5 kg of carbon dioxide gas are released into the air when a fire extinguisher is discharged. What volume does this gas occupy at a pressure of 100,000 Pa and a temperature of 288 K?

Answer

PV $= nRT$

P $= 100,000$ Pa

V $= ?$

n $= 2500 / 44$ moles $= 56.82$ moles

R $= 8.31$ J K^{-1}mol^{-1}

T $= 288$ K

V $= nRT / P = 56.82 \times 8.31 \times 288 / 100,000$ m$^3 = 1.36$ m^3

Question

8.17 20 g of a gas occupies a volume of 5 l at 87°C and 200,000 Pa.

(i) How many moles of the gas are present?

(ii) What is the relative molecular mass of the gas?

Answer

(i) PV $= nRT$

P $= 200,000$ Pa

V $= 5 l = 5 \times 10^{-3}$ m^3

R $= 8.31$ J K^{-1}mol^{-1}

T $= 87°C = 360$ K

n $=$ amount of gas in moles $= PV / RT = \dfrac{200,000 \times 5 \times 10^{-3}}{8.31 \times 360}$

$= 0.334$

(ii) 0.334 moles of the gas $= 20$ g

1 mole has a mass of $20 / 0.334$ g $= 59.88$ g

Experiment

Mandatory Experiment 8.1: Determination of the relative molecular mass (M_r) of a volatile liquid

Procedure

1 Two-thirds fill a beaker with water, and heat to almost boiling with a Bunsen burner. Control the flame so that the temperature remains at about 95°C.

2 Cut a circle of aluminium foil a little more than large enough to cover the mouth of a clean dry conical flask and fold down a little around the sides of the flask.

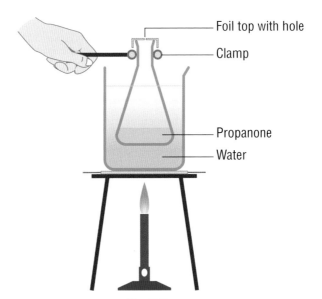

Foil top with hole

Clamp

Propanone

Water

Fig. 8.3

3 Find the total mass of the conical flask, the aluminium foil and a rubber band. Add 3 to 4 cm³ of propanone to the flask.

4 Cover the mouth of the flask with the aluminium foil. Secure it tightly with the rubber band so that no vapour can escape. With a pin, prick one small hole in the centre of the aluminium foil cap. Attach the clamp to the neck of the flask.

5 Immerse the conical flask into the boiling water (Fig. 8.3). Holding the clamp, move the flask up and down periodically to check the liquid level in the flask.

6 The volatile liquid will vaporise and some of it will escape out through the hole in the cap. When the flask appears to be empty (i.e. all the liquid appears to have evaporated), remove the flask from the beaker immediately. Record the exact temperature of the hot water, using the thermometer.

7 Allow the flask to cool – most of the vapour will condense. Then, thoroughly dry the outside of the flask, including the foil. Find the mass of the flask, cap, rubber band and contents. By subtraction, find the mass of liquid vaporised.

8 Remove the cap and rubber band. Find the volume of the flask by completely filling it with water, and then transferring all of the liquid from it to graduated cylinders.

9 Observe the value of atmospheric pressure using a barometer, and record this value.

10 Calculate the value of the relative molecular mass (M_r) of the volatile liquid. A sample calculation is shown in Question 8.18.

Question

8.18 In an experiment to measure the relative molecular mass of a volatile liquid, the following results were obtained:

Mass of condensed vapour of volatile liquid	= 0.75 g
Atmospheric pressure	= 100,705 Pa
Temperature of boiling water (= temperature of vapour)	= 370 K
Volume of flask (= volume of vapour)	= 2.9 x 10^{-4} m^3

What is the relative molecular mass of the volatile liquid?

Answer

$PV = nRT$

$\Rightarrow n = PV / RT$

$\Rightarrow n = 100,705 \times 2.9 \times 10^{-4} / 8.31 \times 370$

$\Rightarrow n = 0.0095$ moles

$n = m / M_r$

$\Rightarrow M_r = m / n$

$\Rightarrow M_r = 0.75 / 0.0095$

$\Rightarrow M_r = 78.95$

Key-points!

- Diffusion is the spontaneous spreading out of a substance due to the natural movement of its particles.

- Boyle's law: At a constant temperature, the volume of a given mass of any gas is inversely proportional to the pressure of the gas.

- Charles's law: At a constant pressure, the volume of a given mass of any gas is directly proportional to the Kelvin temperature.

- Gay-Lussac's law of combining volumes: When gases react, the volumes consumed in the reaction bear a simple whole number ratio to each other and to the volumes of any gaseous product of the reaction, if all volumes are measured under the same conditions of temperature and pressure.

- Avogadro's law: Equal volumes of gases, under the same conditions of temperature and pressure, contain equal numbers of molecules.

- A mole of any substance is defined as the amount of substance that contains as many particles (atoms or molecules or ions) as there are atoms of ^{12}C in 12 g of ^{12}C.

- The relative molecular mass (M_r) of a substance is the average mass of a molecule of the substance relative to one-twelfth of the mass of an atom of ^{12}C.

- The molar mass of a substance is the mass in grams of one mole of the substance.

- An ideal gas is a gas that obeys all of the assumptions of the kinetic theory under all conditions of temperature and pressure.

- A volatile liquid is a liquid that is easily vaporised.

Stoichiometry, Formulas and Equations 9

Formulas for elements

Table 9.1

Element	Formula	Element	Formula
Hydrogen	H_2	Chlorine	Cl_2
Nitrogen	N_2	Bromine	Br_2
Oxygen	O_2	Iodine	I_2
Fluorine	F_2		

Empirical formulas

Key definition

The **empirical formula** of a compound is the formula that gives the simplest whole number ratio in which the atoms of the elements in the compound are present.

9.1 What is the empirical formula of the following compound: ethane (C_2H_6)?

Answer

Ratio of carbon to hydrogen   = 2 : 6

Simplest whole number ratio = 1 : 3

Empirical formula   = CH_3

Empirical formulas from analytical data

Question

9.2 A compound on analysis is found to contain 40% carbon, 6.66% hydrogen and 53.33% oxygen by mass. What is the empirical formula of the compound?

Answer

Element	Percentage	Percentage / A_r	Simplest ratio
Carbon	40	40 / 12 = 3.33	1
Hydrogen	6.66	6.66 / 1 = 6.66	2
Oxygen	53.33	53.33 / 16 = 3.33	1

Empirical formula = CH_2O

Empirical formulas from combination data

Question

9.3 When 0.48 g of magnesium is heated in excess oxygen, 0.8 g of magnesium oxide is formed. What is the empirical formula of magnesium oxide?

Answer

Mass of magnesium consumed	= 0.48 g	
Mass of oxygen consumed	= (0.8 – 0.48) g	= 0.32 g
Moles of magnesium atoms consumed	= 0.48 / 24	= 0.02
Moles of oxygen atoms consumed	= 0.32 / 16	= 0.02
Ratio of magnesium atoms to oxygen atoms	= 0.02 : 0.02	= 1 : 1
Empirical formula of magnesium oxide	= MgO	

Empirical formulas from decomposition data

9.4 11.6 g of an oxide of iron was heated with carbon and 8.4 g of iron was formed. What is the empirical formula of the oxide?

Answer

Mass of iron in the compound	= 8.4 g	
Mass of oxygen in the compound	= (11.6 – 8.4) g	= 3.2 g
Moles of iron atoms in the compound	= 8.4 / 56	= 0.15
Moles of oxygen atoms in the compound	= 3.2 / 16	= 0.2
Ratio of iron atoms to oxygen atoms	= 0.15 : 0.2	= 3 : 4
Empirical formula of iron oxide	= Fe_3O_4	

Molecular formulas

Key definition

The **molecular formula** of a compound is the formula that gives the actual number of atoms of each element present in a molecule of the compound.

The molecular formula of hydrogen peroxide, for example, is H_2O_2. This shows that there are two atoms of hydrogen and two atoms of oxygen in every molecule of the compound.

To find the molecular formula of a compound, both its empirical formula and its relative molecular mass must be known.

Question

9.5 The empirical formula of ethyne is CH and its relative molecular mass is 26. Find the molecular formula of ethyne.

Answer

The formula mass of CH	= 12 + 1	= 13
The relative molecular mass of ethyne	= 26	
Number of CH units in an ethyne molecule	= 26 / 13	= 2
Molecular formula of ethyne	= C_2H_2	

9.6 The relative molecular mass of butanoic acid is found to be 88. On analysis, it is found to contain 54.54% carbon, 9.09% hydrogen and 36.36% oxygen by mass. Find the molecular formula of butanoic acid.

Answer

Element	Percentage	Percentage / A_r	Simplest ratio
Carbon	54.54	54.54 / 12 = 4.545	2
Hydrogen	9.09	9.09 / 1 = 9.09	4
Oxygen	36.36	36.36 / 16 = 2.27	1

Empirical formula of butanoic acid $= C_2H_4O$

Formula mass of C_2H_4O $= 44$

Relative molecular mass of butanoic acid $= 88$

Number of C_2H_4O units in a butanoic acid molecule $= 88 / 44 \ = 2$

Molecular formula of butanoic acid $= C_4H_8O_2$

Percentage composition by mass

If the empirical formula of a compound is known, the percentage by mass of each element present can be calculated. It is useful, for example, to be able to calculate the percentage of nitrogen in a fertiliser, as this is a key nutrient in the fertiliser.

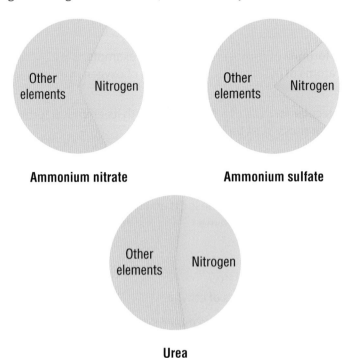

Ammonium nitrate   Ammonium sulfate

Urea

Fig. 9.1

Question

9.7 What is the percentage of nitrogen in ammonium nitrate (NH_4NO_3)?

Answer

Moles of nitrogen per mole of ammonium nitrate = 2

Mass of nitrogen per mole of ammonium nitrate = 28

Molar mass of ammonium nitrate = 80 g mol^{-1}

Percentage of nitrogen in ammonium nitrate = 28 × 100 / 80%

= 35%

Structural formulas

Key definition

The **structural formula** of a compound shows the arrangement of the atoms within a molecule of the compound.

Table 9.2

Substance	Empirical formula	Molecular formula	Structural formula
Ethene	CH_2	C_2H_4	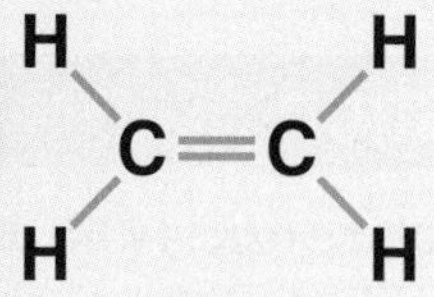
Ethyne	CH	C_2H_2	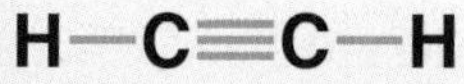

The structural formula of ethene shows that each carbon atom is joined by single bonds to two hydrogen atoms and by a double bond to the other carbon atom.

In ethyne, each carbon atom is joined by a single bond to a hydrogen atom and by a triple bond to the other carbon atom.

9.8 The structural formula of butane is:

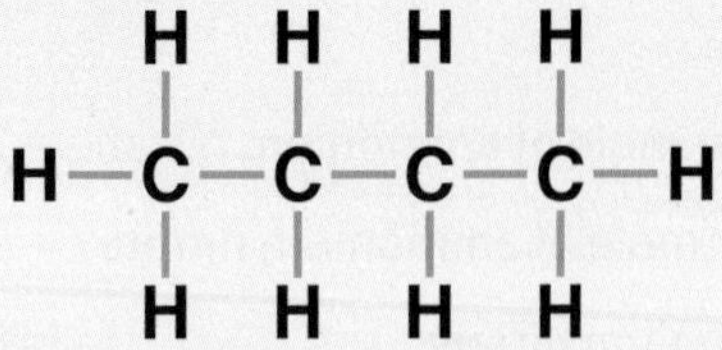

$$\begin{array}{c}\;\;\;H\;\;\;H\;\;\;H\;\;\;H\\\;\;\;|\;\;\;\;|\;\;\;\;|\;\;\;\;|\\H-C-C-C-C-H\\\;\;\;|\;\;\;\;|\;\;\;\;|\;\;\;\;|\\\;\;\;H\;\;\;H\;\;\;H\;\;\;H\end{array}$$

Find (i) its molecular formula and (ii) its empirical formula.

Answer

(i) The molecular formula is found by counting the atoms of each element in the structural formula.
Molecular formula of butane = C_4H_{10}

(ii) Empirical formula of butane = C_2H_5

Balancing chemical equations

Remember

In balancing an equation, formulas cannot be altered in any way, but can only be multiplied by an appropriate number.

9.9 Butane reacts with oxygen, forming carbon dioxide and water vapour only. Write a balanced chemical equation for the reaction.

Answer

The unbalanced equation is:

$$C_4H_{10} + O_2 \rightarrow CO_2 + H_2O$$

To balance the equation, each element is checked in turn to see whether or not there are equal numbers of atoms of that element on the two sides of the equation.

Carbon: There are 4 carbon atoms on the left-hand side of the equation, so CO_2 must be multiplied by 4:

$$C_4H_{10} + O_2 \rightarrow 4CO_2 + H_2O$$

Hydrogen: There are 10 hydrogen atoms on the left-hand side, and only 2 on the right-hand side. H_2O must therefore be multiplied by 5:

$$C_4H_{10} + O_2 \rightarrow 4CO_2 + 5H_2O$$

Oxygen: There are now 2 oxygen atoms on the left-hand side, and 13 on the right-hand side. O_2 must therefore be multiplied by 6.5:

$$C_4H_{10} + 6.5O_2 \rightarrow 4CO_2 + 5H_2O$$

Calculations based on balanced chemical equations

Question

9.10 Ethane burns in air, according to the equation:

$$C_2H_{6(g)} + 3.5O_{2(g)} \rightarrow 2CO_{2(g)} + 3H_2O_{(g)}$$

If 4 moles of ethane are reacted fully with oxygen, calculate (i) the number of moles of carbon dioxide formed, (ii) the number of moles of water vapour formed, and (iii) the number of moles of oxygen consumed.

Answer

From the equation:

$C_2H_{6(g)}$	+	$3.5O_{2(g)}$	$\rightarrow$	$2CO_{2(g)}$	+	$3H_2O_{(g)}$
1 mole		3.5 moles		2 moles		3 moles
Therefore:	$4 \times (1$ mole	3.5 moles		2 moles		3 moles)
= 4 moles		14 moles		8 moles		12 moles

(i) 8 moles of carbon dioxide, (ii) 12 moles of water, (iii) 14 moles of oxygen.

Calculation of masses of reactants or products from balanced chemical equations

Question

9.11 **Magnesium** reacts with water vapour to form magnesium oxide and hydrogen, according to the equation:

$$Mg_{(s)} + H_2O_{(g)} \rightarrow MgO_{(s)} + H_{2(g)}$$

If 60 g of magnesium is reacted with excess water vapour, calculate the mass of magnesium oxide produced.

Answer

$$60 \text{ g Mg} = 60 / 24 \text{ moles Mg}$$
$$= 2.5 \text{ moles Mg}$$

From the equation:

$Mg_{(s)}$	+	$H_2O_{(g)}$	$\rightarrow$	$MgO_{(s)}$	+	$H_{2(g)}$
1 mole		1 mole		1 mole		1 mole

Therefore: 2.5 moles   2.5 moles   2.5 moles   2.5 moles

$$1 \text{ mole MgO} = 40 \text{ g MgO}$$

$$2.5 \text{ moles MgO} = 2.5 \times 40 \text{ g} = 100 \text{ g}$$

Question

9.12 Hydrogen reacts with chlorine to form hydrogen chloride, according to the equation:

$$H_{2(g)} + Cl_{2(g)} \rightarrow 2HCl_{(g)}$$

If 11.2 litres of hydrogen (measured at STP) are used to react with excess chlorine, what mass of hydrogen chloride is formed?

Answer

$$11.2 \text{ litres } H_2 = 11.2 / 22.4 \text{ moles } H_2 = 0.5 \text{ moles } H_2$$

From the equation:

$H_{2(g)}$	+	$Cl_{2(g)}$	$\rightarrow$	$2HCl_{(g)}$
1 mole		1 mole		2 moles

Therefore: 0.5 moles   0.5 moles   1 mole

$$1 \text{ mole HCl} = 36.5 \text{ g HCl}$$

Calculation of volumes of gaseous reactants or products from balanced chemical equations

9.13 Butane burns in air, according to the equation:

$$C_4H_{10(g)} + 6.5O_{2(g)} \rightarrow 4CO_{2(g)} + 5H_2O_{(g)}$$

What volume of oxygen (measured at STP) is needed for complete combustion of 2.9 g of butane?

Answer

$$2.9 \text{ g } C_4H_{10} = 2.9 / 58 \text{ moles } C_4H_{10} = 0.05 \text{ moles } C_4H_{10}$$

$$C_4H_{10(g)} + 6.5O_{2(g)} \rightarrow 4CO_{2(g)} + 5H_2O_{(g)}$$

| 1 mole | 6.5 moles | 4 moles | 5 moles |

Therefore: $0.05 \times$ (1 mole   6.5 moles   4 moles   5 moles)

= 0.05 moles   0.325 moles   0.2 moles   0.25 moles

1 mole of oxygen at STP $= 22.4 \text{ l } O_2$

0.325 moles at STP $= 0.325 \times 22.4 \text{ l} = 7.28 \text{ l}$

Other calculations based on balanced chemical equations

9.14 A solution of sodium hydroxide is reacted with enough nitric acid solution to neutralise it exactly. The equation for the reaction is:

$$NaOH_{(aq)} + HNO_{3(aq)} \rightarrow NaNO_{3(aq)} + H_2O_{(l)}$$

On evaporation of the water, 170 g of sodium nitrate are obtained. Calculate:

(i) The number of moles of nitric acid consumed in the reaction.

(ii) The number of water molecules formed.

(iii) The mass of sodium hydroxide used to make up the solution.

Answer

$$170 \text{ g } NaNO_3 = 170 / 85 \text{ moles } NaNO_3 = 2 \text{ moles } NaNO_3$$

From the eqution:

$$NaOH_{(aq)} \quad + \quad HNO_{3(aq)} \quad \rightarrow \quad NaNO_{3(aq)} \quad + \quad H_2O_{(l)}$$

1 mole	1 mole	1 mole	1 mole

Therefore: 2 moles   2 moles   2 moles   2 moles

(i) Number of moles of nitric acid consumed in the reaction = 2

(ii) 1 mole H_2O $= 6 \times 10^{23}$ molecules of H_2O
     2 moles H_2O $= 2 \times 6 \times 10^{23}$ molecules $= 12 \times 10^{23}$ molecules

                    $= 1.2 \times 10^{24}$ molecules

(iii) 1 mole NaOH   = 40 g NaOH

      2 moles NaOH $= 2 \times 40$ g $= 80$ g

Calculations involving excess of one reactant

It often happens that when a chemical reaction is being carried out, one of the reactants is present in excess. The substance that is not present in excess is called the **limiting reactant**, as the amount of this substance present will dictate how much of each of the products is formed.

Question

9.15 Magnesium reacts with sulfuric acid, according to the equation:

$$Mg_{(s)} + H_2SO_{4(aq)} \rightarrow MgSO_{4(aq)} + H_{2(g)}$$

A 250 cm^3 aqueous solution containing 9.8 g sulfuric acid is added to 6 g magnesium.

(i)   Show that the magnesium is present in excess.

(ii) Calculate the mass of magnesium sulfate formed.

(iii) Calculate the volume of hydrogen (measured at STP) formed.

Answer

(i)   Moles of magnesium present initially = 6 / 24 = 0.25

Moles of sulfuric acid present initially = 9.8 / 98 = 0.1

From the equation:

$$Mg_{(s)} \quad + \quad H_2SO_{4(aq)} \quad \rightarrow \quad MgSO_{4(aq)} \quad + \quad H_{2(g)}$$

1 mole	1 mole	1 mole	1 mole
0.1 moles	0.1 moles	0.1 moles	0.1 moles

Since the 0.1 moles of sulfuric acid that are present initially will react fully with 0.1 moles of magnesium, and there are 0.25 moles of magnesium present initially, it is clear that it is the magnesium that is present in excess. Sulfuric acid is the limiting reagent.

(ii) $Mg_{(s)}$ + $H_2SO_{4(aq)}$ → $MgSO_{4(aq)}$ + $H_{2(g)}$

   0.1 moles   0.1 moles   0.1 moles   0.1 moles

   Amount of magnesium sulfate formed = 0.1 moles
   Mass of magnesium sulfate formed   = 0.1 × 120 g = 12.0 g

(iii) Amount of hydrogen formed   = 0.1 moles
   Volume (at STP) of hydrogen formed   = 0.1 × 22.4 l = 2.24 l

Percentage yields

Question

9.16 In an experiment to prepare ethene (C_2H_4), 6.9 g of ethanol (C_2H_5OH) was heated with aluminium oxide and 0.7 g of ethene was formed. Calculate the percentage yield of ethene. The equation for the reaction is:

$$C_2H_5OH_{(l)} \rightarrow C_2H_{4(g)} + H_2O_{(l)}$$

Answer

   6.9 g C_2H_5OH = 6.9 / 46 moles C_2H_5OH = 0.15 moles

   $C_2H_5OH_{(l)}$ → $C_2H_{4(g)}$ + $H_2O_{(l)}$

   1 mole   1 mole   1 mole

   0.15 moles   0.15 moles   0.15 moles

Theoretical yield   = 0.15 moles C_2H_4 = 0.15 × 28 g C_2H_4 = 4.2 g

Actual yield   = 0.7 g

Percentage yield $= \dfrac{Actual\ yield \times 100}{Theoretical\ yield}\ \% = \dfrac{0.7 \times 100}{4.2}$

$$= 16.7\%$$

Question

9.17 A sample of ethanal was prepared by reacting 9.2 cm³ of ethanol (density 0.8 g cm⁻³) with an acidified solution containing 11 g of sodium dichromate ($Na_2Cr_2O_7.2H_2O$). The reaction may be represented by the equation:

$$3C_2H_5OH_{(l)} + Cr_2O_7{}^{2-}{}_{(aq)} + 8H^+{}_{(aq)} \rightarrow 3CH_3CHO_{(l)} + 2Cr^{3+}{}_{(aq)} + 7H_2O_{(l)}$$

After purification, it was found that 1.2 g of ethanal were formed.

(i) Determine the limiting reactant.

(ii) Calculate the percentage yield of ethanal.

Answer

(i) Density   = mass / volume

Mass   = volume × density

9.2 cm³ of ethanol   = 9.2 × 0.8 g ethanol = 7.36 g ethanol

= 7.36 / 46 moles

= 0.16 moles

11 g sodium dichromate = 11 / 298 = 0.0369 moles

$$3C_2H_5OH_{(l)} + Cr_2O_7{}^{2-}{}_{(aq)} + 8H^+{}_{(aq)} \rightarrow 3CH_3CHO_{(l)} + 2Cr^{3+}{}_{(aq)} + 7H_2O_{(l)}$$

3 moles   1 mole   3 moles   2 moles   7 moles

0.1107   0.0369

Since the 0.0369 moles of sodium dichromate that are present will react fully with 0.1107 moles of ethanol, and there are 0.16 moles of ethanol present initially, it is clear that it is the ethanol that is present in excess. Sodium dichromate is the limiting reagent.

(ii) Actual yield = 1.2 g ethanal

$$3C_2H_5OH_{(l)} + Cr_2O_7{}^{2-}{}_{(aq)} + 8H^+{}_{(aq)} \rightarrow 3CH_3CHO_{(l)} + 2Cr^{3+}{}_{(aq)} + 7H_2O_{(l)}$$

3 moles   1 mole   3 moles   2 moles   7 moles

Theoretical yield of ethanal   = 0.0369 moles × 3   = 0.1107 moles

= 0.1107 × 44 g   = 4.871 g

Percentage yield $= \dfrac{\text{Actual yield} \times 100}{\text{Theoretical yield}} \% = \dfrac{1.2 \times 100}{4.871}$

$= 24.63\%$

Key-points!

- The empirical formula of a compound is the formula that gives the simplest whole number ratio in which the atoms of the elements in the compound are present.

- The molecular formula of a compound is the formula that gives the actual number of atoms of each element present in a molecule of the compound.

- The structural formula of a compound shows the arrangement of the atoms within a molecule of the compound.

- Percentage yield = $\dfrac{\text{Actual yield} \times 100}{\text{Theoretical yield}}$ %

10 Acids and Bases 1

Introduction to acids

Acids are substances that turn blue litmus red and usually react with metals such as zinc, releasing hydrogen. Hydrochloric acid (HCl), sulfuric acid (H_2SO_4) and nitric acid (HNO_3) are examples of acids.

Acids can be classified as monobasic, dibasic or tribasic, depending on the number of hydrogen atoms per molecule that are removable by reaction with a base. For example, hydrochloric acid (HCl) is a **monobasic acid**, while sulfuric acid (H_2SO_4) is **dibasic**.

Introduction to bases

Bases are substances that turn red litmus blue, and neutralise acids. Sodium hydroxide (NaOH), sodium carbonate (Na_2CO_3) and ammonia (NH_3) are examples of bases.

A base that dissolves in water is called an **alkali**. Sodium hydroxide is an alkali; a solution of sodium hydroxide is said to be alkaline.

Household acids and bases

There are many examples of **household acids**. These include: vinegar, which contains the weak acid ethanoic acid

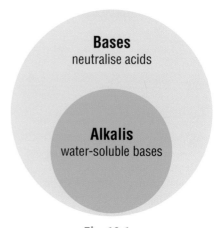

Fig. 10.1

(CH$_3$COOH); lemon juice, containing the weak acid citric acid; and dilute sulfuric acid in car batteries.

Household bases include ammonia (used for cleaning), sodium hydroxide (used in oven cleaners) and magnesium hydroxide (used as a laxative and antacid in Milk of Magnesia).

Neutralisation reactions

When an acid reacts with a base, a **salt** is formed. For example, when hydrochloric acid reacts with sodium hydroxide,

$$HCl + NaOH \rightarrow NaCl + H_2O$$

the salt sodium chloride is formed.

> **Key definition**
>
> A **neutralisation reaction** is one in which an acid and a base react to form a salt and water.

Neutralisation of an acid by a base has many everyday applications. For example, magnesium hydroxide and sodium hydrogencarbonate are bases used in stomach powders to treat acid indigestion. The excess hydrochloric acid is neutralised:

$$2HCl + Mg(OH)_2 \rightarrow MgCl_2 + 2H_2O$$

$$HCl + NaHCO_3 \rightarrow NaCl + H_2O + CO_2$$

Lime (calcium hydroxide) is a base used in agriculture to neutralise acidic soil.

Arrhenius theory of acids and bases

In 1887, the Swedish chemist **Svante Arrhenius** developed a theory of acids and bases.

> **Key definition**
>
> An **Arrhenius acid** is a substance that dissociates in water to form hydrogen ions.

Svante Arrhenius

An **Arrhenius base** is a substance that dissociates in water to form hydroxide ions.

Arrhenius stated that:

1 An acid is a neutral molecule (HX) which **dissociates in water** to form a **hydrogen ion** and an anion:

$$HX \rightarrow H^+ + X^-$$

2 The acidic properties of the solution are due to the presence of H^+ ions.

3 A base (MOH) **dissociates in water** to form a **hydroxide** ion and a cation:

$$MOH \rightarrow OH^- + M^+$$

4 The basic properties of the solution are due to the presence of OH^- ions.

5 In solution, strong acids and bases are fully dissociated.

6 In solution, weak acids and bases are only slightly dissociated.

According to the Arrhenius theory, neutralisation of a solution of a strong acid such as HCl by a solution of a strong base such as NaOH, occurs as follows:

- In solution, the strong acid HCl is fully dissociated into H^+ and Cl^- ions, while the strong base NaOH is fully dissociated into Na^+ and OH^- ions.

- When the two solutions are mixed, the H^+ ions react with the OH^- ions:

$$H^+ + OH^- \rightarrow H_2O$$

- The two other ions present, Na^+ and Cl^-, do not react.

Evidence for the Arrhenius theory

- The Arrhenius theory explains why strong acids only conduct electricity when dissolved in water; there are no ions present in a pure acid.

- The Arrhenius theory also explains why a solution of a weak acid does not conduct electricity as well as a solution of a strong acid of a similar concentration; there are fewer ions present in the weak acid solution.

- For similar reasons, a solution of a weak base does not conduct electricity as well as a solution of a strong base of a similar concentration.

- Acids usually need water before they can show their acidic properties.

Limitations of the Arrhenius theory

- The Arrhenius theory is limited to acid–base reactions that take place in water.

- When an acid dissolves in water, the hydronium ion, H_3O^+, is formed, rather than the hydrogen ion.

- The Arrhenius theory does not explain how certain substances can be amphoteric, i.e. act as an acid with a base **and** as a base with an acid.

Brønsted–Lowry theory of acids and bases

In 1923, Brønsted and Lowry proposed a new and broader theory of acids and bases, called the **Brønsted–Lowry theory**. According to this theory:

1 An acid is a proton donor.

2 A base is a proton acceptor.

3 An acid–base reaction involves transfer of a proton (H^+) from the acid to the base.

4 The stronger the acid, the more readily it transfers a proton.

5 The stronger the base, the more readily it accepts a proton.

6 The weaker the acid, the less readily it transfers a proton.

7 The weaker the base, the less readily it accepts a proton.

Acid–base reactions, according to the Brønsted–Lowry theory, involve proton transfer. When HCl is added to water, the acid (HCl) transfers a proton to water, which in this case, being a proton acceptor, is a base:

$$HCl_{(g)} + H_2O_{(l)} \rightleftharpoons H_3O^+_{(aq)} + Cl^-_{(aq)}$$

hydrogen chloride   hydronium ion

Advantages of the Brønsted–Lowry theory

- The Brønsted–Lowry theory shows how the hydronium ion is formed when an acid reacts with water.

- The Arrhenius theory only deals with reactions in water. The Brønsted–Lowry theory broadens the range of reactions that can be regarded as acid–base reactions. For example, ammonia reacts with hydrogen chloride gas in the absence of water:

$$NH_{3\,(g)} + HCl_{(g)} \rightleftharpoons NH_4^+{}_{(g)} + Cl^-_{(g)} \rightleftharpoons NH_4Cl_{(s)}$$

Ammonia acts as a Brønsted–Lowry base, because it accepts a proton from the Brønsted–Lowry acid, hydrogen chloride.

- The Brønsted–Lowry theory explains how substances can be **amphoteric**. For example, when water reacts with ammonia

$$NH_{3\,(g)} + H_2O_{(l)} \rightleftharpoons NH_4^+{}_{(aq)} + OH^-_{(aq)}$$

it acts as an acid, donating a proton to ammonia.

When it reacts with nitric acid

$$HNO_{3\,(aq)} + H_2O_{(l)} \rightleftharpoons H_3O^+_{(aq)} + NO^-_{3\,(aq)}$$

it acts as a base, accepting a proton from nitric acid.

Remember

The symbol $\rightleftharpoons$ indicates that the reactions are reversible.

Key definition

A **Brønsted–Lowry acid** is a proton donor.

Question

10.1 Identify the Brønsted–Lowry acids in the following reaction:

$$HCO_3^- + H_2O \rightleftharpoons H_2CO_3 + OH^-$$

Answer

When the reaction goes from left to right, H_2O acts as a Brønsted–Lowry acid, as it transfers a proton to HCO_3^-.

When the reaction goes from right to left, H_2CO_3 acts as a Brønsted–Lowry acid, as it transfers a proton to OH^-.

Key definition

A **Brønsted–Lowry base** is a proton acceptor.

Question

10.2 Identify the Brønsted–Lowry bases in the following reaction:

$$HCOOH + H_2O \rightleftharpoons HCOO^- + H_3O^+$$

Answer

When the reaction goes from left to right, H_2O acts as a Brønsted-Lowry base, as it accepts a proton from HCOOH.

When the reaction goes from right to left, $HCOO^-$ acts as a Brønsted-Lowry base, as it accepts a proton from H_3O^+.

Conjugate acids and bases

In the reaction of ammonia with water

$$NH_3 + H_2O \rightleftharpoons NH_4^+ + OH^-$$

ammonia is a base, and accepts a proton to form the ammonium ion (NH_4^+).

An acid and base such as these that differ by the presence or absence of a proton is called a conjugate acid–base pair. In the above reaction, H_2O and OH^- form one conjugate pair, while NH_3 and NH_4^+ form another. NH_4^+ is called the **conjugate acid** of NH_3, while OH^- is the **conjugate base** of H_2O.

Key definition

A **conjugate acid** is formed when a proton (H^+) is added to a Brønsted–Lowry base.

Question

10.3 What is the conjugate acid of HS^-?

Answer

The conjugate acid of HS^- is formed when a proton (H^+) is added to it. Therefore, the conjugate acid of HS^- is H_2S.

Key definition

A **conjugate base** is formed when a proton (H^+) is removed from a Brønsted–Lowry acid.

Question

10.4 What is the conjugate base of H_2SO_4?

Answer

The conjugate base of H_2SO_4 is formed when a proton (H^+) is removed from it. Therefore, the conjugate base of H_2SO_4 is HSO_4^-.

Key definition

A **conjugate acid–base pair** is an acid and base that differ by the presence or absence of a proton.

Question

10.5 In the reaction of ammonia with nitric acid

$$NH_3 + HNO_3 \rightleftharpoons NH_4^+ + NO_3^-$$

identify the conjugate acid–base pairs.

Answer

When NH_3 accepts a proton from HNO_3, it forms its conjugate acid NH_4^+. When HNO_3 donates a proton to NH_3, it forms its conjugate base NO_3^-.

The conjugate acid–base pairs are (i) NH_3 and NH_4^+ and (ii) HNO_3 and NO_3^-.

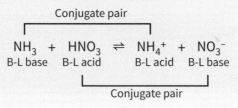

Conjugate pair

$$NH_3 + HNO_3 \rightleftharpoons NH_4^+ + NO_3^-$$

B-L base   B-L acid   B-L acid   B-L base

Conjugate pair

Remember

The stronger an acid, the weaker its conjugate base. The stronger a base, the weaker its conjugate acid.

Key-points!

- A neutralisation reaction is one in which an acid and a base react to form a salt and water.
- An Arrhenius acid is a substance that dissociates in water to form hydrogen ions.
- An Arrhenius base is a substance that dissociates in water to form hydroxide ions.
- A Brønsted–Lowry acid is a proton donor.
- A Brønsted–Lowry base is a proton acceptor.
- A conjugate acid is formed when a proton (H^+) is added to a Brønsted–Lowry base.
- A conjugate base is formed when a proton (H^+) is removed from a Brønsted–Lowry acid.
- A conjugate acid–base pair is an acid and a base that differ by the presence or absence of a proton.

Acid–base Titrations 11

Learning objectives

In this chapter you will learn about:

1 Concentration of solutions

2 Preparation of standard solutions

3 Titrations

4 Standard solutions of acids

Concentration of solutions

Solutions contain at least two substances, a **solute** and a **solvent**. For example, salt water is a solution in which salt is the solute and water is the solvent.

Solutions are described as **concentrated**, if there is a large amount of solute per litre of solution, or **dilute**, if there is not. For accurate work, we need to know the **concentration** of the solution.

The most useful way of expressing the concentration of a solution is in terms of **moles per litre of solution (molarity)**.

If one mole of sodium carbonate is dissolved in water and made up to a total volume of 1 litre with water, a 1 mol l^{-1} solution of sodium carbonate has been made. This may also be written as a 1 M Na_2CO_3 solution.

If 20 g (0.5 moles) of sodium hydroxide is dissolved in water, and more water is then added to make a total volume of 1 litre, a 0.5 M NaOH solution has been made.

Concentration can also be expressed in terms of **grams of solute per litre (g l^{-1})**.

Question

11.1 What is the concentration in grams per litre of a 0.01 M nitric acid (HNO_3) solution?

Answer

Molar mass of HNO_3	= 63 g mol^{-1}
0.01 M HNO_3 solution contains 0.01 moles	= 0.01 × 63 g in 1 litre
Concentration of nitric acid solution	= 0.63 g l^{-1}

Question

11.2 A solution contains 8 g of sodium hydroxide (NaOH) in 250 cm^3 of solution. Calculate the concentration of the solution in moles per litre.

Answer

8 g NaOH in 250 cm^3 of solution is equivalent to 8 × 1000/250

$$= 32 \text{ g in 1 litre}$$

32 g NaOH = 32 / 40 moles NaOH = 0.8 moles NaOH

Concentration of the solution = 0.8 mol l^{-1} (= 0.8 M)

Question

11.3 What mass of sodium hydroxide (NaOH) is contained in 250 cm^3 of 0.02 M sodium hydroxide solution?

Answer

1,000 cm^3 of 0.02 M NaOH solution	= 0.02 moles
250 cm^3 of 0.02 M NaOH	= 0.02 × 250 / 1,000 moles
	= 0.005 moles
Molar mass of NaOH	= 40 g mol^{-1}
Mass of NaOH contained in 250 cm^3 solution	= 40 × 0.005 g = 0.2 g

Question

11.4 How many moles of hydrochloric acid (HCl) are contained in 25 cm^3 of 0.2 M hydrochloric acid solution?

Answer

1,000 cm^3 of 0.2 M HCl solution	= 0.2 moles
1 cm^3 of 0.2 M HCl solution	= 0.2 / 1,000 moles
25 cm^3 of 0.2 M HCl solution	= 0.2 × 25 / 1,000 moles
	= 0.005 moles

Point to note

To solve problems such as those in Question 11.4, there is a formula that may be useful:

Number of moles = volume in cm³ × concentration in moles per litre / 1,000

11.5 How many moles of nitric acid (HNO_3) are contained in 20 cm³ of 0.1 M nitric acid solution?

Answer

Number of moles = volume in cm³ × concentration in moles per litre / 1,000

= 20 × 0.1 / 1,000

= 0.002

Concentration in parts per million

In water analysis, a unit of concentration that is very useful is **parts per million (ppm)**. This is used for very dilute solutions.

1 part per million = 1 milligram per litre

For example, if the concentration of fluoride ion in a water sample is 2 ppm, this means that there are 2 mg of fluoride ion in every litre of the water.

11.6 The concentration of dissolved oxygen in a water sample is 0.0002 M. Calculate the concentration of dissolved oxygen in the water sample in ppm.

Answer

Molar mass of O_2 = 32 g mol^{-1}

There are 0.0002 moles of dissolved oxygen in 1 litre of the water sample.

Mass of O_2 in 1 litre = 0.0002 × 32 g

= 0.0064 g

= 0.0064 × 1,000 mg

= 6.4 mg

Concentration of dissolved oxygen in water sample = 6.4 ppm

Table 11.1

Ways of expressing concentration
Moles per litre of solution
Grams of solute per litre
Parts per million
Percentage weight per volume
Percentage volume per volume
Percentage weight per weight

Concentration expressed in terms of percentages

Concentration can also be expressed in terms of percentage of solute – weight per volume (w/v), volume per volume (v/v) or weight per weight (w/w). Expressing concentration in terms of % (v/v) is useful in everyday life. For example, labels on bottles of wine state the percentage of alcohol in the wine: 11% means 11% (v/v) alcohol in the wine.

Table 11.2

Concentration unit	Example	Meaning
Percentage weight per volume (w/v)	3% (w/v) NaCl solution	3 g NaCl in 100 cm^3 solution
Percentage volume per volume (v/v)	3% (v/v) alcohol solution	3 cm^3 alcohol in 100 cm^3 solution
Percentage weight per weight (w/w)	3% (w/w) sugar solution	3 g sugar in 100 g solution

Question

11.7 A solution contains 20 g potassium hydroxide in 1 litre of solution. Express the concentration of the solution in % (w/v).

Answer

The solution contains 20 g KOH in 1 litre.

100 cm^3 of solution contains 20 × 100 / 1,000 g KOH

$$= 2 \text{ g KOH}$$

Concentration of KOH in solution   = 2% (w/v)

Question

11.8 A bottle of vinegar contains 25 cm^3 ethanoic acid in 500 cm^3 of solution. Express the concentration of ethanoic acid in the solution in % (v/v).

Answer

The solution contains 25 cm^3 CH$_3$COOH in 500 cm^3 of solution.

100 cm^3 of solution contains 25 × 100 / 500 cm^3 CH$_3$COOH

$$= 5 \text{ cm}^3 \text{ CH}_3\text{COOH}$$

Concentration of CH$_3$COOH in solution   = 5% (v/v)

11.9 A solution contains 10 g sodium carbonate in 40 g of solution. Express the concentration of the solution in % (w/w).

Answer

The solution contains 10 g Na_2CO_3 in 40 g of solution.

100 g of solution contains $10 \times 100 / 40$ g Na_2CO_3

$$= 25 \text{ g } Na_2CO_3$$

Concentration of Na_2CO_3 in solution $= 25\%$ (w/w)

Question

11.10 The label on a bottle of wine indicates that the concentration of alcohol in the wine is 9% (v/v). What volume of alcohol is there in 250 cm^3 of the wine?

Answer

100 cm^3 of the wine contains 9 cm^3 alcohol.

250 cm^3 of the wine contains $9 \times 250 / 100$ cm^3 alcohol.

$= 22.5$ cm^3 alcohol

Preparation of standard solutions

> **Key definition**
>
> A **standard solution** is a solution whose concentration is accurately known.

Highly pure substances, called **primary standards**, are needed to make standard solutions. Substances such as anhydrous sodium carbonate are suitable for this purpose. Pure water (deionised or distilled) is used as a solvent.

> **Key definition**
>
> A **primary standard** is a substance that is available in a pure, stable and water-soluble form, so that it can used to make up a solution of accurately known concentration.

Care must be taken when making up a standard solution to minimise error.

- A **volumetric flask** is used because, when it is filled to the calibration mark at the temperature stated on the flask, it contains a specific known volume.

- An analytical balance is used to measure masses of solutes, as it also is extremely accurate.

- Care is taken to ensure that no solution is lost when the solute is being dissolved in a beaker, or when the solution is transferred from the beaker to the volumetric flask.

Experiment

Mandatory Experiment 11.1: Preparation of a standard (0.1 M) solution of sodium carbonate

Procedure

1 Using a balance, measure accurately 2.65 g of pure anhydrous sodium carbonate on a clock glass, and transfer it to a clean 250 cm³ beaker.

2 Add, with stirring, about 50 cm³ of deionised water to the beaker.

3 To ensure that all the sodium carbonate has been transferred from the clock glass, use a wash bottle to rinse the clock glass with deionised water, and add the rinsings to the beaker.

4 Continue stirring the mixture with a stirring rod until the sodium carbonate has fully dissolved.

5 Wash off the solution on the stirring rod with deionised water into the beaker, using a wash bottle.

6 Pour the solution through a clean funnel into the 250 cm³ volumetric flask.

7 Using a wash bottle, rinse out the beaker several times with deionised water, and add the rinsings through the funnel to the solution in the flask.

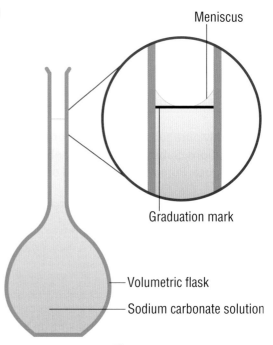

Meniscus

Graduation mark

Volumetric flask

Sodium carbonate solution

Fig. 11.1

8 Rinse the funnel with deionised water, allowing the water to run into the flask.

9 Fill the flask to within about 1 cm of the calibration mark. Then add the water dropwise, using a dropping pipette, until the bottom of the meniscus just rests on the calibration mark.

10 Stopper the flask and invert it several times to ensure an evenly mixed solution.

Effect of dilution on concentration

If a solution is coloured, for example a solution of potassium manganate(VII), then the colour intensity depends on the concentration. Diluting the solution results in a lightening of the colour of the solution.

Calculation of concentrations of diluted solutions

Question

11.11 If 20 cm^3 of a 3 M hydrochloric acid solution is diluted to a volume of 1 l with water, what is the concentration of the diluted acid?

Answer

1,000 cm^3 of 3 M HCl solution contains 3 moles of HCl.

20 cm^3 of 3 M HCl solution contains 3 × 20 / 1,000 moles of HCl.

$$= 0.06 \text{ moles of HCl}$$

1 litre of diluted acid contains 0.06 moles.

Concentration of the diluted acid $= 0.06$ mol l$^{-1} = 0.06$ M

Point to note

To solve problems such as that in Question 11.11, there is a formula that may be useful:

$$V_{dil} \times M_{dil} = V_{conc} \times M_{conc}$$

Question

11.12 If 12 cm^3 of a 0.1 M sodium hydroxide solution is diluted to a volume of 500 cm^3 with water, what is the concentration of the diluted solution?

Answer

$V_{dil} \times M_{dil}$ $= V_{conc} \times M_{conc}$

$500 \times M_{dil}$ $= 12 \times 0.1$

M_{dil} $= 12 \times 0.1 / 500$ mol l$^{-1} = 0.0024$ mol l^{-1}

Concentration of diluted solution $= 0.0024$ mol l^{-1}

11.13 What volume of a 2 M sodium hydroxide solution is needed to make up 100 cm^3 of a 0.1 M sodium hydroxide solution?

Answer

$V_{dil} \times M_{dil}$ $\qquad = V_{conc} \times M_{conc}$

100×0.1 $\qquad = V_{conc} \times 2$

V_{conc} $\qquad = 100 \times 0.1 / 2 \text{ mol l}^{-1} = 5 \text{ cm}^3$

Volume of 2 M NaOH solution needed $= 5 \text{ cm}^3$

Titrations

The concentration of a solution may be found experimentally by **titrating** it with a standard solution.

In a titration:

- A measured volume of one solution is added from a **burette** to a definite known volume of the other solution in a conical flask, until the reaction just reaches completion.

- The end point, at which the reaction just reaches completion, is often detected using an indicator.

- The indicator changes colour at the end point.

- The conical flask is sometimes placed on a white tile during the titration in order that this colour change can be seen more easily.

The instrument used to place a known volume of solution in the conical flask is a **pipette**. This instrument is designed to deliver a specific volume of liquid. When filled to the mark it contains slightly more than this volume; however, some of this liquid is retained after delivery. To ensure that the pipette delivers only the correct amount of liquid, it is allowed to release its contents freely, and then the tip of the pipette is touched to the inside of the conical flask for about 3 seconds.

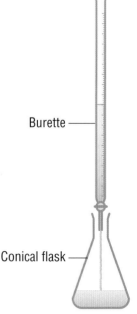

Burette ─

Conical flask ─

Fig. 11.2 A burette and a conical flask in use during a titration

Fig. 11.3 A pipette

Precautions to ensure accurate titration results

- The burette is washed out with pure water and then with the solution that it is to contain. The solution is then added to it, using a beaker and filter funnel.

- The tap of the burette is opened briefly to fill the part of the burette below the tap.

- The burette is then filled up, until the level of the liquid is above the 0 cm^3 mark. The funnel is then removed. The tap of the burette is opened again to allow the level of liquid to fall to a definite mark. The tap is closed and the level is then noted. All burette readings are taken with the surface of the liquid at eye level; the bottom level of the meniscus is then read.

- The conical flask is washed out with pure water only; the pipette is washed out with pure water and then with the second solution.

- The second solution is added to the conical flask using a pipette.

- The conical flask is swirled well after each addition of solution from the burette. Any solution adhering to the sides may be washed down with pure water, using a wash bottle.

- A rough titration is carried out first to determine the approximate end point. The titration is then repeated more accurately, with very careful addition of the solution from the burette as the approximate end point is approached. Two consistent titration results (titres) are got in this way, agreeing within $\pm 0.1 \text{ cm}^3$. The mean of the accurate titres is taken as the final result.

Standard solutions of acids

Standard solutions of the common laboratory acids cannot usually be prepared directly, as these acids are not readily available in a sufficiently pure state. Concentrated hydrochloric acid is volatile – hydrogen chloride gas starts to escape once a bottle of the concentrated acid is opened.

Concentrated nitric acid is volatile and is likely to decompose. Concentrated sulfuric acid is hygroscopic, i.e. it readily absorbs water vapour from the air.

A solution of the acid can be titrated with a standard solution of sodium carbonate. The object of this is to **standardise** the acid, that is, to find its concentration accurately. The mean titration result is used to calculate the concentration of the acid solution.

Acid–base titrations

In straightforward titration calculations, where only the unknown concentration is required, the following formula can be used:

$$V_1 \times M_1 \times n_2 = V_2 \times M_2 \times n_1$$

where

V_1 = volume in cm^3 of the acid solution used in the titration

M_1 = concentration of the acid solution

n_2 = number of moles of the base in the balanced equation for the reaction

V_2 = volume in cm^3 of the basic solution used in the titration

M_2 = concentration of the basic solution

n_1 = number of moles of the acid in the balanced equation for the reaction

Question

11.14 In a titration, 25 cm^3 of a 0.05 M sodium carbonate solution required 22 cm^3 of a hydrochloric acid solution for complete neutralisation. Calculate the concentration of the hydrochloric acid solution. The equation for the reaction is:

$$2HCl_{(aq)} + Na_2CO_{3(aq)} \rightarrow 2NaCl_{(aq)} + H_2O_{(l)} + CO_{2(g)}$$

Answer

$V_1 \times M_1 \times n_2 = V_2 \times M_2 \times n_1$

TV_1 = volume in cm^3 of the acid solution used in the titration = 22 cm^3

M_1 = concentration of the acid solution = ?

n_2 = number of moles of the base in the balanced equation = 1

V_2 = volume in cm^3 of the basic solution used in the titration = 25 cm^3

M_2 = concentration of the basic solution = 0.05 M

n_1 = number of moles of the acid in the balanced equation = 2

$22 \times M_1 \times 1$	= 25 × 0.05 × 2
M_1	= 25 × 0.05 × 2 / (22 × 1)
	= 0.114 mol l^{-1}

Concentration of HCl solution = 0.114 mol l^{-1}

The formula $V_1 \times M_1 \times n_2 = V_2 \times M_2 \times n_1$ may also be used to find the volume of one of the solutions in a titration, provided that the volume of the other solution and the concentrations of both solutions are known.

Question

11.15 In a titration, what volume of a 0.05 M hydrochloric acid is required to neutralise 25 cm^3 of a 0.04 M sodium hydroxide solution? The equation for the reaction is:

$$HCl_{(aq)} + NaOH_{(aq)} \rightarrow NaCl_{(aq)} + H_2O_{(l)}$$

Answer

$V_1 \times M_1 \times n_2 = V_2 \times M_2 \times n_1$

$V_1 \times 0.05 \times 1 = 25 \times 0.04 \times 1$

$V_1 \qquad = 25 \times 0.04 \times 1 / (0.05 \times 1)$

$\qquad = 20$ cm^3 of HCl solution

Experiment

Mandatory Experiment 11.2: Standardisation of a hydrochloric acid solution using a standard solution of sodium carbonate

Methyl orange indicator solution is used. At the end point – when neutralisation just occurs – the indicator changes colour from yellow to peach/pink.

Procedure

1 Rinse the conical flask with deionised water.

2 Rinse the pipette with deionised water and then with sodium carbonate solution.

3 Using the pipette, place 25 cm³ of the sodium carbonate solution in the conical flask. Add 3 drops of methyl orange indicator.

4 Pour about 50 cm³ of the hydrochloric acid solution into a clean dry beaker.

5 Rinse the burette with deionised water and clamp it vertically in the retort stand.

6 Using a funnel, rinse the burette with the hydrochloric acid solution.

7 Fill the burette with hydrochloric acid solution above the zero mark. Remove the funnel. Allow the acid to flow into a beaker until the level of liquid is at the zero mark.

8 Carry out a rough titration by adding hydrochloric acid solution from the burette in approximately 1 cm³ lots to the conical flask, swirling the flask constantly, until the colour of the solution in the conical flask changes. Note the burette reading.

9 Repeat the titration more accurately until two readings agree within 0.1 cm³.

10 Calculate the concentration of the hydrochloric acid solution.

Question

11.16 In a titration, 25 cm³ of a sodium hydroxide solution required 19.5 cm³ of a 0.1 M hydrochloric acid solution for complete neutralisation. Calculate the concentration of the sodium hydroxide solution. The equation for the reaction is:

$$HCl_{(aq)} + NaOH_{(aq)} \rightarrow NaCl_{(aq)} + H_2O_{(l)}$$

Answer

$$V_1 \times M_1 \times n_2 = V_2 \times M_2 \times n_1$$

$$19.5 \times 0.1 \times 1 = 25 \times M_2 \times 1$$

$$M_2 = 19.5 \times 0.1 \times 1 / (25 \times 1)$$

$$= 0.078 \text{ mol } l^{-1}$$

Concentration of NaOH solution $= 0.078 \text{ mol } l^{-1}$

Experiment

Mandatory Experiment 11.2(a): A hydrochloric acid/sodium hydroxide titration and the use of this titration in making the salt sodium chloride

(i) To find the end point accurately

Procedure

1 Rinse the conical flask with deionised water.

2 Rinse the burette with deionised water and then with hydrochloric acid solution.

3 Rinse the pipette with deionised water and then with sodium hydroxide solution.

4 Using the pipette, place 25 cm³ of the unknown sodium hydroxide solution in the conical flask. Add 3 drops of methyl orange indicator.

5 Fill the burette to the 0 cm³ mark with hydrochloric acid solution.

6 Carry out one rough and two accurate titrations.

7 Calculate the concentration of the sodium hydroxide solution.

(ii) To obtain a sample of salt

Procedure

1 Place 25 cm³ of the sodium hydroxide solution in a beaker, without any indicator.

2 Using your results from part (i) of the experiment, add just enough hydrochloric acid to exactly neutralise it.

3 Gently heat the solution until all the water has evaporated to dryness. A sample of sodium chloride will remain in the beaker.

Solving volumetric problems from first principles

In a calculation involving a standard solution where more than just the unknown concentration is required, or where a solid is one of the reactants, an alternative method from first principles should be used. This method can also be used to solve more straightforward problems.

Question

11.17 In a titration, 25 cm³ of a 0.12 M sodium hydroxide solution required 24 cm³ of a sulfuric acid solution for complete neutralisation. Calculate (i) the number of moles of sodium hydroxide consumed, (ii) the number of moles of sulfuric acid consumed, and (iii) the concentration of the sulfuric acid solution. The equation for the reaction is:

$$H_2SO_{4(aq)} + 2NaOH_{(aq)} \rightarrow Na_2SO_{4(aq)} + 2H_2O_{(l)}$$

Answer

(i)   In the titration, 25 cm³ of 0.12 M sodium hydroxide solution were used.

   1,000 cm³ of 0.12 M NaOH solution contains 0.12 moles.

   25 cm³ of 0.12 M NaOH solution contains 0.12 × 25 / 1,000 moles

$$= 0.003 \text{ moles}$$

(ii) The equation for the reaction is:

$$H_2SO_{4(aq)} + 2NaOH_{(aq)} \rightarrow Na_2SO_{4(aq)} + 2H_2O_{(l)}$$

   2 moles of NaOH react with 1 mole of H_2SO_4.

   1 mole of NaOH reacts with 0.5 moles of H_2SO_4.

   0.003 moles of NaOH reacts with 0.003 × 0.5 moles of H_2SO_4.

$$= 0.0015 \text{ moles of } H_2SO_4$$

(iii) In 24 cm³ of the H_2SO_4 solution there are 0.0015 moles of H_2SO_4.

   1,000 cm³ of H_2SO_4 solution contains 0.0015 × 1,000 / 24 moles

$$= 0.0625 \text{ moles}$$

   Concentration of H_2SO_4 solution $= 0.0625$ mol l⁻¹

Question

11.18 What mass of magnesium will react with 20 cm³ of a 0.09 M hydrochloric acid solution? The equation for the reaction is:

$$2HCl_{(aq)} + Mg_{(s)} \rightarrow MgCl_{2(aq)} + H_{2(g)}$$

Answer

$1,000 \text{ cm}^3$ of 0.09 M HCl solution contains 0.09 moles.

20 cm^3 of 0.09 M HCl solution contains $0.09 \times 20 / 1,000$ moles

$$= 0.0018 \text{ moles}$$

From the equation, 1 mole of Mg reacts with 2 moles of HCl.

0.0018 moles of HCl react with $0.0018 / 2 = 0.0009$ moles Mg

Molar mass of Mg	$= 24 \text{ g mol}^{-1}$
0.0009 moles of Mg	$= 0.0009 \times 24 \text{ g} = 0.0216 \text{ g Mg}$
Mass of Mg	$= 0.0216 \text{ g}$

Applications of acid–base titrations

Question

11.19 A sample of vinegar was diluted from 25 cm^3 to 250 cm^3 with water. In a titration, 25 cm^3 of a 0.1 M sodium hydroxide solution required 30 cm^3 of the diluted vinegar for complete neutralisation. Calculate the concentration of ethanoic acid (CH_3COOH) in the vinegar in (i) mol l^{-1} and (ii) % (w/v). The equation for the reaction is:

$$CH_3COOH_{(aq)} + NaOH_{(aq)} \rightarrow CH_3COONa_{(aq)} + H_2O_{(l)}$$

Answer

(i) The formula $V_1 \times M_1 \times n_2 = V_2 \times M_2 \times n_1$ is used first to find the concentration of ethanoic acid in the diluted vinegar.

$V_1 \times M_1 \times n_2 = V_2 \times M_2 \times n_1$

$30 \times M_1 \times 1 = 25 \times 0.1 \times 1$

$M_1 \qquad = 25 \times 0.1 \times 1 / (30 \times 1)$

$\qquad = 0.083 \text{ mol } l^{-1}$

Concentration of CH_3COOH in diluted vinegar $= 0.083 \text{ mol } l^{-1}$

Vinegar was originally diluted from 25 cm^3 to 250 cm^3 with water, i.e. a tenfold dilution.

Concentration of CH_3COOH in vinegar	$= 10 \times 0.083 \text{ mol } l^{-1} = 0.83 \text{ M}$
(ii) Molar mass of CH_3COOH	$= 60 \text{ g mol}^{-1}$
Concentration of CH_3COOH in g l^{-1} in vinegar	$= 0.83 \times 60$
	$= 49.8$
Percentage (w/v) of CH_3COOH in vinegar	$= 49.8 \times 100 / 1,000$
	$= 4.98\%$

Mandatory Experiment 11.3: Determination of the concentration of ethanoic acid in vinegar

Phenolphthalein indicator is used. At the end point, the indicator changes colour from pink to colourless.

Procedure

1 Place 25 cm^3 of 0.1 M sodium hydroxide solution in a conical flask and add 3 drops of phenolphthalein indicator.

2 Place 25 cm^3 of vinegar in a 250 cm^3 volumetric flask and dilute with water to the calibration mark.

3 Stopper the flask and invert several times to ensure an evenly mixed solution.

4 Carry out one rough and two accurate titrations.

5 Calculate the concentration in mol l^{-1} of ethanoic acid in the diluted vinegar solution.

6 Calculate the concentration in mol l^{-1} of ethanoic acid in the vinegar.

7 Calculate the percentage (w/v) of ethanoic acid in the vinegar.

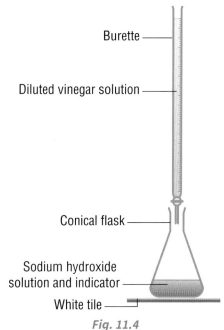

Burette

Diluted vinegar solution

Conical flask

Sodium hydroxide solution and indicator

White tile

Fig. 11.4

Question

11.20 2.91 g of a monobasic acid (HX) were dissolved in water and made up to 250 cm^3 with water. This solution was titrated with 0.108 M sodium hydroxide solution. 25 cm^3 of the sodium hydroxide solution required 22.5 cm^3 of the HX solution for complete neutralisation. The equation for the reaction is:

$$HX_{(aq)} + NaOH_{(aq)} \rightarrow NaX_{(aq)} + H_2O_{(l)}$$

(i) Calculate the concentration in (a) g l^{-1} and (b) mol l^{-1} of the acid.

(ii) Calculate the molar mass of HX.

Answer

(i)

(a) 2.91 g of HX in 250 cm^3 = 2.91 × 4 g = 11.64 g in 1 litre

Therefore: concentration of HX   = 11.64 g l^{-1}

(b) $V_1 × M_1 × n_2$ = $V_2 × M_2 × n_1$

      22.5 × M_1 × 1   = 25 × 0.108 × 1

      M_1 = 25 × 0.108 × 1 / (22.5 × 1)

                            = 0.12 mol l^{-1}

Concentration of HX solution   = 0.12 mol l^{-1}

(ii) 0.12 moles has a mass of 11.64 g.

     1 mole has a mass of 11.64 / 0.12 g   = 97 g

     Molar mass of HX   = 97 g mol^{-1}

Question

11.21 Crystals of hydrated sodium carbonate ($Na_2CO_3.xH_2O$) of mass 3.15 g were dissolved in water and made up to 250 cm^3 in a volumetric flask. 25 cm^3 of this solution required 15 cm^3 of a 0.15 M hydrochloric acid solution for complete neutralisation. The equation for the reaction is:

$$2HCl_{(aq)} + Na_2CO_{3(aq)} → 2NaCl_{(aq)} + H_2O_{(l)} + CO_{2(g)}$$

Find (i) the concentration of the sodium carbonate solution, (ii) the value of x in the formula $Na_2CO_3.xH_2O$, and (iii) the percentage of water of crystallisation in the hydrated sodium carbonate.

Answer

(i) $V_1 × M_1 × n_2$ = $V_2 × M_2 × n_1$

     15 × 0.15 × 1   = 25 × M_2 × 2

     M_2 = 15 × 0.15 × 1 / (25 × 2)

                       = 0.045 mol l^{-1}

Concentration of Na_2CO_3 solution = 0.045 mol l^{-1}

(ii) Molar mass of $Na_2CO_3.xH_2O$

$= 46 + 12 + 48 + 18x$

$= 106 + 18x$

Concentration of Na_2CO_3 in mol l^{-1} $= 0.045$

Concentration of Na_2CO_3 in g l^{-1} $= 3.15 \times 4 = 12.6$

Mass of 0.045 moles of $Na_2CO_3.xH_2O$ $= 12.6$ g

Molar mass of $Na_2CO_3.xH_2O$ $= 12.6 / 0.045$ g mol^{-1}

            $= 280$ g mol^{-1}

$106 + 18x$ $= 280$

$18x$ $= 174$

x $= 9.7$

Remember

Hydrated sodium carbonate gradually loses water of crystallisation over a period of time, so it is not unusual to get a value of x that is not a whole number.

(iii) Molar mass of hydrated sodium carbonate $= 280$ g mol^{-1}

Percentage of water of crystallisation in the compound $= 174 \times 100 / 280\%$

                  $= 62.1\%$

 Experiment

Mandatory Experiment 11.4: Determination of the amount of water of crystallisation in hydrated sodium carbonate

Methyl orange indicator solution is used. At the end point, the indicator changes colour from yellow to peach/pink.

Procedure

1 Weigh accurately about 1.5 g of hydrated sodium carbonate into a beaker.

2 Add about 50 cm^3 of deionised water and stir to dissolve the sample.

3 Using a funnel, transfer all of the solution into a 250 cm^3 volumetric flask. Rinse the beaker with deionised water and add the washings to the volumetric flask.

Procedure

4 Carefully make up the volumetric flask to the mark. Stopper the flask and invert several times.

5 Titrate the sodium carbonate solution against 0.1 M hydrochloric acid, using 25 cm^3 of sodium carbonate solution in the conical flask and methyl orange as indicator.

6 Repeat the titrations more accurately until two titrations agree to within 0.1 cm^3.

7 Calculate the concentration of the sodium carbonate solution.

8 Find the formula of hydrated sodium carbonate.

9 Find the percentage of water of crystallisation present in hydrated sodium carbonate.

Key-points!

- Concentration is defined as the amount of solute in a specified amount of solution. It is expressed in moles per litre of solution (molarity).

- Concentration can also be expressed in grams of solute per litre (g l^{-1}).

- A standard solution is a solution whose concentration is accurately known.

- A primary standard is a substance that is available in a pure, stable and water-soluble form, so that it can used to make up a solution of accurately known concentration.

Oxidation Numbers and Redox Titrations

12

Oxidation numbers

Key definition

The **oxidation number** of an atom is defined as the charge that an atom appears to have when the electrons are distributed according to certain rules.

1 In free elements, each atom has an oxidation number of 0. For example, in a nitrogen molecule (N_2) each nitrogen atom has an oxidation number of 0.

2 The sum of the oxidation numbers of all the atoms in a molecule is 0. For example, in the water molecule (H_2O), where hydrogen has an oxidation number of +1 and oxygen has an oxidation number of –2, the oxidation numbers add up to 0:

$$H_2O$$

$$2(+1) - 2 = 0$$

3 The oxidation number of a simple ion containing one atom is equal to the charge on the ion. For example, in a chloride ion (Cl^-) the oxidation number of chlorine is –1.

4   The sum of the oxidation numbers of all the atoms in a complex ion is equal to the charge on the ion. For example, in a nitrate ion (NO_3^-), where nitrogen has an oxidation number of +5 and oxygen has an oxidation number of −2, the oxidation numbers add up to −1:

$$NO_3^-$$

$$+5 + 3(-2) = -1$$

5   Hydrogen has an oxidation number of +1 in its compounds, except in metallic hydrides, where it is −1.

6   Oxygen has an oxidation number of −2 in its compounds, except in hydrogen peroxide where it is −1, and when bonded to fluorine it is +2.

7   The oxidation number of Group 1 elements in their compounds is always +1, and the oxidation number of Group 2 elements in their compounds is always +2.

8   The oxidation number of a halogen when bonded to a less electronegative atom is −1. Fluorine is the most electronegative element and always has an oxidation number of −1 in its compounds. Chlorine has an oxidation number of −1 in compounds where it is not bonded to oxygen or fluorine.

Oxidation states

Oxidation numbers represent the oxidation state of an element. As indicated in rule 7, Group 1 and 2 elements in their compounds have just one normal oxidation state each (1 and 2, respectively). With the exception of fluorine, the halogens in their compounds have several oxidation states.

Remember

All elements have an oxidation state of 0 when uncombined.

The transition metals each have a number of different oxidation states in their compounds.

Table 12.1 Oxidation states for transition metals

Element	Oxidation states
Chromium	2, 3, 6
Manganese	2, 3, 4, 6, 7
Iron	2, 3, 6
Copper	1, 2

Calculation of oxidation numbers

Question

12.1 What is the oxidation number of the sulfur atom in the H_2SO_4 molecule?

Answer

Let the oxidation number of S $= x$

The oxidation number of H $= +1$ (from rule 5)

The oxidation number of O $= -2$ (from rule 6)

Therefore: $2(+1) + x + 4(-2)$ $= 0$ (from rule 2)

Therefore: x $= -2 + 8 = +6$

Naming of transition metal compounds

Oxidation numbers are used when naming compounds of transition metals systematically. In the case of a compound containing two elements only, the ending '–ide' is used as usual, and the oxidation number of the metal is indicated by a roman number in brackets after the name of that metal. An example of this is copper(II) oxide.

If the compound contains a complex ion, for example $CuNO_3$, then the name ends with the name of the complex ion – copper(I) nitrate in this case. If the compound contains water of crystallisation, then the number of molecules of water of crystallisation is indicated at the end of the name, as shown for $CuSO_4.5H_2O$. The systematic name of this compound is copper(II) sulfate-5-water.

Question

12.2 What is the systematic name of $MnCl_2$?

Answer

Let the oxidation number of Mn $= x$

The oxidation number of Cl $= -1$ (from rule 8)

Therefore: $x + 2(-1)$ $= 0$ (from rule 2)

Therefore: x $= 2$

The name of the compound is therefore manganese(II) chloride.

Question

12.3 What is the formula of iron(II) sulfate-7-water?

Answer

The iron(II) ion has a charge of +2.

The sulfate ion has a charge of –2.

The formula is $FeSO_4.7H_2O$

Oxidation and reduction in terms of oxidation numbers

In terms of oxidation numbers, oxidation is an increase in oxidation number, while reduction is a decrease in oxidation number.

In working out what is oxidised and what is reduced in a reaction, the oxidation number should be written below the atom to which it applies, as shown in the following examples:

$$H_2O \qquad Cr_2O_7^{2-} \qquad OH^-$$
$$+1\,-2 \qquad +6\,-2 \qquad -2\,+1$$

Remember

When doing redox equations, the oxidation number for only a single atom of each element should be written directly underneath.

Key definition

Oxidation is an increase in oxidation number.

Key definition

Reduction is a decrease in oxidation number.

Question

12.4 What is (i) oxidised, (ii) reduced, (iii) the oxidising agent, and (iv) the reducing agent in the following redox reaction?

$$As_2O_3 + 2I_2 + 2H_2O \rightarrow As_2O_5 + 4I^- + 4H^+$$

Answer

Assign oxidation numbers to all of the atoms in the equation, using the rules:

$$As_2O_3 + 2I_2 + 2H_2O \rightarrow As_2O_5 + 4I^- + 4H^+$$
$$+3\,-2 \quad 0 \quad +1\,-2 \quad +5\,-2 \quad -1 \quad +1$$

(i) The oxidation number of arsenic increases from +3 to +5. Therefore, arsenic is oxidised.

(ii) The oxidation number of iodine decreases from 0 to −1. Therefore, iodine is reduced.

(iii) Iodine is the oxidising agent because it is reduced itself.

(iv) Arsenic is the reducing agent because it is oxidised itself.

Everyday examples of oxidising and reducing agents

Bleaching is a redox reaction. Many domestic bleaches contain sodium hypochlorite (NaOCl). This is an example of an oxidising bleach. When it bleaches by oxidation, it is reduced to sodium chloride:

$$NaOCl \rightarrow NaCl$$
$${+1\ -2\ +1}{+1\ -1}$$

Reducing bleaches include sodium sulfite (Na_2SO_3), used for example in the paper industry, and sulfur dioxide (SO_2), used in solution where it forms sulfite ions (SO_3^{2-}). When sulfite ions bleach by reduction, they are converted to sulfate ions:

$$SO_3^{2-} \rightarrow SO_4^{2-}$$
$${+4\ -2}{+6\ -2}$$

Balancing redox equations using oxidation numbers

Question

12.5 Balance the following redox equation:

$$Cr_2O_7^{2-} + Fe^{2+} + H^+ \rightarrow Cr^{3+} + Fe^{3+} + H_2O$$

Answer

1. Assign oxidation numbers to all the atoms in the equation.

$$Cr_2O_7^{2-} + Fe^{2+} + H^+ \rightarrow Cr^{3+} + Fe^{3+} + H_2O$$
$${+6\ -2}\phantom{O_7^{2-}}{+2}{+1}{+3}\phantom{Cr^{3+}}{+3}\phantom{+Fe^{3+}}{+1\ -2}$$

2. Identify atoms that are oxidised or reduced, include any subscripts attached to them, and indicate the extent of the change in oxidation numbers:

    Cr_2: $2(+6 \rightarrow +3)$, i.e. decrease of $2 \times 3 = 6$ Reduction

    Fe: $+2 \rightarrow +3$, i.e. increase of 1   Oxidation

3. Since the total increase in oxidation number must equal the total decrease, the ratio of chromium to iron must be Cr_2 : Fe = 1 : 6

4. Rewrite the original equation and apply the ratio Cr_2 : Fe = 1 : 6

$$Cr_2O_7^{2-} + 6Fe^{2+} + H^+ \rightarrow 2Cr^{3+} + 6Fe^{3+} + H_2O$$

5. Balance the rest by inspection:

$$Cr_2O_7^{2-} + 6Fe^{2+} + 14H^+ \rightarrow 2Cr^{3+} + 6Fe^{3+} + 7H_2O$$

Redox titrations with potassium manganate(VII)

In redox titrations, potassium manganate(VII) is a very useful oxidising agent.

- It has the advantage of (1) reacting completely and (2) acting as its own indicator, giving a sharp end point.

- It has the disadvantage in solution of not being very stable. As a result, solutions of potassium manganate(VII) have to be standardised shortly before use by titration against a standard solution of a substance such as ammonium iron(II) sulfate.

Ammonium iron(II) sulfate is a primary standard.

- It is stable and available in a high state of purity.

- In acidic conditions, it reacts readily with a solution of potassium manganate(VII), and the reaction goes to completion.

- Standard solutions of ammonium iron(II) sulfate are stable. Dilute sulfuric acid is used along with deionised water in making up these solutions. This ensures stability by inhibiting premature oxidation of iron(II) in the solutions by air to iron(III).

Potassium manganate(VII) contains manganese in the highly coloured (VII) oxidation state.

- Manganese in this state is a good oxidising agent because it is very easily reduced.

- If acidic conditions are used, it undergoes complete reduction to the (II) oxidation state, which is almost colourless.

- The end point of a titration involving the

$$Mn(VII)_{(aq)} \rightarrow Mn(II)_{(aq)}$$

reaction is therefore easily detectable – no indicator is necessary. Before the end point, all added potassium manganate(VII) solution is decolourised by reaction with iron(II) ions:

$$MnO_4^-{}_{(aq)} + 5Fe^{2+}{}_{(aq)} + 8H^+{}_{(aq)} \rightarrow Mn^{2+}{}_{(aq)} + 5Fe^{3+}{}_{(aq)} + 4H_2O_{(l)}$$

- At the end point, all of the iron(II) ions have reacted, and added potassium manganate(VII) solution is no longer decolourised.

If acidic conditions are not used in the titration, the reaction will not be according to the above equation.

- Instead, manganese is likely to be reduced to intermediate oxidation states – for example, Mn(IV) which appears as a brown precipitate – and not directly to the (II) oxidation state.

- To prevent this happening, dilute sulfuric acid is used to enable complete reduction of the manganese from Mn(VII) to Mn(II) to occur. Unlike hydrochloric acid, it does not react with potassium manganate(VII). Nitric acid cannot be used to lower the pH in a redox titration, as it is a powerful oxidising agent itself.

Manganate(VII)–iron(II) titrations

In redox titrations involving potassium manganate(VII), the manganate(VII) solution is placed in the burette and the reducing agent solution and sulfuric acid solution are placed in the conical flask. Because the dark colour of the manganate(VII) solution makes the meniscus difficult to see, burette readings are taken from the top of the liquid level.

Question

12.6 24 cm³ of a potassium manganate(VII) solution required 25 cm³ of a 0.0108 M ammonium iron(II) sulfate solution for complete reaction. Calculate the concentration in mol l⁻¹ of the potassium manganate(VII) solution.

Answer

$$MnO_4^-{}_{(aq)} + 5Fe^{2+}{}_{(aq)} + 8H^+{}_{(aq)} \rightarrow Mn^{2+}{}_{(aq)} + 5Fe^{3+}{}_{(aq)} + 4H_2O_{(l)}$$

$$V_1 \times M_1 \times n_2 \quad = V_2 \times M_2 \times n_1$$

$$24 \times M_1 \times 5 \quad = 25 \times 0.0108 \times 1$$

$$M_1 \quad = 25 \times 0.0108 \times 1 / (24 \times 5)$$

$$= 0.00225 \text{ mol } l^{-1}$$

Concentration of potassium manganate(VII) solution = 0.00225 mol l⁻¹

 Experiment

Mandatory Experiment 12.1: A potassium manganate(VII)–ammonium iron(II) sulfate titration

No indicator is needed as the manganate(VII) ions are decolourised in the reaction until the end point, when a pale pink colour persists.

Procedure

1 Wash the pipette, burette and conical flask with deionised water.

2 Rinse the burette with the potassium manganate(VII) solution and the pipette with the iron(II) solution.

3 Place 25 cm³ of the iron(II) solution in the conical flask using the pipette. Add about 10 cm³ of dilute sulfuric acid.

4 Using a funnel, fill the burette with potassium manganate(VII) solution, making sure that the part below the tap is filled before adjusting to zero (Fig. 12.1). Because of the dark colour of the potassium manganate(VII) solution, take readings from the top of the meniscus.

5 Carry out a rough titration and a number of accurate titrations until two titres agree to within 0.1 cm^3. The end point of the titration is detected by the first persisting pale pink colour.

6 Calculate the concentration of the potassium manganate(VII) solution.

Applications of manganate(VII)–iron(II) titrations

A standard solution of potassium manganate(VII) can be used to find the amount of iron in an iron tablet. These tablets are commonly used in the treatment of anaemia.

- To find the iron(II) content of an iron tablet, a known number of tablets are first dissolved in dilute sulfuric acid.

- This solution is then titrated against a standardised potassium manganate(VII) solution. The reaction is represented by the equation:

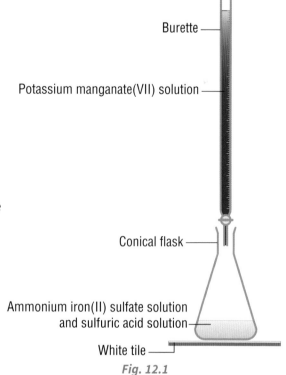

Burette

Potassium manganate(VII) solution

Conical flask

Ammonium iron(II) sulfate solution and sulfuric acid solution

White tile

Fig. 12.1

$$MnO_4^-{}_{(aq)} + 5Fe^{2+}{}_{(aq)} + 8H^+{}_{(aq)} \rightarrow Mn^{2+}{}_{(aq)} + 5Fe^{3+}{}_{(aq)} + 4H_2O_{(l)}$$

Question

12.7 In an experiment to determine the mass of iron in an iron tablet, five iron tablets of total mass 1.8 g were dissolved in dilute sulfuric acid and the solution made up to 250 cm^3 with deionised water. 25 cm^3 of this solution required 16.5 cm^3 of a 0.005 M potassium manganate(VII) solution for complete reaction. Calculate (i) the mass of iron in one iron tablet and (ii) the percentage of iron in the tablet.

Answer

$$MnO_4^-{}_{(aq)} + 5Fe^{2+}{}_{(aq)} + 8H^+{}_{(aq)} \rightarrow Mn^{2+}{}_{(aq)} + 5Fe^{3+}{}_{(aq)} + 4H_2O_{(l)}$$

$V_1 \times M_1 \times n_2$	$= V_2 \times M_2 \times n_1$
$16.5 \times 0.005 \times 5$	$= 25 \times M_2 \times 1$
M_2	$= 16.5 \times 0.005 \times 5 / (25 \times 1)$

	= 0.0165 mol l^{-1}
Concentration of iron(II) solution	= 0.0165 mol l^{-1}
Volume of iron(II) solution in total	= 250 cm^3
Moles of iron in this volume	= 0.0165 / 4 = 0.004125
Mass of iron in this volume	= 0.004125 × 56 = 0.231 g
(i) Mass of iron in each tablet	= 0.231 / 5 = 0.0462 g
Mass of each tablet	= 1.8 / 5 = 0.36 g
(ii) Percentage of iron in each tablet	= 0.0462 × 100 / 0.36%
	= 12.8%

Experiment

Mandatory Experiment 12.2: Determination of iron(II) in an iron tablet using a standard solution of potassium manganate(VII)

Procedure

1 Find the mass of five iron tablets.

2 Crush the weighed tablets in a mortar and pestle. Transfer all the ground material to a beaker and stir to dissolve it in about 100 cm^3 of dilute sulfuric acid.

3 Transfer all of this solution (including washings) to a 250 cm^3 volumetric flask and make the solution up to the mark with deionised water. Stopper the flask and invert it several times.

4 Wash the pipette, burette and conical flask with deionised water.

5 Rinse the burette with the potassium manganate(VII) solution and the pipette with the iron tablets solution.

6 Place 25 cm^3 of the iron tablets solution in the conical flask using the pipette. Add about 10 cm^3 of dilute sulfuric acid.

7 Using a funnel, fill the burette with potassium manganate(VII) solution, making sure that the part below the tap is filled before adjusting to zero. Because of the dark colour of the potassium manganate(VII) solution, take readings from the top of the meniscus.

8 Carry out a rough titration and a number of accurate titrations until two titres agree to within 0.1 cm^3. The end point of the titration is detected by the first persisting pale pink colour.

9 Calculate the concentration of iron(II) in the solution of iron tablets.

10 Calculate the mass of iron in an iron tablet.

Iodine–thiosulfate titrations

Iodine reacts with sodium thiosulfate according to the equation:

$$I_{2(aq)} + 2S_2O_3{}^{2-}{}_{(aq)} \rightarrow 2I^-{}_{(aq)} + S_4O_6{}^{2-}{}_{(aq)}$$

Iodine is reduced and is therefore the oxidising agent. The thiosulfate ion is oxidised.

- This reaction is useful in volumetric analysis, as the reaction goes to completion and the end point can be easily detected.

- Neither iodine nor sodium thiosulfate is a primary standard. Iodine is too volatile, while sodium thiosulfate is not sufficiently pure.

- However, a standard solution of iodine can be used to standardise a sodium thiosulfate solution. Also, a standard solution of sodium thiosulfate can be used to standardise an iodine solution.

- In an iodine–thiosulfate titration, the iodine solution is placed in the conical flask.

- The thiosulfate solution is added from the burette until the colour of the mixture in the flask changes from brown to pale yellow.

- A freshly prepared solution of starch is then added. The starch acts as an indicator.

- When it is added, it forms a blue-black colour with iodine. This colour disappears at the end point.

Question

12.8 25 cm^3 of an iodine solution required 24.5 cm^3 of a 0.01 M sodium thiosulfate solution for complete reaction. Calculate the concentration in mol l^{-1} of the iodine solution.

Answer

$$I_{2(aq)} + 2S_2O_3{}^{2-}{}_{(aq)} \rightarrow 2I^-{}_{(aq)} + S_4O_6{}^{2-}{}_{(aq)}$$

$$V_1 \times M_1 \times n_2 \quad = V_2 \times M_2 \times n_1$$

$$25 \times M_1 \times 2 \quad = 24.5 \times 0.01 \times 1$$

$$M_1 \quad = 24.5 \times 0.01 \times 1 / 50$$

$$= 0.0049 \text{ M}$$

Concentration of iodine solution $= 0.0049$ mol l^{-1}

Experiment

Mandatory Experiment 12.3: An iodine–thiosulfate titration

Before each titration, a standard (0.06 M) solution of iodine is generated in the conical flask by reacting a standard (0.02 M) solution of potassium iodate, for each titration, with excess potassium iodide. Iodine is liberated from iodate and iodide according to the equation:

$$IO_3^-{}_{(aq)} + 5I^-{}_{(aq)} + 6H^+{}_{(aq)} \rightarrow 3I_{2(aq)} + 3H_2O_{(aq)}$$

Excess potassium iodide is used because potassium iodide acts to keep the iodine in solution.

Iodine reacts with sodium thiosulfate according to the equation:

$$I_{2(aq)} + 2S_2O_3^{2-}{}_{(aq)} \rightarrow 2I^-{}_{(aq)} + S_4O_6^{2-}{}_{(aq)}$$

Procedure

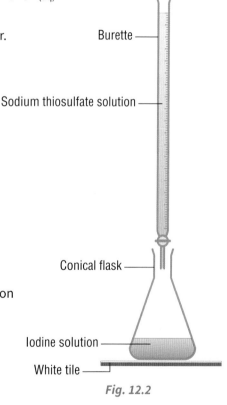

1 Wash the pipette, burette and conical flask with deionised water.

2 Rinse the pipette with potassium iodate solution and the burette with the sodium thiosulfate solution.

3 Place 25 cm³ of the potassium iodate solution in the conical flask using the pipette, and add 20 cm³ of dilute sulfuric acid, followed by 10 cm³ of 0.5 M potassium iodide solution.

4 Using a funnel, fill the burette with sodium thiosulfate solution. (Fig. 12.2)

5 Add the sodium thiosulfate solution from the burette to the flask.

6 Add a few drops of the starch indicator solution just prior to the end point, when the colour of the solution fades to pale yellow. Upon addition of the indicator a blue-black colour should appear.

7 The end point of the titration is detected by a colour change from blue-black to colourless. Note the burette reading.

8 Carry out a number of accurate titrations, adding the sodium thiosulfate solution dropwise approaching the end point, until two titres agree to within 0.1 cm³.

9 Calculate the concentration of the sodium thiosulfate solution.

Burette

Sodium thiosulfate solution

Conical flask

Iodine solution

White tile

Fig. 12.2

Applications of iodine–thiosulfate titrations

Many commercial bleaches are simply solutions of hypochlorite salts, such as sodium hypochlorite (NaOCl) or calcium hypochlorite ($Ca(OCl)_2$).

- To determine the amount of hypochlorite in bleach, the bleach is first diluted.

- Hypochlorite ion then is reacted with excess iodide ion in the presence of acid to generate an iodine solution:

$$ClO^-_{(aq)} + 2I^-_{(aq)} + 2H^+_{(aq)} \rightarrow Cl^-_{(aq)} + I_{2(aq)} + H_2O_{(l)}$$

- The iodine solution produced is titrated against sodium thiosulfate solution using starch solution as indicator. Iodine reacts with sodium thiosulfate according to the equation:

$$I_{2(aq)} + 2S_2O_3^{2-}_{(aq)} \rightarrow 2I^-_{(aq)} + S_4O_6^{2-}_{(aq)}$$

Question

12.9 25 cm³ of bleach was diluted to 250 cm³ with deionised water. It was found that the iodine solution produced by the reaction of 25 cm³ of the diluted bleach with acidified potassium iodide solution required 18.5 cm³ of a 0.1 M sodium thiosulfate solution for complete reaction. Calculate (i) the concentration in mol l^{-1} of the iodine solution, (ii) the concentration of hypochlorite in the bleach, and (iii) the percentage (w/v) of hypochlorite in the bleach.

Answer

$$I_{2(aq)} + 2S_2O_3^{2-}_{(aq)} \rightarrow 2I^-_{(aq)} + S_4O_6^{2-}_{(aq)}$$

$$V_1 \times M_1 \times n_2 = V_2 \times M_2 \times n_1$$

$$25 \times M_1 \times 2 = 18.5 \times 0.1 \times 1$$

$$M_1 = 18.5 \times 0.1 \times 1 / 50$$

$$= 0.037 \text{ M}$$

(i) Concentration of iodine solution   = 0.037 M

    Concentration of hypochlorite in diluted bleach solution   = 0.037 M

(ii) Concentration of hypochlorite in undiluted bleach solution   = 0.037 × 10 M

$$= 0.37 \text{ M}$$

$$= 74.5 \times 0.37 \text{ g l}^{-1}$$

$$= 27.565 \text{ g l}^{-1}$$

(iii) Percentage (w/v) of hypochlorite in bleach = 27.565 × 100 / 1000 = 2.76%

Experiment

Mandatory Experiment 12.4: Determination of the percentage (w/v) of hypochlorite in bleach

Procedure

1 Using a pipette, add 25 cm³ of bleach to a 250 cm³ volumetric flask, and make the solution up to the mark with deionised water. Stopper the flask and invert it several times.

2 Wash the pipette, burette and conical flask with deionised water.

3 Rinse the pipette with the diluted bleach solution and the burette with the sodium thiosulfate solution.

4 Place 25 cm³ of the diluted bleach solution in the conical flask using the pipette.

5 Add 10 cm³ of dilute sulfuric acid and 1 g potassium iodide to the conical flask – an iodine solution is formed.

6 Using a funnel, fill the burette with sodium thiosulfate solution, making sure that the part below the tap is filled before adjusting to zero.

7 Carry out a rough titration and a number of accurate titrations until two titres agree to within 0.1 cm³. Each time, add a few drops of the starch indicator solution just prior to the end point, when the colour of the solution fades to pale yellow. The end point of the titration is detected by a colour change from blue-black to colourless.

8 Calculate the concentration of the iodine solution.

9 Calculate the concentration and percentage of hypochlorite in the bleach solution.

Key-points!

- The oxidation number of an atom is defined as the charge that an atom appears to have when the electrons are distributed according to certain rules.
- Oxidation is an increase in oxidation number.
- Reduction is a decrease in oxidation number.

13 Fuels and Heats of Reaction

Sources of hydrocarbons

Key definition

Hydrocarbons are compounds consisting of carbon and hydrogen only.

Methane (CH_4), the main component of natural gas, is a hydrocarbon. The fossil fuels crude oil, natural gas and coal are sources of hydrocarbons.

Methane can be produced by the anaerobic decomposition of animal waste and vegetation. It is produced in an uncontrolled way in slurry pits and refuse dumps.

Methane is also produced in large quantities in the digestive tracts of animals such as cattle.

Aliphatic hydrocarbons

Hydrocarbons are part of a large branch of chemistry called **organic chemistry**. This is the chemistry of carbon compounds, excluding carbon dioxide, carbon monoxide, carbonates and hydrogencarbonates.

Key definition

Hydrocarbons that consist of straight and branched chains of carbon atoms, or rings of carbon atoms other than those containing a special ring called a benzene ring, are called **aliphatic hydrocarbons**.

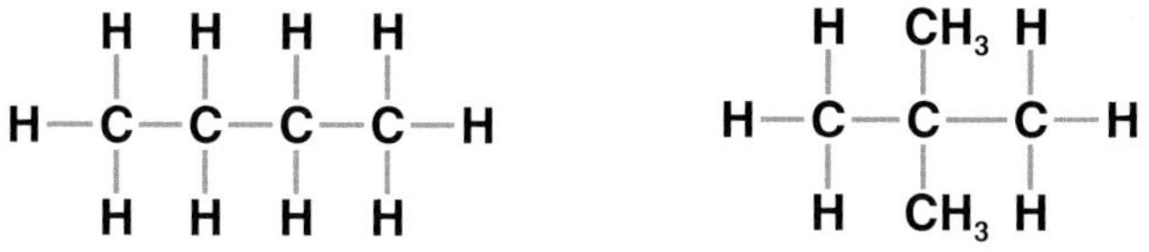

Butane   2,2-dimethylpropane
Fig. 13.1 Structural formulas of some aliphatic compounds

Key definition

Hydrocarbons that contain a benzene ring are called **aromatic** hydrocarbons.

Homologous series

Key definition

A **homologous series** is a family of compounds with:
- The same general formula
- Successive members differing by CH_2
- Similar chemical properties.

Question

13.1 Use the general formula C_nH_{2n+2} to work out the molecular formulas of the first five members of the alkanes.

Answer

Substituting $n = 1$ into the formula as follows gives the formula of methane, the first member of the series:

$$C_nH_{2n+2} \rightarrow C_1H_{2(1)+2} \rightarrow C_1H_4 \rightarrow CH_4$$

Substituting $n = 2, 3, 4$ and 5 in turn produces the formulas C_2H_6 for ethane, C_3H_8 for propane, C_4H_{10} for butane and C_5H_{12} for pentane.

Naming system

In the IUPAC naming system, each hydrocarbon name consists of two parts: the root and the suffix. The roots correspond with the number of carbon atoms in the longest chain present. The first 10 roots are shown in Table 13.1.

Table 13.1

No. of carbons	Root	No. of carbons	Root
1	Meth–	6	Hex–
2	Eth–	7	Hept–
3	Prop–	8	Oct–
4	But–	9	Non–
5	Pent–	10	Dec–

The suffix depends on the homologous series to which the compound belongs. For example, each alkane has the suffix **–ane**, each alkene has the suffix **–ene**, and each alkyne has the suffix **–yne**.

Question

13.2 Write the names of the following: (i) the alkene with two carbons, (ii) the alkyne with three carbons, and (iii) the alkane with six carbons in its longest chain.

Answer

(i) Two carbons mean that the root is eth–, and alkenes have the suffix –ene. Thus, the name is ethene.

(ii) Three carbons mean that the root is prop–, and alkynes have the suffix –yne. Thus, the name is propyne.

(iii) Six carbons mean that the root is hex–, and alkanes have the suffix –ane. Thus, the name is hexane.

Alkanes

The alkanes form a homologous series of aliphatic hydrocarbons of general formula C_nH_{2n+2}.

Table 13.2

No. of carbons	Name	Formula	No. of carbons	Name	Formula
1	Methane	CH_4	5	Pentane	C_5H_{12}
2	Ethane	C_2H_6	6	Hexane	C_6H_{14}
3	Propane	C_3H_8	7	Heptane	C_7H_{16}
4	Butane	C_4H_{10}	8	Octane	C_8H_{18}

The formula shown in each case is the **molecular formula**. The structural formulas of the first four alkanes are shown in Table 13.3.

Table 13.3

Name	Molecular formula	Structural formula
Methane	CH_4	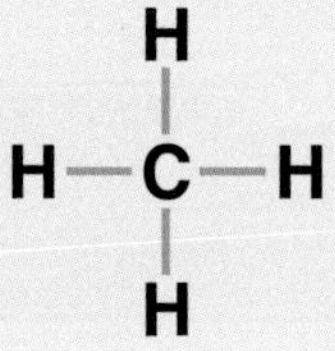
Ethane	C_2H_6	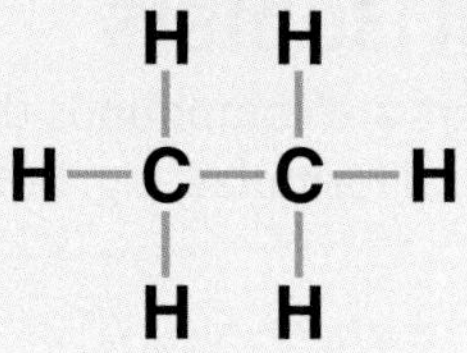
Propane	C_3H_8	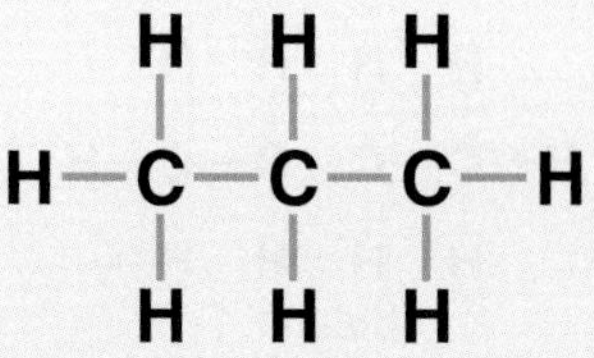
Butane	C_4H_{10}	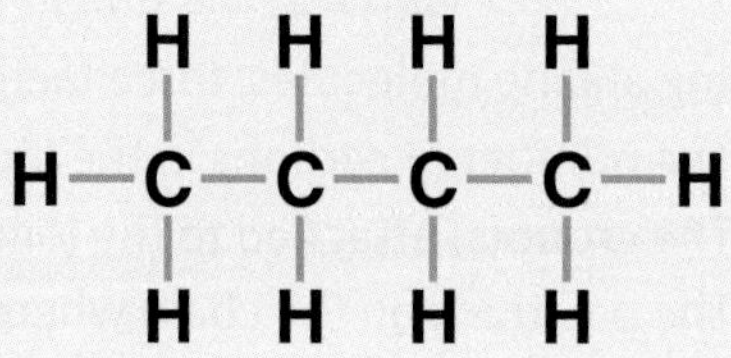

13.3 Draw the structural formula of pentane, hexane, heptane and octane, respectively.

Answer

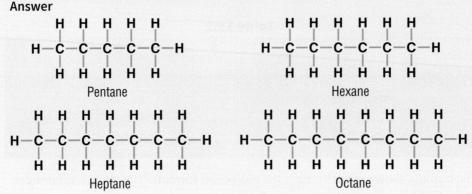

Pentane   Hexane

Heptane   Octane

In the alkanes, each carbon atom forms four separate single bonds to satisfy the valency of carbon. All of the compounds discussed so far are referred to as straight-chain molecules, given the absence of any branches or rings. In the alkane molecules, all of the bonds are single bonds.

Key definition

Molecules that contain only single bonds are said to be **saturated**.

Structural isomers

Structural isomers are compounds that have the same molecular formula but different structural formulas, e.g. butane and 2-methylpropane.

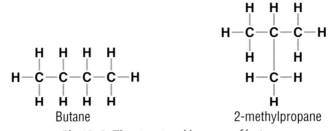

Butane   2-methylpropane

Fig 13. 2 The structural isomers of butane

When naming alkane molecules, three factors are taken into account:

1 The number of carbons in the longest straight chain in the molecule.
2 The group(s) attached to the longest chain.
3 The positions on the chain where the group(s) are attached.

The structural isomer of butane is named as follows:

1 Since there are three carbons in the longest chain, the molecule is regarded as a propane derivative.
2 The presence of a methyl group attached to the longest straight chain means that the compound is called methylpropane.

3 Since the methyl group is attached to the second carbon in the chain, the compound is called 2-methylpropane.

Question

13.4 Draw the structural formulas and write the names of the structural isomers of pentane (C_5H_{12}).

Answer

The use of molecular models will help in working out the required structures.

(i)

$$\begin{array}{c} \text{H} \quad \text{H} \quad \text{H} \quad \text{H} \quad \text{H} \\ | \quad | \quad | \quad | \quad | \\ \text{H—C—C—C—C—C—H} \\ | \quad | \quad | \quad | \quad | \\ \text{H} \quad \text{H} \quad \text{H} \quad \text{H} \quad \text{H} \end{array}$$

Pentane

- Since there are five carbon atoms in the longest chain, the molecule is called pentane.

(ii)

$$\begin{array}{c} \text{H} \quad \text{H} \quad \text{H} \quad \text{H} \\ | \quad | \quad | \quad | \\ \text{H—C—C—C—C—H} \\ | \quad | \quad | \quad | \\ \text{H} \quad \text{CH}_3 \quad \text{H} \quad \text{H} \end{array}$$

2-methylbutane

- Since there are four carbons in the longest chain, the molecule is regarded as a butane derivative.
- The presence of a methyl group attached to the longest straight chain means that the compound is called methylbutane.
- Since the methyl group is attached to the second carbon in the chain, the compound is called 2-methylbutane.

(iii)

$$\begin{array}{c} \text{H} \quad \text{CH}_3 \quad \text{H} \\ | \quad | \quad | \\ \text{H—C—C—C—H} \\ | \quad | \quad | \\ \text{H} \quad \text{CH}_3 \quad \text{H} \end{array}$$

2,2-dimethylpropane

- Since there are three carbons in the longest chain, the molecule is regarded as a propane derivative.
- The presence of two methyl groups attached to the propane chain means that the compound is called dimethylpropane. The prefix *di-* is used to indicate that there are two methyl groups attached to the straight chain.
- Since the methyl groups are both attached to the second carbon in the chain, the compound is called 2,2-dimethylpropane.

Question

13.5 Draw the structural formula of 2,2,4-trimethylpentane.

Answer

(i) The compound is a derivative of pentane, so there are five carbon atoms in the longest straight chain:

$$- C - C - C - C - C -$$

(ii) *Trimethyl* indicates that there are three methyl groups (CH_3) attached to the straight chain.

(iii) The numbers *2,2,4–* indicate the positions on the chain at which the methyl groups are attached. Two methyl groups are attached to the second carbon in the chain, and the third methyl group is attached to the fourth carbon.

The structural formula of 2,2,4-trimethylpentane is:

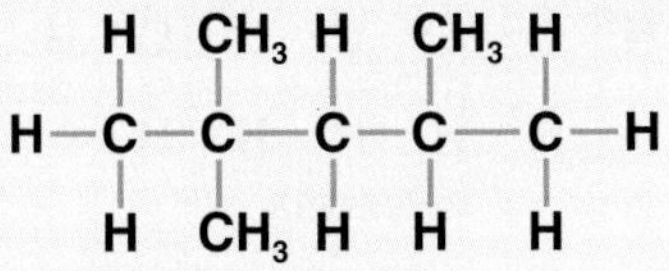

2,2,4-trimethylpentane

The traditional name of 2,2,4-trimethylpentane is iso-octane.

Sometimes the structural formula is written in abbreviated or condensed form.

Question

13.6 Draw the structural formula and name the compound $CH_3C(CH_3)_2CH_3$.

Answer

The methyl groups in brackets form the branches or side chains. The remaining three carbons form the longest straight chain, so the compound is a derivative of propane. The side-chain methyl groups are written after the second carbon in the chain, which means that they are attached to this carbon. Thus the compound is 2,2-dimethylpropane. Its structural formula is:

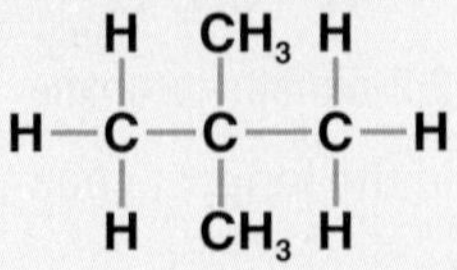

2,2-dimethylpropane

Physical properties of alkanes

The lower members of the alkanes, those up to and including butane, are gases at normal temperatures. Alkanes from pentane up to alkanes containing 15 carbon atoms per molecule are liquids; those with more carbon atoms per molecule than this are waxy solids.

Alkanes are non-polar substances. Because of this, they are insoluble in water but soluble in non-polar solvents, such as cyclohexane and methylbenzene.

Alkenes

The alkenes form a homologous series of aliphatic hydrocarbons of general formula C_nH_{2n}. Each alkene molecule contains a carbon–carbon double bond, C=C, which is the reactive portion or functional group of the molecule. The lowest member of the series has two carbon atoms.

Alkenes are unsaturated compounds.

> **Key definition**
>
> Molecules that contain a double or triple bond are **unsaturated**.

Question

13.7 Use the general formula, C_nH_{2n}, to work out the molecular formulas of the first two members of the alkenes. Name the compounds and draw their structural formulas.

Answer

(i) The first member of the alkenes has two carbon atoms. Substituting $n = 2$ into the formula as follows gives the required molecular formula:

$$C_nH_{2n} \rightarrow C_2H_{2(2)} \rightarrow C_2H_4$$

All alkenes have a carbon–carbon double bond, so the structural formula is:

Ethene

(ii) The second member of the alkenes has three carbon atoms. Substituting $n = 3$ into the formula as follows gives the required molecular formula:

$$C_nH_{2n} \rightarrow C_3H_{2(3)} \rightarrow C_3H_6$$

All alkenes have a carbon–carbon double bond, so the structural formula is:

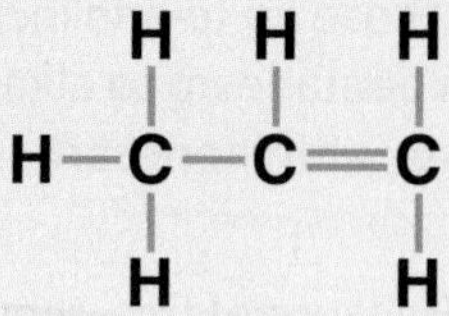

Propene

Table 13.4

No. of carbons	Name	Molecular formula
2	Ethene	C_2H_4
3	Propene	C_3H_6
4	Butene	C_4H_8

Structural isomers of alkenes, which contain four or more carbon atoms, exist.

Question

13.8 Draw the structural formula, write the condensed formula and name the structural isomers of butene.

Answer

(i)

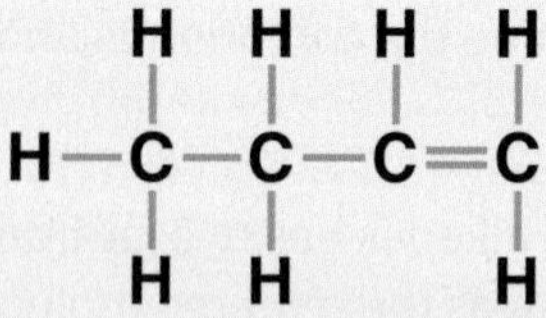

But-1-ene

In this case the double bond is formed between the first two carbons in the chain. Since this bond starts at the first carbon in the chain, the molecule is called but-1-ene. The condensed formula is $CH_2=CHCH_2CH_3$.

(ii)

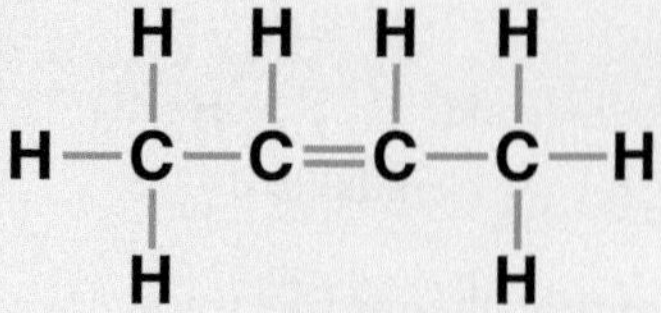

But-2-ene

In this case the double bond is formed between the second and third carbons in the chain. Since this bond starts at the second carbon in the chain, the molecule is called but-2-ene. The condensed formula is $CH_3CH=CHCH_3$.

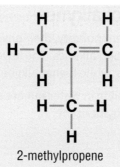

2-methylpropene

Since the longest straight chain of carbons containing the carbon–carbon double bond is three, the molecule is regarded as propene with a branch or side chain. The methyl group is attached to the second carbon in the chain, so the compound is called 2-methylpropene. The condensed formula is $CH_2=C(CH_3)CH_3$.

Physical properties of alkenes

The lower members of the alkenes, those up to and including butene, are gases at normal temperatures. Higher alkenes are liquids or solids.

Alkenes are either non-polar or only slightly polar substances. Because of this, they have a very low solubility in water but are soluble in non-polar solvents, such as cyclohexane and methylbenzene.

Alkynes

The alkynes form a homologous series of aliphatic hydrocarbons of general formula C_nH_{2n-2}. Each alkyne molecule contains a carbon–carbon triple bond, $C\equiv C$, and this is the functional group of the series. The lowest member of the series has two carbon atoms.

Alkynes are said to be unsaturated due to the presence of a triple bond.

Question

13.9 Use the general formula, C_nH_{2n-2}, to work out the molecular formula of the first member of the alkynes. Name the compound and draw its structural formula.

Answer

The first member of the alkynes has two carbon atoms. Substituting $n = 2$ into the formula as follows gives the required molecular formula:

$$C_nH_{2n-2} \rightarrow C_2H_{2(2)-2} \rightarrow C_2H_{(4-2)} \rightarrow C_2H_2$$

All alkynes have a carbon–carbon triple bond, so the structural formula is:

$$H-C\equiv C-H$$

Ethyne

Physical properties of alkynes

Being compounds of low or zero polarity, their physical properties are essentially the same as those of alkanes and alkenes. The lower members of the alkynes are gases at normal temperatures, while higher alkynes are liquids or solids.

Alkynes have a very low solubility in water but are soluble in non-polar solvents, such as cyclohexane and methylbenzene.

 Experiment

Specified Demonstration: The solubility properties of methane, ethene and ethyne

Procedure

1 Three-quarters fill a test tube with water.

2 Fit the stopper and delivery tubes to the test tube as illustrated. The short leg does not reach the surface of the water and the long leg dips well below the surface.

3 Empty syringe A of any air by pushing the piston in as far as possible. Connect it to the short-legged delivery tube.

4 Fill syringe B with methane gas as far as the 10 cm³ mark. Connect syringe B to the other delivery tube.

5 Slowly force the methane gas into the water by pushing on the piston of syringe B.

6 Note the extent, if any, to which the piston in syringe A is pushed back by gas emerging from the water. Note the degree of solubility of methane in water.

7 Repeat steps 1–6 using ethene and ethyne gases, with water as the solvent.

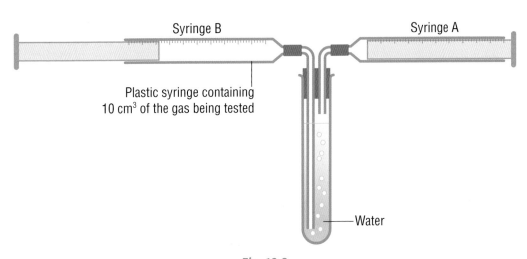

Syringe B

Syringe A

Plastic syringe containing
10 cm³ of the gas being tested

Water

Fig. 13.3

8 Repeat the experiment for all three gases using cyclohexane and methylbenzene in turn as solvents.

9 It will be found that methane, ethene and ethyne are insoluble in water but soluble in cyclohexane and methylbenzene.

Chemical reactions of ethyne

Like most hydrocarbons, ethyne gas burns in air to form carbon dioxide and water vapour.

$$C_2H_{2(g)} + 2\frac{1}{2}O_{2(g)} \rightarrow 2CO_{2(g)} + H_2O_{(g)}$$

The carbon dioxide may be detected using the limewater test.

 **Experiment**

Mandatory Experiment 13.1: Preparation and properties of ethyne

Calcium dicarbide reacts with water, producing ethyne and calcium hydroxide:

$$CaC_{2(s)} + 2H_2O_{(l)} \rightarrow C_2H_{2(g)} + Ca(OH)_{2(aq)}$$

Impurities present in the gas, such as hydrogen sulfide and phosphine, can be removed by bubbling the gas through acidified copper sulfate solution.

The impurities are caused by the hydrolysis of traces of calcium sulfide and calcium phosphide present in the calcium dicarbide.

Procedure **Preparation**

1 Place a few pieces of calcium dicarbide (a grey solid) in a Büchner flask and set up the apparatus as in Fig. 13.4.

2 Add water from the dropping funnel, a few drops at a time.

3 Collect the gas produced in test tubes by displacement of water. Stopper each gas-filled test tube under water. Discard the first test tube filled, as it contains a mixture of air and ethyne.

Investigation of properties

1 Ignite a test tube of the gas. The flame will be very sooty. Add a few drops of limewater to the test tube, stopper and shake well. The limewater turns milky.

2 Add a few drops of a solution of bromine water to a test tube of gas, stopper quickly and shake well. The red/brown bromine water decolourises, indicating that ethyne is unsaturated.

3 Add a few drops of acidified potassium manganate solution to a test tube of gas, stopper quickly and shake well. The purple potassium manganate solution decolourises, indicating that ethyne is unsaturated.

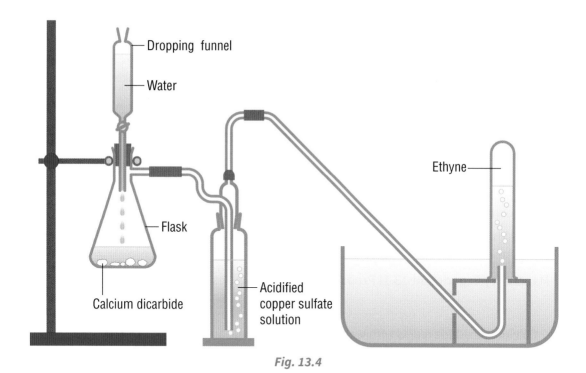

Fig. 13.4

Uses of ethyne

- When mixed with pure oxygen, ethyne produces a clear flame at a very high temperature.
- Because of this it is used in oxyacetylene torches for cutting and welding metals.

Aromatic hydrocarbons

Key definition

Aromatic hydrocarbons are compounds that contain a benzene-type ring.

Benzene itself (C_6H_6) is the most important aromatic compound.

The benzene molecule consists of six carbon atoms joined to form a ring. There is one hydrogen atom attached to each carbon.

In benzene, the carbon–carbon bonds are intermediate between carbon–carbon single and double bonds. This special type of bonding is indicated in the structural formula of benzene by a circle drawn inside a regular hexagon. Each corner of the hexagon represents a carbon atom bonded to a hydrogen atom.

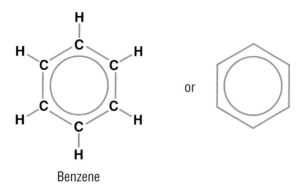

or

Benzene

In methylbenzene, an organic solvent, the methyl group (CH_3) replaces a hydrogen atom in the benzene molecule. In ethylbenzene, a hydrogen atom in benzene is replaced by the ethyl group (C_2H_5).

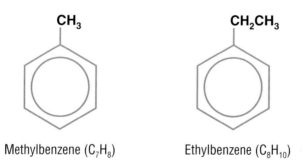

Methylbenzene (C_7H_8)

Ethylbenzene (C_8H_{10})

Physical properties of aromatic hydrocarbons

The physical properties of the aromatic hydrocarbons are similar to those of the aliphatic hydrocarbons. Being non-polar, they do not dissolve to any extent in water, but do dissolve in non-polar solvents. Liquid aromatic hydrocarbons, such as methylbenzene, are themselves good non-polar solvents, dissolving non-polar solutes readily.

Aromatic hydrocarbons of lower relative molecular mass, such as benzene, methylbenzene and ethylbenzene, are liquids at room temperature, while those of higher relative molecular mass are solids.

 Experiment

Specified Demonstration: Solubility properties of methylbenzene, using cyclohexane, water, sodium chloride, ethyl ethanoate, cooking oil and iodine crystals as solutes

Procedure

1 Approximately half fill a test tube with methylbenzene.

2 Add a small quantity of one of the solutes – a few crystals in the case of the solids, a few drops in the case of the liquids.

3 Stopper the test tube and shake vigorously.

4 Open the test tube carefully in case there is a build-up of pressure.

5 Decide by inspection whether or not the solute has dissolved.

6 Repeat in turn for each of the solutes.

7 It will be observed that only non-polar solutes such as cyclohexane will have dissolved in methylbenzene.

Exothermic and endothermic reactions

Energy is needed to break bonds and is given out when new bonds form.

If the amount of heat produced in forming bonds is greater than the amount needed to break bonds, heat is given out and the temperature of the reaction mixture increases. Such a reaction is said to be **exothermic**. Most chemical reactions are of this type, e.g. burning fuels.

Key definition

An **exothermic reaction** is a reaction that gives out heat to the surroundings.

If the amount of heat produced in forming bonds is less than the amount needed to break bonds, heat is taken in from the surroundings and the temperature of the reaction mixture decreases. Such a reaction is said to be **endothermic**, e.g. the manufacture of hydrogen by the steam reforming of natural gas.

Key definition

An **endothermic reaction** is a reaction that takes in heat from the surroundings.

One of the most important properties of hydrocarbons is that they burn in air or oxygen, producing carbon dioxide and water vapour. Heat is produced in combustion reactions, so they are classified as exothermic reactions. The large amount of heat produced when alkanes burn makes them particularly suitable as fuels.

Methane, the first member of the alkanes, is the principal component of natural gas. Propane and butane are used as bottled gas and are the main components of liquid petroleum gas (LPG) for use in cars. Petrol is made up of a large number of different compounds, mostly alkanes.

Specified Demonstration: Demonstration of (i) an exothermic reaction and (ii) an endothermic reaction.

(i) Exothermic reaction

Procedure
1 Place about 5 cm^3 of hydrochloric acid in a test tube and record its temperature.

2 Drop in a few pieces of magnesium.

3 When the reaction has stopped, take the temperature again.

Remember

The temperature of the water has risen because the reaction of magnesium metal with hydrochloric acid is an exothermic reaction.

(ii) Endothermic reaction

Procedure
1 Place about 5 cm3 of water in a test tube and record its temperature.

2 Add a few crystals of ammonium nitrate.

3 Stir gently until the crystals have dissolved.

4 Take the temperature again.

Remember

The temperature of the mixture has fallen because dissolving ammonium nitrate in water is an endothermic process.

Heat of reaction

Key definition

The **heat of reaction** (ΔH) of a chemical reaction is the heat in kilojoules released or absorbed when the number of moles of reactants indicated in the balanced equation describing the reaction react completely.

The heat change depends on the amounts of reactants involved, which is indicated by the balanced equation. If 1 mole of hydrogen gas burns in oxygen to form water:

$$H_{2(g)} + \tfrac{1}{2}O_{2(g)} \rightarrow H_2O_{(g)}$$

242 kilojoules of heat are produced.

As this is an exothermic reaction, the ΔH is negative because heat energy has been lost from the chemical reactants to the surroundings, i.e. ΔH = –242 kJ mol^{-1}.

For endothermic reactions, ΔH is positive because the chemical reactants are gaining energy from the surroundings. For example, to break 1 mole of water in the liquid state into hydrogen and oxygen gas:

$$H_2O_{(l)} \rightarrow H_{2(g)} + \tfrac{1}{2}O_{2(g)}$$

286 kilojoules are required, i.e. ΔH = +286 kJ mol^{-1}.

Question

13.10 When 200 cm^3 of 1 M nitric acid solution (HNO_3) react with 200 cm^3 of 1 M sodium hydroxide solution (NaOH), the temperature rises by 6.7 kelvins. Calculate the heat of reaction described by the equation:

$$HNO_{3(aq)} + NaOH_{(aq)} \rightarrow NaNO_{3(aq)} + H_2O_{(l)}$$

Answer

The amount of heat produced in the reaction can be calculated from the formula:

$$\text{Heat change} = mc\,\Delta T$$

where

m = the mass in kg of liquid heated by the reaction

c = the specific heat capacity of the liquid

ΔT = the rise in temperature

As the reactants and products are very dilute solutions, it is assumed that their densities and specific heat capacities are the same as those of water. Thus, 200 cm^3 of each reacting solution can be taken to have a mass of 0.2 kilograms. The specific heat capacity of water is 4.2 kJ kg^{-1} K^{-1}.

Heat change = $mc\,\Delta T$

= 0.4 × 4.2 × 6.7

= 11.256 kJ

The number of moles of HNO_3 in 200 cm^3 of 1 M nitric acid solution is calculated as follows:

No. of moles = volume in litres × molarity

= 0.2 × 1

= 0.2 moles

Since 0.2 moles of HNO_3 produce 11.256 kJ of heat when reacted with NaOH, 1 mole, the quantity indicated by the balanced equation, produces 56.28 kJ mol^{-1}. In other words, the heat of reaction ΔH = –56.28 kJ mol^{-1}, the minus sign indicating that the reaction is exothermic, with heat being produced.

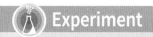

Mandatory Experiment 13.2: Determination of the heat of reaction of hydrochloric acid with sodium hydroxide

Hydrochloric acid reacts with sodium hydroxide, producing sodium chloride and water:

$$HCl_{(aq)} + NaOH_{(aq)} \rightarrow NaCl_{(aq)} + H_2O_{(l)}$$

Procedure

1 Place 50 cm^3 of the 1 M hydrochloric acid solution into a polystyrene cup.

2 Place 50 cm^3 of the 1 M sodium hydroxide solution into another polystyrene cup.

3 Measure the temperature of each solution. The average of the two temperatures is taken as the initial temperature.

4 Quickly add the base to the acid, stirring with an accurate thermometer.

5 Record the maximum temperature reached.

6 By subtraction find the rise in temperature.

7 Calculate the heat of reaction, i.e. the heat liberated when 1 mole of acid reacts fully. A value close to -57 kJ mol^{-1} should be the result.

Bond energy

In chemical reactions, energy must be supplied to break bonds, and energy is given out when new bonds are formed.

The energy needed to break bonds is called the **bond energy**.

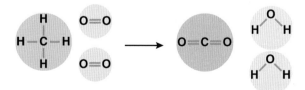

These bonds are broken.
Energy is taken in.

These bonds are made.
Energy is given out.

Fig. 13.5 Bond energy

Key definition

Bond energy is the amount of energy in kJ needed to break 1 mole of bonds of the same type, where all species are in the gaseous state.

The heat change for the reaction

$$CH_{4(g)} \rightarrow C_{(g)} + 4H_{(g)}$$

is found to be 1664 kJ mol^{-1}. In this reaction, four C – H bonds are broken, and no other bonds are formed or broken. Thus, the C – H bond energy in methane is a quarter of 1664 kJ mol^{-1}, since there are four bonds present in each molecule, i.e.

$$E(C - H) = \tfrac{1}{4}(1664) = 416 \text{ kJ mol}^{-1}$$

The energy of a particular type of bond can vary depending on the molecule that the bond is in. It is usual to quote average bond energies, which do not take into account the environment that the bond is in.

Heat of combustion

Key definition

The **heat of combustion** of a substance is the heat change in kilojoules when 1 mole of the substance is completely burned in excess oxygen.

Question

13.11 When 1 mole of methane gas is burned completely in excess oxygen, carbon dioxide and water vapour are formed and 890 kilojoules of heat energy are released. Use this information to write an equation for the heat of combustion of methane.

Answer

The balanced equation for the reaction is:

$$CH_{4(g)} + 2O_{2(g)} \rightarrow CO_{2(g)} + 2H_2O_{(g)}$$

Since 890 kilojoules of heat energy are released, the reaction is exothermic and $\Delta H = -890$ kJ mol^{-1}. The equation describes the complete combustion of 1 mole of methane, so the equation for the heat of combustion of methane is:

$$CH_{4(g)} + 2O_{2(g)} \rightarrow CO_{2(g)} + 2H_2O_{(g)} \quad \Delta H = -890 \text{ kJ mol}^{-1}$$

Accurate values of heats of combustion can be obtained using a **bomb calorimeter**.

Table 13.5

Uses of a bomb calorimeter
Measure the calorific value of foods
Measure the heat of combustion of fuels
Measure the kilogram calorific value of fuels

Key definition

The **kilogram calorific value** of a fuel is defined as the heat energy produced per kilogram of fuel.

Kilogram calorific values are also measured using a bomb calorimeter.

Heat of formation

Key definition

The **heat of formation** is defined as the heat change in kilojoules when 1 mole of a substance is formed from its elements in their standard states.

The standard state of an element is its common form at 298 K and 101,325 Pa. For example, the standard state of hydrogen is $H_{2(g)}$ and that of magnesium is $Mg_{(s)}$.

Question

13.12 When 1 mole of carbon dioxide gas is formed from its elements in their standard states, 393 kilojoules of heat energy are released. Use this information to write an equation for the heat of formation of carbon dioxide.

Answer

The balanced equation for the reaction is:

$$C_{(s)} + O_{2(g)} \rightarrow CO_{2(g)}$$

Since 393 kilojoules of heat energy are produced, the reaction is exothermic and $\Delta H = -393$ kJ mol^{-1}. Carbon and oxygen are in their standard states, so the heat of formation is -393 kJ mol^{-1} and the complete equation is:

$$C_{(s)} + O_{2(g)} \rightarrow CO_{2(g)} \quad \Delta H = -393 \text{ kJ mol}^{-1}$$

Hess's law

The Russian chemist **G.H. Hess** modified this law in terms of heat changes.

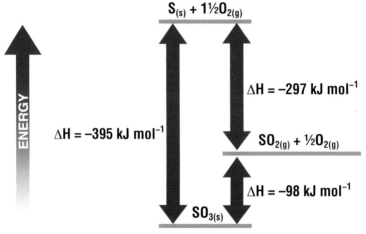

Fig. 13.6 *An illustration of Hess's law*

Problems based on Hess's law may be solved using the fact that for a reaction described by a given equation, the heat of reaction equals the sum of the heats of formation of the products of the reaction less the sum of the heats of formation of the reactants of the reaction. In symbols:

$$\Delta H_r = \Sigma \, \Delta H_f[\text{products}] - \Sigma \, \Delta H_f[\text{reactants}]$$

Question

13.13 Calculate the heat of combustion of ethane

$$C_2H_{6(g)} + 3½O_{2(g)} \rightarrow 2CO_{2(g)} + 3H_2O_{(l)} \; \Delta H_c = ?$$

given the heats of formation of ethane gas, carbon dioxide gas and liquid water are -84.7 kJ mol^{-1}, -393.5 kJ mol^{-1} and -285.8 kJ mol^{-1}, respectively.

Answer

$$C_2H_{6(g)} + 3½O_{2(g)} \rightarrow 2CO_{2(g)} + 3H_2O_{(l)} \; \Delta H_c = ?$$

$\Delta H_r \qquad = \Sigma \; \Delta H_f[\text{products}] - \Sigma \; \Delta H_f[\text{reactants}]$

$\Rightarrow \Delta H_c(C_2H_6) = 2 \times \Delta H_f(CO_2) + 3 \times \Delta H_f(H_2O) - \Delta H_f(C_2H_6) - 3½ \times \Delta H_f(O_2)$

$\Rightarrow \Delta H_c(C_2H_6) = 2 \times (-393.5 \text{ kJ mol}^{-1}) + 3 \times (-285.8 \text{ kJ mol}^{-1})$

$\qquad\qquad\qquad - (-84.7 \text{ kJ mol}^{-1}) - 3½ \times (0 \text{ kJ mol}^{-1})$

$\Rightarrow \Delta H_c(C_2H_6) = -1559.7 \text{ kJ mol}^{-1}$

In Example 13.14, the heat of combustion of one substance is given together with all the heats of formation, except the one required to be calculated.

Question

13.14 The heat of combustion of propane is $-2,220$ kJ mol^{-1} and the heats of formation of carbon dioxide gas and liquid water are -393.5 kJ mol^{-1} and -285.8 kJ mol^{-1}, respectively. Calculate the heat of formation of propane.

Answer

The equation for the heat of combustion of propane is:

$$C_3H_{8(g)} + 5O_{2(g)} \rightarrow 3CO_{2(g)} + 4H_2O_{(l)} \; \Delta Hc = -2,220 \text{ kJ mol}^{-1}$$

$\Delta H_r \qquad\qquad = \Sigma \; \Delta H_f[\text{products}] - \Sigma \; \Delta H_f[\text{reactants}]$

$\Rightarrow \Delta H_c(C_3H_8) \qquad = 3 \times \Delta H_f(CO_2) + 4 \times \Delta H_f(H_2O)$

$\qquad\qquad\qquad\qquad - \Delta H_f(C_3H_8) - 5 \times \Delta H_f(O_2)$

$\Rightarrow -2,220 \text{ kJ mol}^{-1} = 3 \times (-393.5 \text{ kJ mol}^{-1}) + 4 \times (-285.8 \text{ kJ mol}^{-1})$

$\qquad\qquad\qquad\qquad - \Delta H_f(C_3H_8) - 5 \times (0 \text{ kJ mol}^{-1})$

$\Rightarrow -2,220 \text{ kJ mol}^{-1} = -1180.5 - 1143.2 - \Delta H_f(C_3H_8) - 0$

$\Rightarrow \Delta H_f(C_3H_8) \qquad = -1180.5 - 1143.2 + 2220$

$\Rightarrow \Delta H_f(C_3H_8) \qquad = -103.7 \text{ kJ mol}^{-1}$

Oil refining and its products

When crude oil is brought to an oil refinery, the many compounds in the crude oil mixture are separated according to their different boiling points. This is done in a process of fractionation or fractional distillation. Fractional distillation of crude oil results in a series of fractions, each consisting of a mixture of hydrocarbons boiling within a given temperature range.

Table 13.6

Fraction	Boiling range	Carbon atoms per molecule	Typical uses
Refinery gas	<300 K	1–4	Liquefied petroleum gas (LPG)
Light gasoline	300–350 K	5–8	Petrol
Naphtha	350–435 K	8–10	Petrol and organic chemicals
Kerosene	435–525 K	10–14	Central heating fuel, jet fuel
Gas oil	525–625 K	14–19	Diesel fuel
Fuel oil and residue	>625 K	>19	Power station fuel, bitumen, lubricating oil, greases

Natural gas

Natural gas is a mixture consisting mostly of methane (CH_4 – at least 85%), ethane (C_2H_6 – up to 10%), and smaller amounts of propane (C_3H_8) and butane (C_4H_{10}). Trace amounts of other substances may also be present. Natural gas is an extremely important fuel both for domestic and industrial use.

Like LPG, natural gas is almost odourless. As both are highly inflammable and explosive when mixed with air, undetected leaks present a serious hazard. Very smelly organic sulfur compounds called mercaptans are added to the gas so that leaks can be detected almost instantly by smell.

Petrol and the internal combustion engine

Petrol is a complex mixture of at least 100 different compounds, mostly hydrocarbons. Most of these are branched-chain alkanes and some are aromatic compounds.

When petrol is pumped into the engine of a vehicle – an internal combustion engine – the petrol is first vaporised and then mixed with air. The petrol/air mixture is compressed by the piston and then ignited by a spark from the spark plug and burned. The gases produced by the combustion reaction expand and cause the piston to move. In effect, kinetic energy is produced and this is transmitted to the wheels to make the car move.

The more gases are compressed, the more they tend to heat up. Sometimes this causes ignition before the spark is produced. This is intended in a diesel engine, where there is no spark plug, but in a petrol engine the occurrence is called **auto-ignition** or **knocking** or pinking. This is quite a problem as it can cause loss of power, with obvious danger, or damage to the engine.

> **Key definition**
>
> **Auto-ignition** is ignition in an internal combustion engine before a spark is produced.

Octane numbers

> **Key definition**
>
> The **octane number** (or octane rating) is a measure of the tendency of a fuel to auto-ignite or cause knocking.

The lower the octane rating, the more likely it is that auto-ignition will occur. Clearly, high-octane fuels are more desirable.

In devising a scale, two compounds were chosen, heptane (C_7H_{16}) and 2,2,4-trimethylpentane ($CH_3C(CH_3)_2CH_2CH(CH_3)CH_3$). Heptane has a high tendency to auto-ignite, so it was given an octane number of 0. On the other hand, 2,2,4-trimethylpentane has a low tendency to auto-ignite, so it was given a rating of 100.

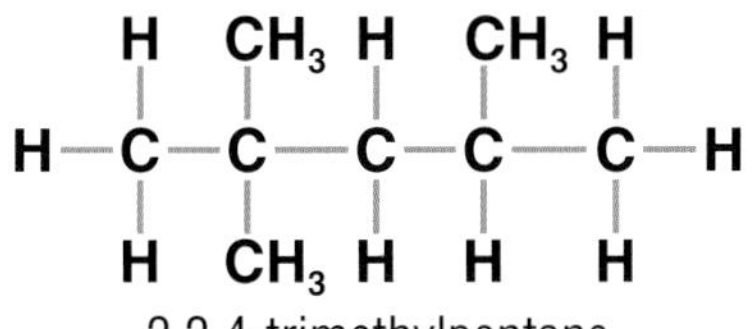

2,2,4-trimethylpentane
Octane number = 100

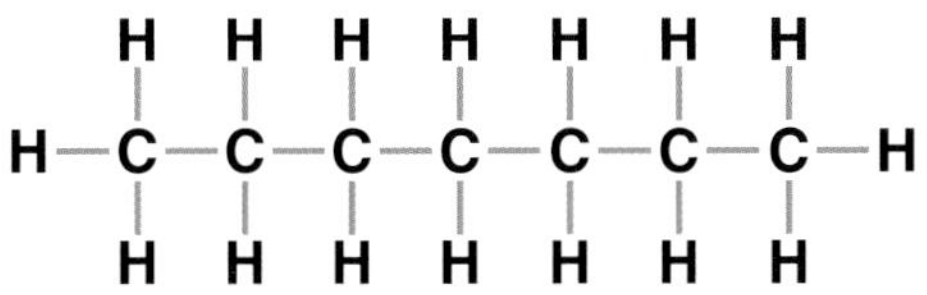

Heptane
Octane number = 0

Fig. 13.7

A mixture of these two compounds containing 95% 2,2,4-trimethylpentane is said to have an octane number of 95. (2,2,4-trimethylpentane is also known as iso-octane, hence the terms 'octane numbers' or 'octane rating'.)

Petrol with an identical tendency to auto-ignite as this mixture, under the same conditions, would thus also be given an octane rating of 95. A compound less likely to auto-ignite than pure iso-octane would have an octane number of more than 100.

Additives

One method of preventing knocking is the use of additives in petrol manufacture. Two types of additive have been in use in recent decades: lead compounds and oxygenates.

Lead compounds work by preventing the type of reactions that cause auto-ignition. However, the lead compounds present in exhaust fumes are toxic. Leaded petrol also became unsuitable for use in modern vehicles because the lead compounds acted as catalyst poisons in the catalytic converters of vehicles. Leaded petrol has been phased out in many countries, and has been banned in Ireland since 2000.

Adding compounds called oxygenates prevents knocking by raising the octane number of the fuel. They have the added benefit of causing less pollution because, apart from not containing lead, they produce lower levels of carbon monoxide when they burn. The most commonly used oxygenate is methyl tertiary butyl ether (MTBE). Its octane rating is 118.

High-octane compounds

Apart from additives, using a mixture of high-octane compounds in petrol manufacture also prevents knocking. Compounds with certain structural features are found to have high-octane numbers, which make them suitable for petrol manufacture. These features are: **a high degree of branching, short-chain length and the existence of rings in the molecule.**

Table 13.7

Methods of increasing octane number
Isomerisation
Dehydrocyclisation
Catalytic cracking

Isomerisation

When certain compounds are heated in the presence of a suitable catalyst, a different structural isomer of the particular compound is formed. Pentane (C_5H_{12}) is a straight-chain alkane that has an octane number of 62. If pentane is heated in the presence of a suitable catalyst, the chain breaks and the fragments rejoin to form a branched compound, 2-methylbutane ($CH_3CH(CH_3)CH_2CH_3$).

This compound has the same molecular formula as pentane, so they are structural isomers of each other. Since the product has an octane number of 93, it is a much more suitable component of petrol than the original pentane.

Dehydrocyclisation

This process involves the formation of a ring compound, accompanied by the removal of hydrogen gas, which is a valuable by-product. A straight-chain alkane such as hexane (C_6H_{14}), which has an octane number of 25, is heated in the presence of a suitable catalyst. The catalyst causes the hexane to change to cyclohexane, which is a cycloalkane, that is, an alkane containing a carbon ring.

This step alone causes an increase in octane number from the 25 of hexane to the 83 of cyclohexane.

The catalyst then causes the cycloalkane to change further to an aromatic compound, benzene, which has an octane number greater than 100.

In terms of octane numbers, the overall effect is to increase from 25 to a number greater than 100.

Catalytic cracking

This process involves taking heavy oil such as kerosene or diesel and heating it to a high temperature in the presence of a catalyst. The large molecule breaks down into several smaller ones: some saturated, some unsaturated. For example:

The unsaturated products are used as feedstock for the polymer industry. The saturated products are usually high-octane branched-chain alkanes suitable for making petrol.

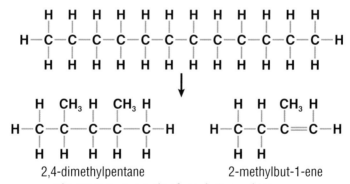

2,4-dimethylpentane   2-methylbut-1-ene

Fig. 13.8 An example of catalytic cracking

Table 13.8

Advantages of catalytic cracking
Long-chain compounds are converted to more useful compounds
Branched-chain alkanes with shorter chain length are formed that have high octane numbers and are used for making petrol
Alkenes are formed which are the starting compounds for the manufacture of polymers

Hydrogen

Hydrogen (H_2) is a colourless, odourless gas, which is almost insoluble in water. It is the least dense of all gases.

Hydrogen is used in large quantities in the chemical industry in processes such as:

- The manufacture of ammonia
- The hydrogenation of vegetable oils to make margarine
- The manufacture of hydrochloric acid.

Hydrogen has great potential as a motor fuel. It burns more efficiently than petrol and is non-polluting. Water is the only product, apart from trace quantities of nitrogen oxides.

Steam reforming

Natural gas is an important industrial source of hydrogen. Methane, the major component of natural gas, is reacted with steam:

$$CH_{4(g)} + H_2O_{(g)} \rightleftharpoons CO_{(g)} + 3H_{2(g)}$$

The mixture is then reacted with more steam and the carbon monoxide is oxidised to carbon dioxide, producing more hydrogen in the process:

$$CO_{(g)} + H_2O_{(g)} \rightleftharpoons CO_{2(g)} + H_{2(g)}$$

The process successfully converts about 70% of the methane to hydrogen.

Electrolysis of water

Electrolysis of water is an expensive method of producing hydrogen as it uses a large amount of electricity. Pure water itself is not an electrolyte, that is, it will not conduct electricity. Instead, dilute sulfuric acid is added. Inert electrodes of platinum or carbon are used. Hydrogen is liberated at the negative electrode, the cathode, while oxygen is liberated at the positive electrode, the anode. The overall reaction is:

$$H_2O_{(l)} \rightarrow H_{2(g)} + \tfrac{1}{2}O_{2(g)}$$

Key-points!

- Hydrocarbons are compounds consisting of carbon and hydrogen only.

- Hydrocarbons that contain a benzene-type ring are called aromatic hydrocarbons.

- A homologous series is a family of compounds with: (1) the same general formula, (2) successive members differing by CH_2 and (3) similar chemical properties.

- Molecules that contain only single bonds are said to be saturated.

- Structural isomers are compounds that have the same molecular formula but different structural formulas.

- Molecules that contain a double or triple bond are unsaturated.

- An exothermic reaction is a reaction that gives out heat to the surroundings.

- An endothermic reaction is a reaction that takes in heat from the surroundings.

- The heat of reaction (ΔH) of a chemical reaction is the heat in kilojoules released or absorbed when the number of moles of reactants indicated in the balanced equation describing the reaction react completely.

- Bond energy is the amount of energy in kJ needed to break 1 mole of bonds of the same type, where all species are in the gaseous state.

- The heat of combustion of a substance is the heat change in kilojoules when 1 mole of the substance is completely burned in excess oxygen.

- The kilogram calorific value of a fuel is defined as the heat energy produced per kilogram of fuel.

- The heat of formation is defined as the heat change in kilojoules when 1 mole of a substance is formed from its elements in their standard states.

- The law of conservation of energy states that energy cannot be created or destroyed, but only changed from one form to another.

- Hess's law states that the heat change of a reaction depends only on the initial and final states of the reaction and is independent of the route by which the reaction may occur.

- Auto-ignition is ignition in an internal combustion engine before a spark is produced.

- The octane number (or octane rating) is a measure of the tendency of a fuel to auto-ignite or cause knocking.

14 Rates of Reaction

Rates of reaction

The rate of a chemical reaction is a measure of how quickly the reaction proceeds. It may be defined as the change in concentration in unit time of any one reactant or product, i.e.

$$\text{Rate} = \frac{\text{Change in concentration}}{\text{Time taken}}$$

Key definition

The **rate of a chemical reaction** is the change in concentration in unit time of any one reactant or product.

Experiment

Mandatory Experiment 14.1: Monitoring the rate of production of oxygen from hydrogen peroxide, using manganese dioxide as a catalyst

Hydrogen peroxide decomposes into water and oxygen as follows:

$$H_2O_{2(l)} \rightarrow H_2O_{(l)} + \tfrac{1}{2}O_{2(g)}$$

Manganese dioxide acts as a suitable catalyst and, when it is added, the reaction occurs at a measurable rate.

Procedure

1 Place 50 cm³ of 2 volumes hydrogen peroxide in a conical flask.

2 Weigh about 0.5 g manganese(IV) oxide into a small test tube. Suspend the test tube in the conical flask using the thread. The manganese(IV) oxide and the hydrogen peroxide should not come into contact until the stop clock is started.

3 Fill the graduated cylinder with water from the trough, and invert it onto the beehive shelf.

4 Assemble the apparatus for the collection of the oxygen produced, by displacement of water.

5 Bring the manganese(IV) oxide into contact with the hydrogen peroxide by loosening the stopper sufficiently to allow the thread to fall into the flask. Shake vigorously, starting the stop clock as the manganese(IV) oxide comes into contact with the hydrogen peroxide solution. Record the volume of oxygen in the graduated cylinder every 30 seconds.

6 Draw a graph of total volume of oxygen against time, putting time on the horizontal axis.

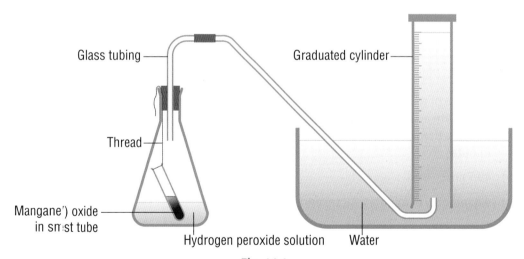

Glass tubing — Graduated cylinder —

Thread —

Mangane') oxide in sm st tube

Hydrogen peroxide solution   Water

Fig. 14.1

Question

14.1 When a hydrogen peroxide (H_2O_2) solution was decomposed in the presence of a suitable catalyst, the oxygen gas produced was collected and its volume measured every 3 minutes until the reaction was complete. The data obtained are shown in the table.

Time (min)	0	3	6	9	12	15	18	21
Volume (cm³)	0	30	45	53	57	59	60	60

(i)   Give the name and formula of a suitable catalyst for this reaction.

(ii)   Plot a graph of the volume of oxygen gas collected against time.

(iii)   Is the rate of reaction faster after 3 minutes or after 9 minutes? Justify your answer from the shape of the graph.

(iv)   What volume of oxygen had been collected after 7.5 minutes?

(v)   How long did it take to collect exactly 40 cm³?

(vi)   After how many minutes was the reaction finished? Explain your answer.

Answer

(i)   Manganese dioxide (MnO_2).

(ii)

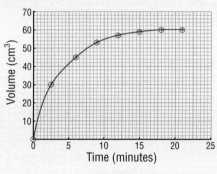

Fig. 14.2

(iii)   The rate of reaction is faster after 3 minutes. The slope of the graph is a measure of the rate at any point in time. The slope of the graph is much steeper at 3 minutes than it is at 9 minutes, so it can be deduced that the rate is faster at 3 minutes.

(iv)   49.7 cm³.

(v)   4.8 minutes (4 minutes, 48 seconds).

(vi)   The reaction was finished after 18 minutes because no further oxygen was produced after this time.

Average and instantaneous rates

In Question 14.1, 60 cm³ of oxygen gas were produced in 18 minutes. The **average rate** of production of oxygen is volume/time = 60 cm³/18 minutes = 3.3 cm³ min⁻¹. However, the rate is not constant throughout the reaction. For example, the average rate for the first 3 minutes is volume/time = 30 cm³/3 minutes = 10 cm³ min⁻¹.

The **instantaneous rate of reaction** is the rate at a particular point in time during the reaction.

The rate at a particular point in time is known as the **instantaneous rate**. It can be found by drawing a tangent to the curve at the appropriate point on the curve. The slope of the curve, which is calculated as shown in Question 14.2, is a measure of the reaction rate.

Question

14.2 In the experiment described in Question 14.1, calculate the instantaneous rate of reaction after 4.5 minutes.

Answer

(i)

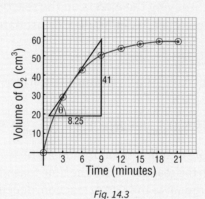

Fig. 14.3

(ii) A tangent to the curve is drawn at the point where time $t = 4.5$ minutes.

(iii) A right-angled triangle is drawn with the tangent as hypotenuse, and the other two sides, of lengths Δt and Δv, respectively, parallel to the horizontal and vertical axes of the graph.

(iv) The angle θ equals the angle made by the tangent with the horizontal axis.

(v) Slope $= \tan \theta = \Delta v / \Delta t = 41.0 / 8.25 = 4.97$ cm^3 min^{-1}

Factors affecting reaction rates

There are a number of factors which can influence the rate of a chemical reaction:

- Concentration of reactants
- Temperature of the reaction
- Particle size of solid reactants
- Nature of reactants, i.e. whether ionic or covalent
- Presence of a catalyst

Concentration of reactants

An increase in the concentration of the reactants usually increases the rate of the reaction.

In the decomposition of hydrogen peroxide using manganese(IV) oxide as a catalyst,

$$H_2O_{2(aq)} \rightarrow H_2O_{(l)} + \frac{1}{2}O_{2(g)}$$

the more concentrated the peroxide solution, the more rapidly the oxygen gas is produced. The peroxide concentration decreases as the reaction proceeds, so the reaction rate decreases.

Temperature

An increase in temperature usually brings about an increase in reaction rate.

Experiment

Mandatory Experiment 14.2: Studying the effects on the reaction rate of (i) concentration and (ii) temperature, using sodium thiosulfate solution and hydrochloric acid

Sodium thiosulfate solution reacts with hydrochloric acid solution according to the following equation:

$$2HCl_{(aq)} + Na_2S_2O_{3(aq)} \rightarrow 2NaCl_{(aq)} + SO_{2(aq)} + S_{(s)}\downarrow + H_2O_{(l)}$$

The pale yellow precipitate of sulfur formed gradually obscures a cross marked on paper placed beneath the reaction flask. The time taken to obscure the cross, which is inversely proportional to the rate of reaction, depends on variables such as temperature and concentration.

(i) Effect of concentration

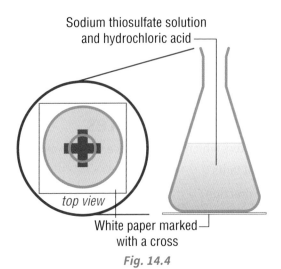

Sodium thiosulfate solution and hydrochloric acid

top view

White paper marked with a cross

Fig. 14.4

1 Place 100 cm^3 of a 0.1 M sodium thiosulfate solution in a conical flask (Fig. 14.4).

2 Add 10 cm^3 of 3 M hydrochloric acid to the flask and swirl, starting the stop clock at the same time.

3 Place the flask on a piece of white paper marked with a cross.

4 Stop the clock when the cross disappears completely and record the time taken in seconds. Calculate the rate as the inverse of the time, i.e. 1/time (s^{-1}).

5 Repeat the experiment using 80 cm^3 of sodium thiosulfate solution mixed with deionised water to make the volume up to 100 cm^3.

6 Repeat step 5 using 60, 40 and 20 cm^3 of sodium thiosulfate solution, respectively, in turn.

7 Draw a graph of reaction rate, i.e. 1/time (vertical axis) against concentration of thiosulfate solution (horizontal axis).

(ii) Effect of temperature

Procedure

1 Place 100 cm^3 of 0.05 M sodium thiosulfate solution into a conical flask at room temperature.

2 Add 5 cm^3 of 3 M HCl, starting a stop clock at the same time.

3 Swirl the flask immediately and place it on a piece of white paper marked with a cross. Record the exact temperature of the contents of the flask.

4 Record the time in seconds taken for the cross to disappear. Calculate the rate as the inverse of the time, i.e. 1/time (s^{-1}).

5 Repeat the experiment, heating the thiosulfate solution to temperatures of approximately 30°C, 40°C, 50°C and 60°C, respectively (before adding the HCl and taking the exact temperature).

6 Draw a graph of reaction rate, i.e. 1/time (vertical axis) against temperature of reaction mixture (horizontal axis).

Particle size

In reactions where one of the reactants is a solid and the other reactant is a liquid, the particle size of the solid has a marked effect on the rate of reaction. The more finely divided the solid, the faster the reaction.

For example, in the reaction of marble (calcium carbonate) with dilute hydrochloric acid solution, powdered marble reacts much more quickly than marble chips.

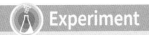

Specified Demonstration: The effect on reaction rate of particle size

The reaction between calcium carbonate and dilute hydrochloric acid is used in this demonstration:

$$CaCO_{3(s)} + 2HCl_{(aq)} \rightarrow CaCl_{2(s)} + H_2O_{(l)} + CO_{2(g)}$$

Procedure

1 Place 5 g of powdered calcium carbonate in a conical flask (Fig.14.5).

2 Place 50 cm³ of hydrochloric acid solution in a graduated cylinder.

3 Pour the acid into the conical flask and swirl, starting a stop clock as the substances come into contact.

4 Stop the clock when the reaction has ended, i.e. when gas bubbles are no longer produced. Record the reaction time.

5 Repeat steps 1–4, this time using 5 g of marble chips.

6 It will be found that the time taken for the powdered calcium carbonate to react completely will be less than that for the marble chips.

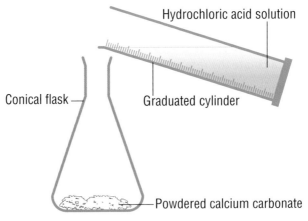

Hydrochloric acid solution

Conical flask

Graduated cylinder

Powdered calcium carbonate

Fig. 14.5

Dust explosions

Dust explosions are a hazard in coalmines, grain silos and other industrial situations. Any solid material that can burn in air will do so at a rate that increases with increased surface area. If the heat released is sufficiently great, then an explosion will occur.

Table 14.1

Conditions needed for a dust explosion to occur
Combustible dust particles
Source of ignition
Dryness
Sufficient oxygen

Nature of reactants

Reactions of covalent compounds are generally slow. In this type of reaction, bonds have to be broken before new bonds are formed. For example, water vapour and carbon dioxide are formed in a reaction between methane gas and oxygen gas.

In this case, C – H bonds and O $=$ O bonds must be broken before the O – H bonds in water vapour and C $=$ O bonds in carbon dioxide can be formed.

Reactions of ionic compounds normally take place in aqueous solution. When an ionic compound is being dissolved in water, the constituent ions are pulled apart by water molecules and surrounded by them.

Thus, when two reacting solutions are mixed, the bonds are already broken, and so when the ions collide they react immediately. For example:

$$Ag^+_{(aq)} + Cl^-_{(aq)} \rightarrow AgCl_{(s)}$$

A white precipitate of silver chloride is formed.

Catalysts

Key definition

A **catalyst** is a substance that alters the rate of a chemical reaction but is not consumed in the reaction.

Types of catalyst

Heterogeneous	Homogeneous
Reaction occurs at a surface	All reactants and catalyst are in the same phase

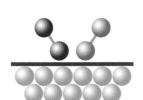
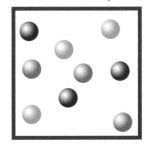

Fig. 14.6

Catalysts are often transition metals or their compounds, which speed up reactions in solution or in the gas phase. Catalysts work by lowering the energy needed to start a reaction – the activation energy – so the operating temperature can be lowered and costs reduced as a result.

In reactions such as the decomposition of hydrogen peroxide into oxygen and water, using manganese(IV) dioxide as a catalyst, the catalyst is in a different phase to the reactant. This type of catalysis is **heterogeneous**.

Key definition

A **heterogeneous catalyst** is a catalyst that is in a different phase to the reactants.

In **homogeneous catalysis**, the catalyst is in the same phase as the reactants. For example, aqueous potassium iodide solution catalyses the decomposition of hydrogen peroxide to water and oxygen:

$$H_2O_{2(aq)} \xrightarrow{\text{KI}_{(aq)}} H_2O_{(l)} + \tfrac{1}{2}O_{2(g)}$$

Key definition

A **homogeneous catalyst** is a catalyst that is in the same phase as the reactants.

Enzymes act as homogeneous catalysts in living systems. Examples include catalase, an enzyme found in the livers of mammals, and zymase, a series of enzymes found in microscopic fungi called yeasts. Zymase helps control the fermentation of sugar to alcohol in the production of alcoholic drinks.

Autocatalysis occurs when a product of a reaction increases the rate of the reaction. For example, in the reduction of manganate(VII) ions

$$MnO_4^-{}_{(aq)} + 8H^+{}_{(aq)} + 5Fe^{2+}{}_{(aq)} \rightarrow Mn^{2+}{}_{(aq)} + 5Fe^{3+}{}_{(aq)} + 4H_2O_{(l)}$$

the $Mn^{2+}{}_{(aq)}$ ions produced catalyse the reaction. The first few drops of the purple $MnO_4^-{}_{(aq)}$ solution added to the $Fe^{2+}{}_{(aq)}$ solution are decolourised slowly, while subsequent drops are decolourised rapidly. The $Mn^{2+}{}_{(aq)}$ formed by the initial slow reaction catalyses the subsequent reaction, the rate of which is increased.

Specified Demonstration: The effect on reaction rate of a catalyst

Hydrogen peroxide decomposes into water and oxygen gas. The reaction proceeds extremely slowly in the absence of a catalyst. However, if a few grains of manganese dioxide are added, bubbles of gas are immediately formed.

$$2H_2O_{2(l)} \xrightarrow{MnO_2} O_{2(g)} + 2H_2O_{(l)}$$

Procedure

1 Place about 25 cm³ of hydrogen peroxide solution in the beaker. Note that there is no significant formation of bubbles.

2 Using the spatula, sprinkle a few grains of manganese dioxide on the surface of the hydrogen peroxide. Note that a vigorous reaction takes place, with the production of bubbles of gas.

Pollution caused by car engines

- Carbon monoxide is formed by the incomplete combustion of petrol vapour:

$$C_8H_{18(g)} + 8\tfrac{1}{2}O_{2(g)} \rightarrow 8CO_{(g)} + 9H_2O_{(g)}$$

This is the reason why running a car engine in an enclosed space may be lethal, as carbon monoxide poisoning may result.

- Nitrogen monoxide is formed when the spark from the spark plug causes the petrol/air mixture to explode. The very high temperature causes nitrogen and oxygen from the air in the mixture to react:

$$N_{2(g)} + O_{2(g)} \rightarrow 2NO_{(g)}$$

- Nitrogen monoxide reacts readily with oxygen to form nitrogen dioxide, which in turn reacts with water and oxygen to form nitric acid:

$$2NO_{(g)} + O_{2(g)} \rightarrow 2NO_{2(g)}$$

$$4NO_{2(g)} + 2H_2O_{(g)} + O_{2(g)} \rightarrow 4HNO_{3(g)}$$

- These reactions occurring in the atmosphere cause acid rain. In sunlight, nitrogen dioxide also reacts with oxygen or hydrocarbons to form an irritating photochemical smog.

- Incomplete combustion of petrol vapour can also result in the emission of unburned hydrocarbons, which can act as greenhouse gases.

Catalytic converters

The catalytic converters in car exhaust systems help to reduce the emission of gases such as nitrogen monoxide, carbon monoxide and hydrocarbons.

The catalyst is a mixture of transition metals – platinum, rhodium and palladium – in the form of a very fine powder. The catalyst is spread in a very thin layer over a ceramic support material full of tiny holes that provide a large surface area.

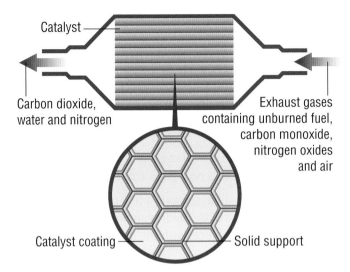

Fig. 14.7 A catalytic converter

As the catalyst is solid and the reactants are gaseous, this is an example of heterogeneous catalysis.

Reactions catalysed

- Carbon monoxide is converted into carbon dioxide by reaction with oxygen:

$$CO_{(g)} + \tfrac{1}{2}O_{2(g)} \rightarrow CO_{2(g)}$$

- Carbon monoxide is also converted into carbon dioxide in a reaction with nitrogen monoxide:

$$2CO_{(g)} + 2NO_{(g)} \rightarrow 2CO_{2(g)} + N_{2(g)}$$

- This reaction has the advantage of reducing the pollutant nitrogen monoxide to nitrogen gas. By catalysing both of these reactions, the converter removes two pollutants quite effectively from exhaust gases.

- Unburned hydrocarbons are also oxidised to carbon dioxide and water, e.g. octane:

$$C_8H_{18(g)} + 12\tfrac{1}{2}O_{2(g)} \rightarrow 8CO_{2(g)} + 9H_2O_{(g)}$$

Environmental benefits of catalytic converters

- Reduction of emissions of carbon monoxide
- Reduction of emissions of nitrogen oxides, removing one cause of acid rain, and reducing the amount of photochemical smog in large cities
- Reduction of emissions of other toxic gases such as unburned hydrocarbons

Activation energy

Molecules must collide with sufficient energy for reaction to take place. The minimum energy needed is called the **activation energy** (E_A), measured in kilojoules per mole (kJ mol^{-1}).

If the reactants collide with energy at least equal to the activation energy, the collision is successful and products will form. Otherwise the molecules will simply rebound without reaction.

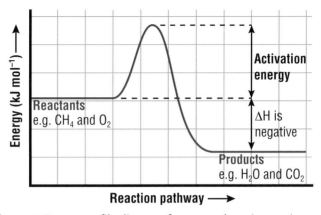

Fig. 14.8 *Energy profile diagram for an exothermic reaction*

The difference between the energy of the reactants and the energy of the products is the heat of reaction (ΔH), and it has a negative value (Fig. 14.8). The E_A is shown as a hump that must be overcome for the reaction to proceed.

The heat of reaction (ΔH) in this case has a positive value (Fig. 14.9). The E_A is again shown as a hump that must be overcome for the reaction to proceed.

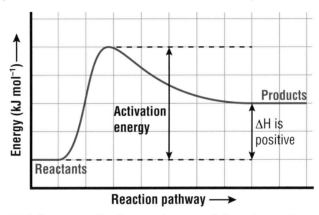

Fig. 14.9 *Energy profile diagram for an endothermic reaction*

Influence of temperature on reaction rate

Reactions occur faster at higher temperatures. The higher the temperature, the greater the energy of the molecules and the greater their average speed. This has two consequences, each of which increases the rate of reaction:

   (a) The number of collisions per second is increased.

   (b) Each collision is more energetic, and a higher proportion of collisions have the necessary activation energy for reaction to occur.

Factor (b) is much more significant in increasing reaction rate than (a).

Influence of concentration on reaction rate

The consequence of increased concentration of reactants is that the number of collisions per second is increased, so increasing the rate of reaction. As the reaction progresses, the reactants become used up and their concentrations decrease. The reaction rate decreases, because of the consequent reduction in collisions per second.

Theories of catalysis

Catalysts work by providing an alternative reaction route with lower activation energy.

By lowering the activation energy, a catalyst can make it possible to carry out a reaction at a lower temperature, with consequent savings in energy costs.

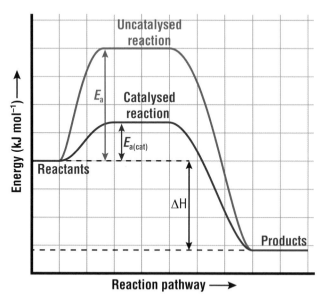

Fig. 14.10 A catalyst lowers the activation energy for the reaction

Intermediate formation theory of catalysis

Homogeneous catalysts sometimes work by reacting with reactants to form unstable intermediate products. These intermediates decompose readily, forming products and regenerating the catalyst.

Specified Demonstration to be observed using an animation or video clip: Oxidation of potassium sodium tartrate by hydrogen peroxide, catalysed by cobalt(II) salts

Potassium sodium tartrate ions ($C_4H_4O_6^{2-}$) are oxidised by hydrogen peroxide to carbon dioxide and water:

$$C_4H_4O_6^{2-} + H_2O_2 \rightarrow CO_2 + H_2O$$

The reaction is catalysed by Co^{2+} ions.

At the start of the reaction, the mixture will have the pink colour of the cobalt(II) ions. During the course of the reaction, which is indicated by vigorous bubbling, a green colour, that of an intermediate complex, will be seen. However, as the reaction nears its conclusion, the pink colour will be restored showing that the catalyst is being regenerated.

Procedure
1. Dissolve about 5 g of potassium sodium tartrate in 65 cm³ of water, which has been heated to about 50°C.

2. Dissolve about 0.2 g of cobalt chloride crystals in water and add this to the potassium sodium tartrate solution.

3. Add 20 cm³ of 100 volume hydrogen peroxide.

4. The initial pink colour changes to green, before reverting to pink.

Surface adsorption theory of catalysis

The heterogeneous catalysis of gaseous reactions by metals is believed to involve adsorption. This is where some sort of bond or attachment is formed between one or more of the reactants and the surface of the catalyst.

A given catalyst has a number of active sites at which the reactants may adsorb. The bond must be strong enough to hold the reactants to the surface of the catalyst, but weak enough to break and release the products, so making sites available for more reactants to adsorb.

The addition reaction of hydrogen to ethene, forming ethane, is catalysed by nickel. An ethene molecule is believed to adsorb onto the surface of the nickel, as does a molecule of hydrogen, which splits into two atoms in the process. The two hydrogen atoms add on in turn to the ethene, forming a molecule of ethane, which then desorbs from the nickel surface.

Catalyst poisons

Catalysts can be poisoned so that they no longer function at full efficiency. In heterogeneous catalysis, the particles that poison the catalyst, e.g. lead, arsenic and compounds of sulfur, are adsorbed more strongly onto the catalyst surface than the actual reactant particles. This is the reason why cars fitted with catalytic converters cannot use leaded petrol. The lead atoms bond strongly to the platinum/rhodium surface of the converter, poisoning it and making it ineffective.

Catalyst poisons can block the active sites of enzymes. This can inhibit vital biochemical reactions.

 **Experiment**

Specified Demonstration: Demonstration of the oxidation of methanol using a hot platinum catalyst

This is an example of heterogeneous catalysis, where methanol, an alcohol, is oxidised to methanal, an aldehyde. The oxygen in the air removes hydrogen atoms from the methanol. The rate is extremely slow in the absence of a catalyst. However, in the presence of hot platinum, the reaction proceeds rapidly and is so exothermic that the wire glows.

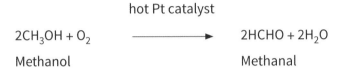

$$2CH_3OH + O_2 \xrightarrow{\text{hot Pt catalyst}} 2HCHO + 2H_2O$$

Methanol   Methanal

Procedure

1 In the fume cupboard add 25 cm³ of methanol to a warm conical flask with the cardboard insert as in Fig. 14.11.

2 Warm slowly to about 60°C on a hot plate.

3 Place the flask on a heat-resistant mat.

4 Heat a spiral of platinum wire to red heat in a Bunsen flame (making sure that the naked flame is well away from the methanol).

5 Quickly lower the spiral into the flask on one side of the cardboard insert, using a piece of nichrome wire to suspend it from the neck of the conical flask.

6 The spiral, which will have cooled to below red hot during the transfer, should begin to glow again.

7 There may be a number of mild explosions.

8 These may become cyclic, i.e. the spiral glows, the mixture explodes, the spiral cools, then heats up again until a further explosion occurs.

9 This should continue as long as there is a supply of methanol.

10 The card allows more air to flow in and allows the waste gases to be swept away.

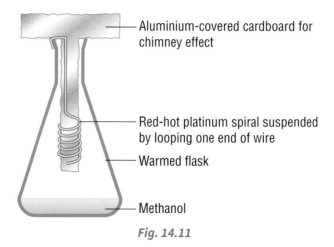

Aluminium-covered cardboard for chimney effect

Red-hot platinum spiral suspended by looping one end of wire

Warmed flask

Methanol

Fig. 14.11

Key-points!

- The rate of a chemical reaction is the change in concentration in unit time of any one reactant or product.
- The instantaneous rate of reaction is the rate at a particular point in time during the reaction.
- A catalyst is a substance that alters the rate of a chemical reaction but is not consumed in the reaction.
- A heterogeneous catalyst is a catalyst that is in a different phase to the reactants.
- A homogeneous catalyst is a catalyst that is in the same phase as the reactants.
- Activation energy is the minimum energy with which particles need to collide to cause a reaction.

15 Organic Compounds

Tetrahedral carbon

> **Point to note**
>
> In saturated organic compounds, all of the carbon atoms are tetrahedral.

In alkanes, chloroalkanes and alcohols, all of the carbon atoms are tetrahedral.

Chloroalkanes — *compounds where chlorine replaces one or more hydrogens.*

A chloroalkane is an alkane in which one or more hydrogen atoms are replaced with chlorine atoms.

Chloroalkanes are named after the alkane from which they are derived. The prefix *chloro–* indicates the presence of a chlorine atom.

Table 15.1

No. of chlorine atoms	Name of compound	Chemical formula	Structural formula
1	Chloromethane	CH_3Cl	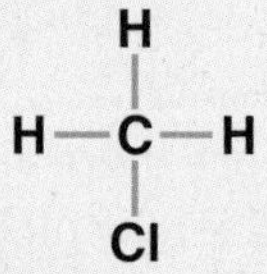
2	Dichloromethane	CH_2Cl_2	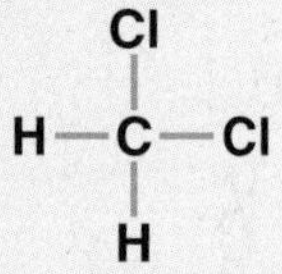
3	Trichloromethane	$CHCl_3$	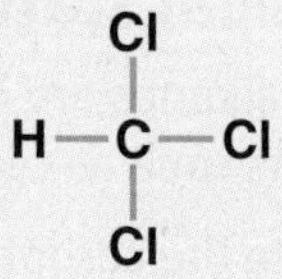
4	Tetrachloromethane	CCl_4	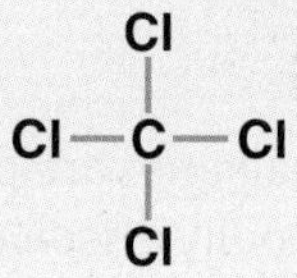

Question

15.1 Name and draw the structural formulas of (i) CH_2ClCH_2Cl and (ii) CH_3CCl_3.

Answer

(i) CH_2ClCH_2Cl

Since there are two chlorine atoms, the prefix *di*– is used, hence dichloroethane. There is one chlorine atom on each of the two carbons, so the numbers 1 and 2 are listed as a further prefix, to indicate the chlorine positions. The full name is therefore 1,2-dichloroethane.

1,2-Dichloroethane

(ii) CH_3CCl_3

Since there are three chlorine atoms, the prefix *tri–* is used, hence trichloroethane. All three chlorine atoms are on the same carbon, which is designated number 1, so as to give the lowest number to the position of the chlorine atoms. The full name is therefore 1,1,1-trichloroethane.

1,1,1-Trichloroethane

Physical state and properties

Chloroalkanes are insoluble in water. However, they are very soluble in non-polar solvents such as cyclohexane and methylbenzene.

Because the carbon–chlorine bond has slightly greater polarity than the carbon–hydrogen bond, chloroalkanes have higher boiling points than the corresponding alkanes. Most chloroalkanes are liquids at room temperature, with just chloromethane and chloroethane being gaseous.

Uses

Chloroalkanes are particularly useful as solvents. Because of their lack of polarity, they readily dissolve grease and oil and other substances that are insoluble in water. For this reason, they have been used extensively in the dry cleaning of clothes.

Alcohols

The alcohols form a homologous series of organic compounds of general formula $C_nH_{2n+1}OH$. All the alcohols possess a hydroxyl group (–OH) as the functional group. The carbon atoms, including that bonded directly to the hydroxyl group, are all tetrahedral.

Alcohols are named by replacing the –e at the end of the corresponding alkane name with –*ol*.

Question

15.2 Write the name, chemical formula and structural formula of the alcohol derived from ethane (C_2H_6).

Answer

The name of the alcohol is ethanol. The chemical formula is C_2H_5OH. The structural formula is:

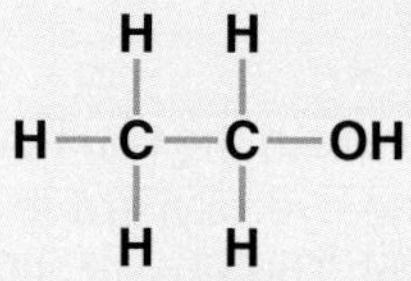

$$H-\overset{\overset{\displaystyle H}{|}}{\underset{\underset{\displaystyle H}{|}}{C}}-\overset{\overset{\displaystyle H}{|}}{\underset{\underset{\displaystyle H}{|}}{C}}-OH$$

Ethanol

The position of the hydroxyl group on the carbon chain must be given when the chain contains three or more carbons. In alcohols with the hydroxyl group at the end of the carbon chain, the carbon attached to the hydroxyl group will be bonded to one carbon atom. Such alcohols are classed as **primary** alcohols.

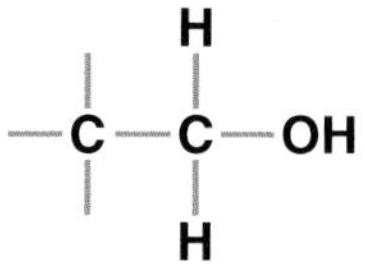

$$-\overset{|}{\underset{|}{C}}-\overset{\overset{\displaystyle H}{|}}{\underset{\underset{\displaystyle H}{|}}{C}}-OH$$

Fig. 15.1 Primary alcohols

Propan-1-ol is an example of a primary alcohol:

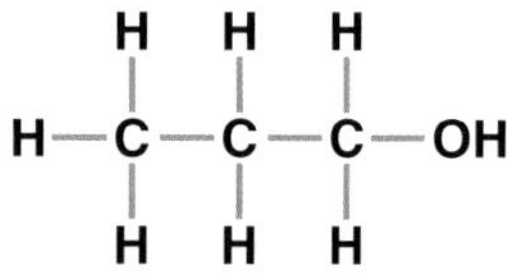

$$H-\overset{\overset{\displaystyle H}{|}}{\underset{\underset{\displaystyle H}{|}}{C}}-\overset{\overset{\displaystyle H}{|}}{\underset{\underset{\displaystyle H}{|}}{C}}-\overset{\overset{\displaystyle H}{|}}{\underset{\underset{\displaystyle H}{|}}{C}}-OH$$

Propan-1-ol

Secondary alcohols, for example propan-2-ol, have two carbon atoms attached to the carbon with the hydroxyl group.

$$-\overset{|}{\underset{|}{C}}-\overset{\overset{\displaystyle H}{|}}{\underset{\underset{\displaystyle OH}{|}}{C}}-\overset{|}{\underset{|}{C}}-$$

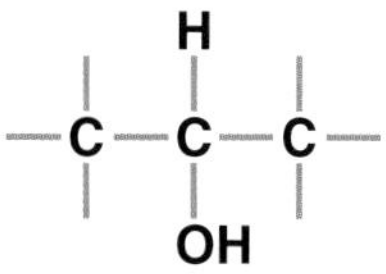

Fig. 15.2 Secondary alcohols

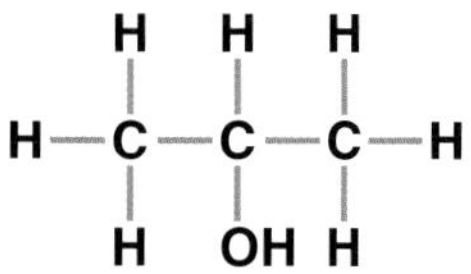

$$H-\overset{\overset{\displaystyle H}{|}}{\underset{\underset{\displaystyle H}{|}}{C}}-\overset{\overset{\displaystyle H}{|}}{\underset{\underset{\displaystyle OH}{|}}{C}}-\overset{\overset{\displaystyle H}{|}}{\underset{\underset{\displaystyle H}{|}}{C}}-H$$

Fig. 15.3 Propan-2-ol

15.3 Write the name, chemical formula and structural formula of the secondary alcohol containing four carbon atoms.

Answer

Since there are four carbon atoms in the chain, whichever of the middle two carbon atoms is attached to the hydroxyl group is designated position 2. Thus, the alcohol is named butan-2-ol. The chemical formula is:

$$CH_3CH(OH)CH_2CH_3$$

Butan-2-ol

Physical state and properties

Fig. 15.4 shows that alcohols have higher boiling points than alkanes of similar relative molecular mass. Methanol, ethanol and the isomers of propanol and butanol are all liquids at room temperature.

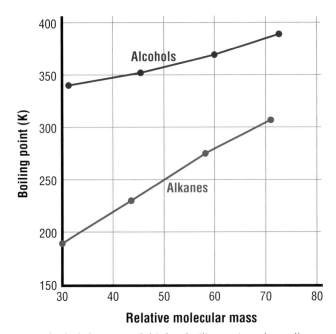

Fig. 15.4 Alcohols have much higher boiling points than alkanes of comparable relative molecular mass

The presence of the polar –OH group in alcohols results in hydrogen bonding between neighbouring molecules. These strong hydrogen bonds have to be broken before the alcohol boils, so more energy must be supplied and the boiling point is correspondingly raised.

Wine and beer are mixtures of ethanol, water and some other substances. The ethanol molecules and the water molecules mix completely because hydrogen bonds form between the hydroxyl groups in ethanol and the hydroxyl groups in water.

Methanol and propan-1-ol also mix with water in all proportions. However, the solubility decreases as the hydrocarbon chain gets bigger and becomes more significant.

Occurrence and uses

- Most of the world's supply of ethanol is made by the hydration of ethene.

- However, the ethanol in alcoholic drinks is made by fermentation of sugars in fruits such as grapes, as in wine making. In fermentation, enzymes in yeast break down the sugar to give carbon dioxide and ethanol.

$$C_6H_{12}O_{6(aq)} \rightarrow 2C_2H_5OH_{(l)} + 2CO_{2(g)}$$

- Fermentation is used in the brewing industry to make beer and in the distilling industry to make spirits.

- Ethanol is used extensively as a solvent for paints, glues, perfumes and aftershaves.

- It is the major component of methylated spirits. However, a small amount of methanol, which is poisonous, and a dye are added to the ethanol to make it undrinkable. Methanol used in this way is said to be a **denaturing agent**.

Planar carbon

Planar carbon atoms feature in a number of homologous series – those whose compounds have a carbon–carbon ($C = C$) or carbon–oxygen ($C = O$) double bond. **The atoms in the double bond are planar**, although other carbon atoms in the molecule may be tetrahedral. The presence of a double bond means that these compounds are **unsaturated**.

All compounds of the homologous series of alkenes, aldehydes, ketones, carboxylic acids, esters and aromatic compounds possess one or more planar carbon atoms.

Aldehydes

Aldehydes form a homologous series of compounds of general formula $C_nH_{2n+1}CHO$. All aldehydes contain the **carbonyl group**, which consists of an oxygen atom attached to a carbon atom by a polar double covalent bond, $C = O$. In aldehydes, there is always a hydrogen atom bonded to the carbonyl carbon. The carbonyl carbon is a planar carbon atom. The functional group of the aldehydes is –CHO.

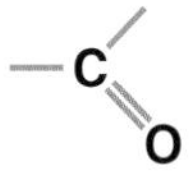

Fig. 15.5 The carbonyl group

Aldehydes are named by replacing the –e at the end of the corresponding alkane name with –*al*.

Question

15.4 Write the name, chemical formula and structural formula of the aldehyde containing three carbon atoms.

Answer

The corresponding alkane is propane, $CH_3CH_2CH_3$. The name of the aldehyde is therefore propanal. The chemical formula is CH_3CH_2CHO. The structural formula is:

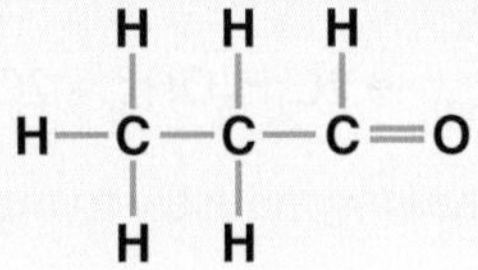

$$
\begin{array}{ccccc}
 & H & H & H & \\
 & | & | & | & \\
H\!-\!&C&\!-\!C&\!-\!C&\!=\!O \\
 & | & | & & \\
 & H & H & &
\end{array}
$$

Propanal

Physical state and properties

The carbon–oxygen double bond (C = O) in the carbonyl group is quite polar. As a result, dipole–dipole attractions exist between adjacent aldehyde molecules. This leads to boiling points that are higher than those of the alkanes of similar relative molecular mass, but lower than those of comparable alcohols. Apart from methanal, which is a gas at room temperature, the other lower members of the aldehyde series are liquids.

The polarity of the carbon–oxygen double bond (C = O) means that water molecules can form hydrogen bonds with the carbonyl group. Consequently, the lower aldehydes dissolve in water. Aldehydes are soluble in non-polar solvents such as cyclohexane.

Occurrence and uses

Benzaldehyde is found in almond kernels and contributes to the flavouring of this fruit.

Ketones

Like aldehydes, all ketones contain the carbonyl group (C = O). But unlike aldehydes, the carbonyl group is in the middle of a carbon chain, which means that there cannot be a hydrogen atom bonded to the carbonyl carbon. The functional group of the ketones is C = O.

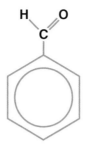

Fig. 15.6 Benzaldehyde

Ketones are named by replacing the –e at the end of the corresponding alkane name with –*one*. Given that a ketone consists of two alkyl groups as well as the carbonyl group, there must be at least three carbons present.

Questions

15.5 Write the name, chemical formula and structural formula of the ketone containing three carbon atoms.

Answer

The corresponding alkane is propane, $CH_3CH_2CH_3$.

The name of the ketone is therefore propanone. The chemical formula is CH_3COCH_3. The structural formula is:

Propanone

Physical state and properties

Ketones have similar physical properties to aldehydes, due to the influence of the polar carbonyl group. The lower ketones are liquids at room temperature and are soluble in water. All ketones are soluble in organic solvents, and ketones have higher boiling points than alkanes of similar relative molecular mass.

Uses

Propanone is widely used as a solvent and has been used in nail varnish remover.

Carboxylic acids

Carboxylic acids form a homologous series of compounds of general formula $C_nH_{2n+1}COOH$. The carboxyl group (–COOH) is the functional group of carboxylic acids. The structural formula of the carboxyl group is shown in Fig. 15.7. The carboxyl carbon atom is a planar carbon.

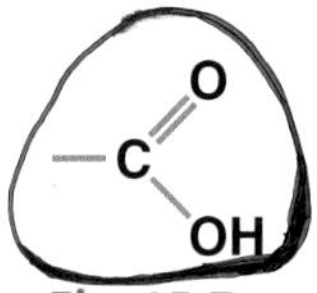

Fig. 15.7

The carboxyl group

Carboxylic acids are named by replacing the –e at the end of the corresponding alkane name with –oic acid.

Question

15.6 Write the name, chemical formula and structural formula of the carboxylic acid containing three carbon atoms.

Answer

The corresponding alkane is propane, $CH_3CH_2CH_3$. The name of the carboxylic acid is propanoic acid. The chemical formula is CH_3CH_2COOH. The structural formula is:

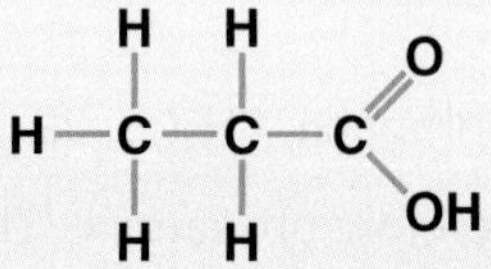

Propanoic acid

Physical state and properties

The lower carboxylic acids are colourless liquids, usually with sharp or distinctive smells. Boiling points are higher than even those of alcohols of similar relative molecular mass. These relatively high boiling points result from the formation of *dimers*, where two carboxylic acid molecules are held together by two hydrogen bonds.

Hydrogen bonding can also occur between water molecules and the lower carboxylic acids. As a result, acids containing up to four carbon atoms are highly soluble in water.

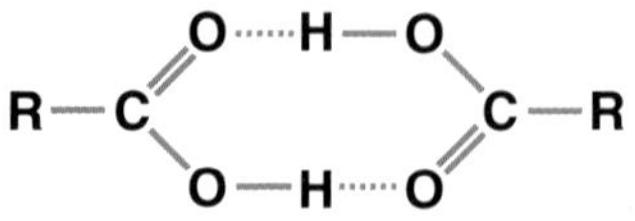

R = alkyl group or H

Fig. 15.8

Occurrence and uses

- Methanoic acid (HCOOH) is an irritant fluid emitted by some ants and is also found in nettles.
- Ethanoic acid (CH_3COOH) is the principal acid found in vinegar.
- Ethanoic acid is also used in the manufacture of cellulose acetate, which is used in lacquers, varnishes, photographic film, non-shatter glass and as rayon fibre.
- Propanoic acid (CH_3CH_2COOH), benzoic acid (C_6H_5COOH) and some of their salts are used in the preservation of food. Sodium benzoate is a particularly widely used food preservative.

Esters

Esters are compounds derived from carboxylic acids. The formula of an ester can be represented as RCOOR', where R could be a hydrogen atom or an alkyl group, and R' is an alkyl group. All esters contain the ester linkage – COO –, which contains a planar carbon.

The name of each ester has two parts: (1) the alkyl group derived from the alcohol and (2) the name of the acid, with the ending –oic replaced by –*oate*.

Question

15.7 Write the name, chemical formula and structural formula derived from methanoic acid (HCOOH) and ethanol (C_2H_5OH).

Answer

The alcohol, ethanol, provides the first part of the name, ethyl. The carboxylic acid, methanoic acid, provides the second part of the name, methanoate. Thus, the ester is ethyl methanoate.

In writing the chemical formula of the ester, the formula of the acid is written first with the carboxyl hydrogen atom omitted, HCOO–. The alkyl group from the alcohol is then added in place of the omitted hydrogen, so the completed formula is $HCOOC_2H_5$.

The structural formula is built up in the same way.

Ethyl methanoate

Physical state and properties

Esters of lower relative molecular mass are liquids. The carbon–oxygen double bond (C = O) in the ester linkage is polar, leading to intermolecular forces – but not hydrogen bonds – between adjacent ester molecules. Thus, the boiling points of esters are similar to those of aldehydes and ketones of similar relative molecular mass.

The polarity of the C = O group allows hydrogen bonding to occur with water molecules, so esters with fewer than five carbon atoms are water soluble. Esters are soluble in non-polar solvents.

Occurrence and uses

- Members of the ester family have strong and often pleasant, fruity smells. Many of them occur naturally and are responsible for the smells of flowers and the flavour in fruits, e.g. mangos.

- Ethyl ethanoate is used as a solvent for printing inks and paints.

- Fats and oils are naturally occurring esters of long-chain carboxylic acids.

Aromatic compounds

Compounds that contain a benzene ring are called aromatic compounds. Benzene itself (C_6H_6) is the most important aromatic compound.

The benzene molecule consists of six carbon atoms joined to form a hexagonal planar ring. Each carbon atom has four valence electrons. One of these is used to bond with a hydrogen atom, and two others are used to form sigma bonds with the carbon atoms on either side. This leaves one valence electron, which is not involved in sigma bonding, on each carbon atom.

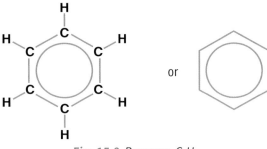

or

Fig. 15.9 Benzene, C_6H_6

The six valence electrons not involved in sigma bonding are delocalised in a pi-type bond, which is spread around the six atoms in the ring.

The structure of benzene is represented as in Fig. 15.9. The circle emphasises the delocalisation involved.

Physical properties

Being non-polar, aromatic hydrocarbons do not dissolve to any extent in water, but dissolve in non-polar solvents. Liquid aromatic hydrocarbons, such as methylbenzene, are themselves good non-polar solvents, dissolving non-polar solutes readily. Methylbenzene ($C_6H_5CH_3$) is a widely used industrial solvent.

Occurrence and uses

- Some aromatic compounds, including benzene, are carcinogens. This means that they are capable of causing cancer in humans.

- However, many other aromatic compounds are non-carcinogenic. The common painkiller, aspirin, is an example.

- Aromatic compounds are in widespread use in a range of different applications. They are used in the manufacture of dyes, detergents, garden chemicals such as herbicides, and many medicines.

- The acid–base indicators phenolphthalein and methyl orange, are also aromatic compounds.

Experiment

Specified Demonstration: Solubility of liquid organic compounds in cyclohexane and in water

The solubility of liquid organic compounds, such as methanol, ethanol, propan-1-ol, butan-1-ol, ethanol, propanone, methanoic acid, ethanoic acid, ethyl ethanoate and methylbenzene, in cyclohexane and water, respectively, can be investigated. For each solute, the following steps are carried out and the results summarised in a table.

Procedure
1 About half fill a test tube with cyclohexane and add 1 cm³ of one of the solutes.

2 Stopper the test tube and shake vigorously.

3 Open carefully to release pressure and allow to stand.

4 The formation of separate layers will indicate insolubility.

5 Repeat using water as the solvent.

Organic natural products

A natural product is any chemical produced in nature, either by plants or by animals. Perfumes, dyes and medical potions can all be obtained in the form of plant extracts. Examples of well-known natural products include codeine, morphine, paracetamol, aspirin, quinine, nicotine, cocaine, strychnine and caffeine.

Experiment

Mandatory Experiment 15.1: The extraction of clove oil from cloves by steam distillation followed by solvent extraction of eugenol

Steam distillation allows substances to be distilled that, if heated on their own to higher temperatures, might partially decompose. The natural product eugenol is the main constituent of clove oil. Its structure is:

Eugenol

Procedure

1 Set up the Quickfit apparatus as in Fig. 15.10.

2 Weigh out about 5–10 g of whole cloves, and place them in the pear-shaped flask. Cover with a little warm water.

3 Connect the steam generator to the rest of the apparatus and heat it to boiling point. Regulate the heat so that a constant supply of steam is supplied to the pear-shaped flask. If Quickfit apparatus is used for steam generation, use anti-bumping granules in the steam generator.

4 Monitor the level of boiling water in the steam generator during the experiment, topping it up with **hot** water if necessary.

5 Collect the distillate. It should have a pale milky appearance. Note the strong smell of clove oil.

6 When sufficient product has been collected, disconnect the steam generator to prevent suck-back, and turn off the heat.

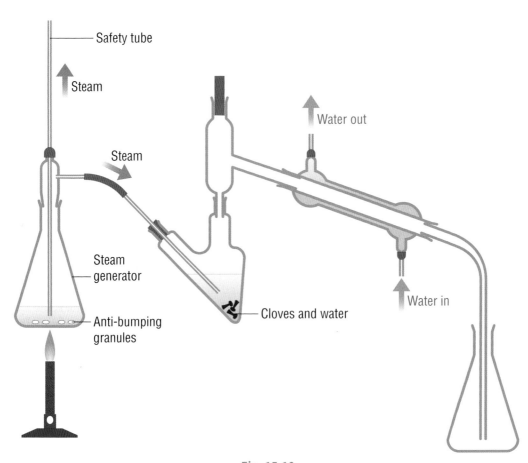

Fig. 15.10

Solvent extraction

The clove oil is separated from the water in the emulsion by solvent extraction (Fig. 15.11). The distillate is shaken up in a separating funnel with the solvent cyclohexane. The non-polar clove oil will dissolve in the cyclohexane, which is a non-polar solvent. The funnel is allowed to stand until the aqueous and non-aqueous layers have separated. The layers are run into separate beakers. The top layer is the solution of clove oil in cyclohexane. The clove oil is recovered by evaporating off the cyclohexane on a hot plate in a fume cupboard.

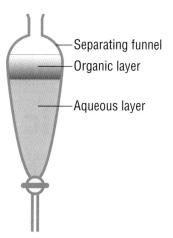

Separating funnel
Organic layer
Aqueous layer

Fig. 15.11

Key-points!

- In saturated organic compounds, all of the carbon atoms are tetrahedral.
- The alkanes form a homologous series of aliphatic hydrocarbons of general formula C_nH_{2n+2}.
- A chloroalkane is an alkane in which one or more hydrogen atoms are replaced with chlorine atoms.
- The alcohols form a homologous series of organic compounds of general formula $C_nH_{2n+1}OH$.
- The alkenes form a homologous series of aliphatic hydrocarbons of general formula C_nH_{2n}.
- Aldehydes form a homologous series of compounds of general formula $C_nH_{2n+1}CHO$.
- Ketones contain the carbonyl group ($C = O$), located in the middle of a carbon chain.
- Carboxylic acids form a homologous series of compounds of general formula $C_nH_{2n+1}COOH$.
- The formula of an ester can be represented as RCOOR', where R could be a hydrogen atom or an alkyl group, and R' is an alkyl group.
- Compounds that contain a benzene ring are called aromatic compounds, e.g. benzene (C_6H_6).
- All compounds of the homologous series of alkenes, aldehydes, ketones, carboxylic acids, esters and aromatic compounds possess one or more planar carbon atoms.

16 Organic Chemical Reactions

Learning objectives

In this chapter you will learn about:

1 Addition reactions

2 Reaction mechanism: ionic addition

3 Polymerisation

4 Substitution reactions: halogenation of alkanes

5 Other substitution reactions

6 Elimination reactions

7 Redox reactions

8 Reactions as acids

9 Organic synthesis

Addition reactions

> ### Key definition
>
> An **addition reaction** is a reaction in which two molecules add together to form one larger molecule.

Addition reactions are typical of unsaturated compounds, such as alkenes.

The planar, unsaturated alkene molecule changes into a tetrahedral, saturated molecule in the process. In general, an **addition reaction involves a change in structure from planar to tetrahedral**.

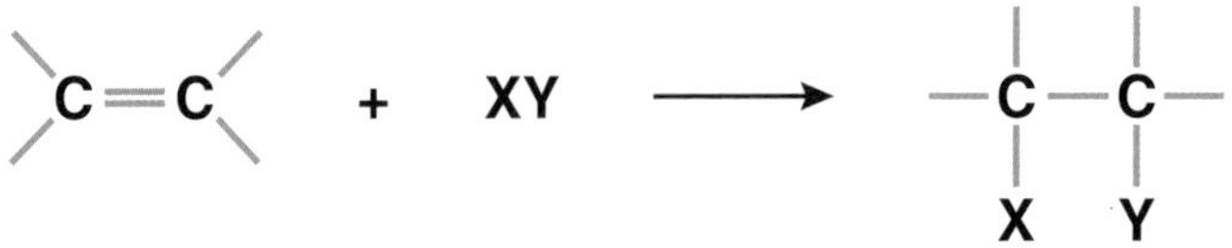

$$\text{C=C} \quad + \quad \text{XY} \quad \longrightarrow \quad \overset{|}{\underset{X}{C}}-\overset{|}{\underset{Y}{C}}$$

Fig 16.1

(i) Addition of hydrogen

Hydrogenation of double bonds is used in industry to convert vegetable oils, which are unsaturated, into solid saturated materials used in margarine and dairy spreads.

$$
\underset{\text{Ethene}}{\overset{\displaystyle H \quad\quad H}{\underset{\displaystyle H \quad\quad H}{C=C}}} \quad + \quad H_2 \quad \xrightarrow[\text{heat}]{\text{Ni}} \quad \underset{\text{Ethane}}{H-\overset{\displaystyle H}{\underset{\displaystyle H}{C}}-\overset{\displaystyle H}{\underset{\displaystyle H}{C}}-H}
$$

(ii) Addition of chlorine

This product, 1,2-dichloroethane, is used in industry to make chloroethene, the raw material for the manufacture of the important plastic PVC.

$$
\overset{\displaystyle H \quad\quad H}{\underset{\displaystyle H \quad\quad H}{C=C}} \quad + \quad Cl_2 \quad \longrightarrow \quad \underset{\text{1,2-dichloroethane}}{H-\overset{\displaystyle H}{\underset{\displaystyle Cl}{C}}-\overset{\displaystyle H}{\underset{\displaystyle Cl}{C}}-H}
$$

(iii) Addition of bromine

$$
\overset{\displaystyle H \quad\quad H}{\underset{\displaystyle H \quad\quad H}{C=C}} \quad + \quad Br_2 \quad \longrightarrow \quad \underset{\text{1,2-dibromoethane}}{H-\overset{\displaystyle H}{\underset{\displaystyle Br}{C}}-\overset{\displaystyle H}{\underset{\displaystyle Br}{C}}-H}
$$

(iv) Addition of water

The addition of water is called a **hydration** reaction.

$$
\overset{\displaystyle H \quad\quad H}{\underset{\displaystyle H \quad\quad H}{C=C}} \quad + \quad HOH \quad \longrightarrow \quad \underset{\text{Ethanol}}{H-\overset{\displaystyle H}{\underset{\displaystyle H}{C}}-\overset{\displaystyle H}{\underset{\displaystyle OH}{C}}-H}
$$

(v) Addition of hydrogen chloride

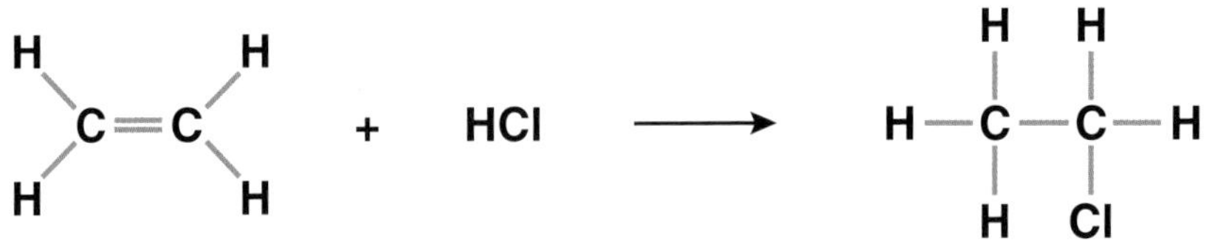

$$H_2C=CH_2 \quad + \quad HCl \quad \longrightarrow \quad \text{Chloroethane}$$

Chloroethane

Stability of benzene

Benzene is a planar, unsaturated molecule. However, it does not readily take part in addition reactions. It is a stable and relatively unreactive molecule. This stability is caused by the very different delocalised pi bonding in benzene.

Reaction mechanism: ionic addition

The movement of electrons involved in bond breaking and bond making is shown by using curved arrows (Fig. 16.2).

Movement of
one electron

Movement of a
pair of electrons

Fig. 16.2

The bromination of ethene is the example used to illustrate the mechanism of an addition reaction.

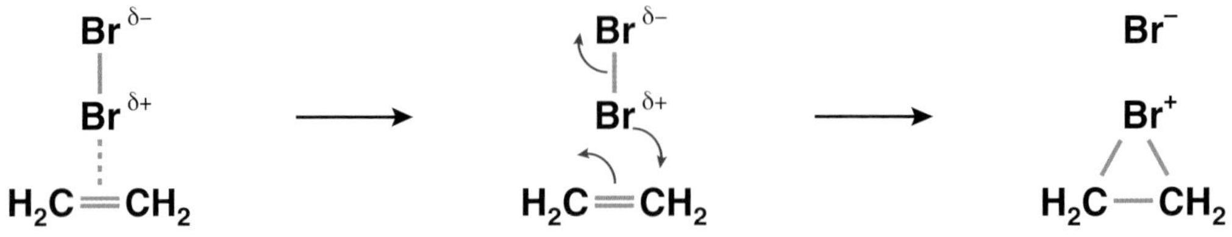

The first step is the approach of a bromine molecule at right angles to the plane of an ethene molecule. The electron-rich double bond induces polarity in the bromine molecule. This results in a weak attraction between the partially positive bromine atom ($Br^{\delta+}$) and the double bond region of the ethene molecule.

Electron movement follows, causing the breaking of the bromine–bromine bond. The bromide ion (Br^-) breaks away, while the positive ion (Br^+) bonds to the ethene molecule, forming a positively charged bridged structure.

In the last step of the reaction, the Br^- attacks the positively charged intermediate from the opposite side to where the bridge is located.

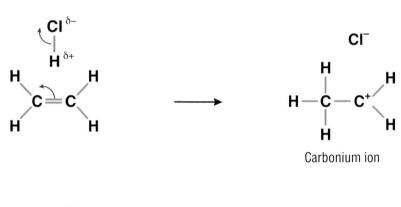

Evidence for mechanism

Evidence for the ionic addition mechanism is found if sodium chloride (NaCl) is added to the mixture for the reaction of bromine water, which contains BrOH, to ethene. Mixed products result, including 2-bromoethanol, 1-bromo-2-chloroethane and 1,2-dibromoethane.

Mechanisms of other ionic addition reactions

Fig 16.3 Mechanism of the reaction of ethene with hydrogen chloride

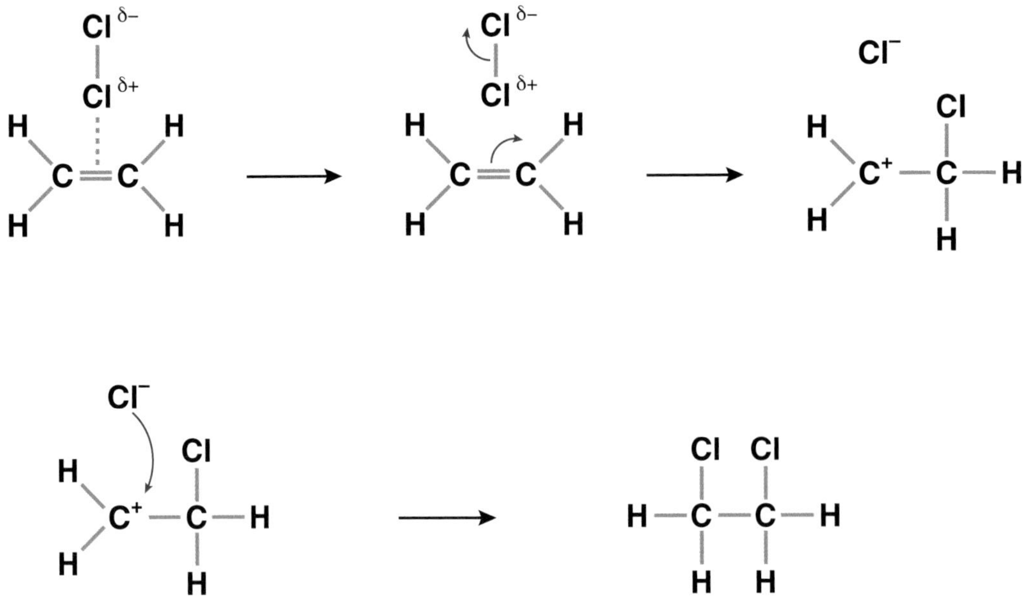

Fig. 16.4 *Mechanism of the reaction of ethene with chlorine*

Polymerisation

Alkenes are the raw materials in the industrial manufacture of plastics. In the polymerisation of ethene, the molecule **adds to itself** to produce a saturated hydrocarbon chain that consists of repeating $-CH_2CH_2-$ units.

The resulting solid substance is called poly(ethene) and has many uses, such as in plastic bags and in food-wrapping films. Polythene is an example of a **polymer**, a large molecule made up of many identical repeating units called **monomers**. Physical properties, such as hardness, depend on the number of carbon atoms in the polymer chain.

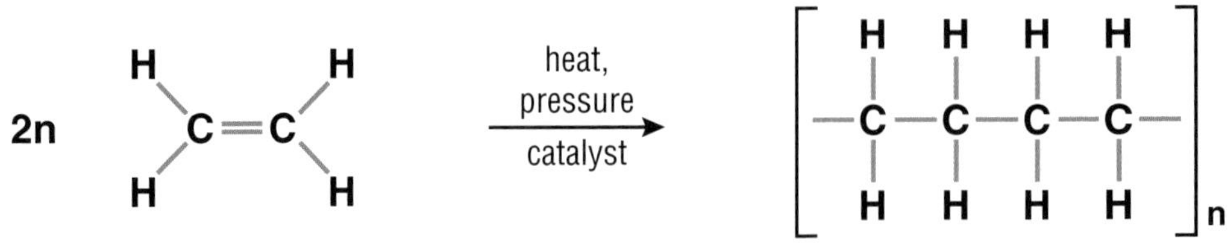

Key definition

A **polymer** is a large molecule made up of many repeating units called monomers.

If a different alkene is used, a similar reaction occurs, but the product will have different atoms or groups bonded to the carbon chain. For example, propene ($CH_2= CHCH_3$) polymerises to form poly(propene). This product differs from polythene in that every second carbon in the chain has a methyl group attached. Poly(propene) is used to make crates, stacking chairs and ropes.

Polythene and poly(propene) are but two of a very large number of products of the petrochemical industry. Other products include other plastics and various dyes, pharmaceuticals, fabrics and solvents.

Substitution reactions: halogenation of alkanes

Key definition

A **substitution reaction** is a reaction in which an atom or group of atoms in a molecule is replaced by another atom or group of atoms.

In these reactions, one or more atoms of a halogen such as chlorine replace hydrogen atoms in the alkane molecule. Ultraviolet light or high temperatures are usually required for these reactions to take place. The chlorination of methane is used to illustrate the reaction:

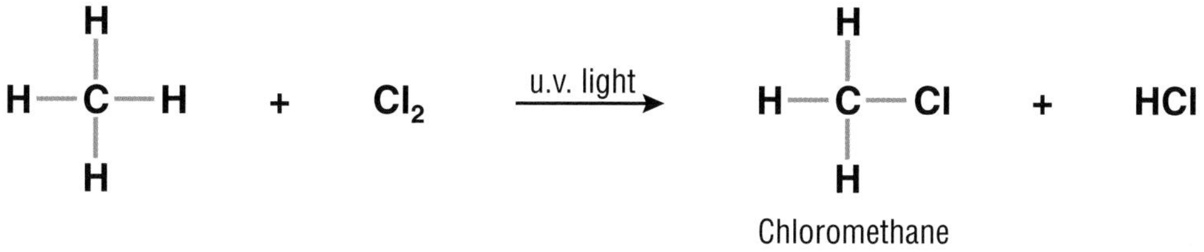

H
H — C — H
H
+
Cl_2
u.v. light
H
H — C — Cl
H
+
HCl
Chloromethane

Fig. 16.5 Chlorination of methane

Reaction mechanism: free radical substitution

Initiation

In the first step of the reaction, the ultraviolet light causes splitting of the chlorine molecules into two identical chlorine atoms. The chlorine atoms are highly reactive, due to having an unpaired electron each. The dot on the symbol indicates an unpaired electron.

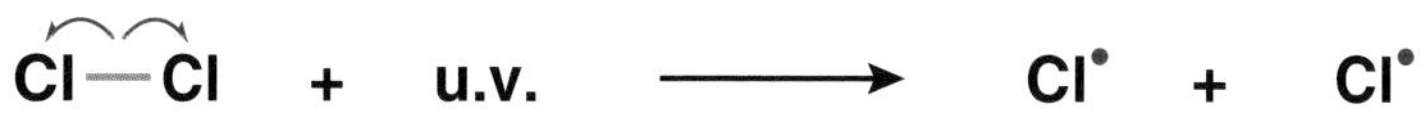

Cl — Cl
+
u.v.
Cl•
+
Cl•

Fig. 16.6 Initiation

Propagation

Each chlorine atom reacts with a methane molecule, removing a hydrogen atom to form hydrogen chloride (HCl). This leaves the methyl **free radical**, $CH_3^{\bullet}$, which is highly reactive due to the presence of an unpaired electron. It reacts immediately with a chlorine molecule, generating another chlorine atom. This atom can react with another methane molecule, so the two propagation steps can be repeated indefinitely in a chain reaction (Fig. 16.7).

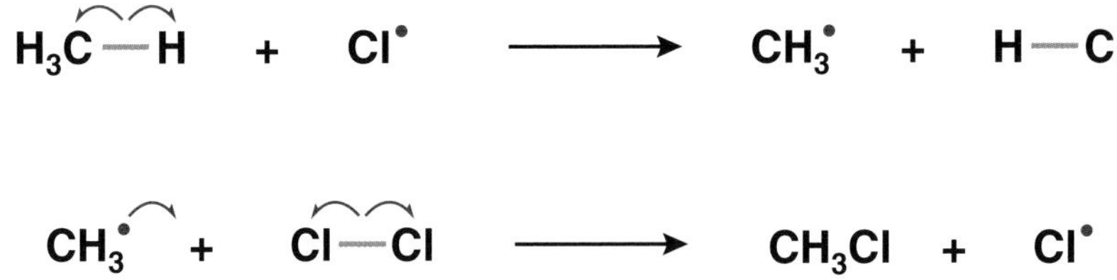

Fig. 16.7 *Propagation*

Termination

As the concentration of chlorine molecules drops, other reactions become more likely, where two radicals combine in termination reactions. These are bond-forming reactions, using up the reactive species.

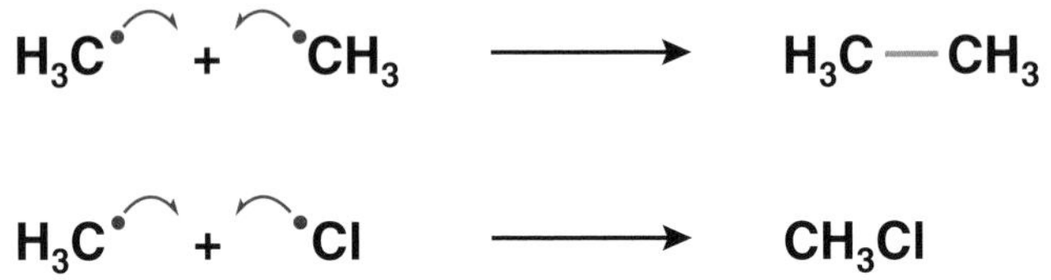

Fig. 16.8 *Termination*

Evidence for mechanism

- When a mixture of an alkane and chlorine is irradiated with ultraviolet light, a chain reaction occurs.

- The formation of ethane is evidence of the termination steps.

- These reactions are speeded up by the addition of known sources of free radicals such as tetraethyllead.

Other substitution reactions

Esterification

Ester formation is an example of a substitution reaction. For example, ethanoic acid (CH_3COOH) reacts with ethanol (C_2H_5OH) to form ethyl ethanoate ($CH_3COOC_2H_5$) and water.

This is a reversible reaction, which proceeds very slowly in the absence of a catalyst. It is catalysed by hydrogen ions (H^+), which are supplied by adding sulfuric acid. There is no change in structure, as the carboxyl carbon atom remains planar.

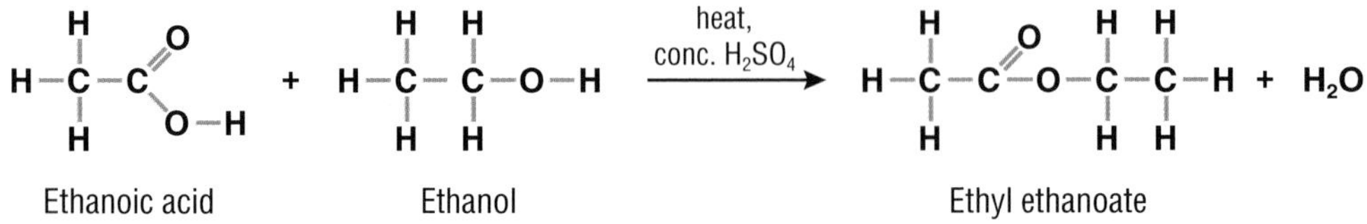

Fig. 16.9

Base hydrolysis of esters

Reactions of substances with water are called **hydrolysis** reactions. For example, if an ester such as ethyl ethanoate reacts with water, the reverse of ester formation occurs.

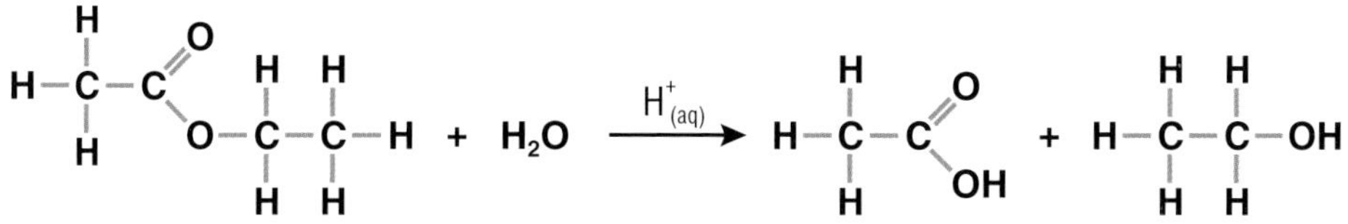

Fig. 16.10 The reaction of ethyl ethanoate with water

A similar reaction occurs when a base such as sodium hydroxide reacts with an ester. However, one of the products this time is the sodium salt of the carboxylic acid.

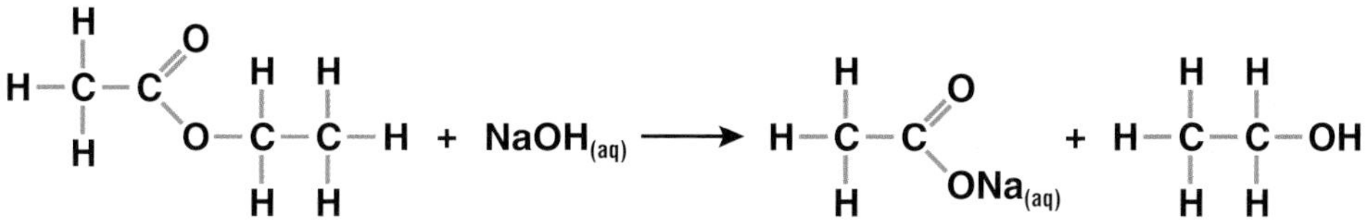

Fig. 16.11 The reaction of ethyl ethanoate with sodium hydroxide solution

These are further examples of substitution reactions. There is no change in structure, as the carbon atom in the ester linkage remains planar. It is called a **base hydrolysis of an ester**, or a **saponification** reaction, and occurs in soap making.

Soap

Soaps are the sodium or potassium salts of long-chain carboxylic acids. Soap is generally made by the base hydrolysis of the esters present in vegetable oils or animal fats.

Animal fats and vegetable oils are esters of long-chain carboxylic acids and of the alcohol propane-1,2,3-triol (glycerol). The base hydrolysis of these substances produces glycerol and the salt of the acid present, i.e. soap. For example, if the animal fat contains esters of stearic acid, the reaction is as follows:

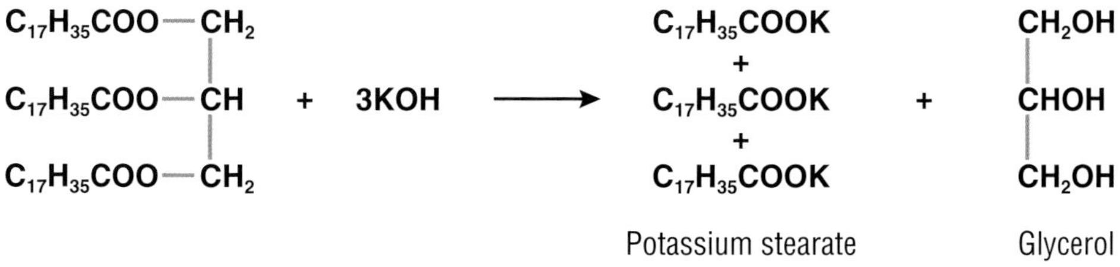

$C_{17}H_{35}COO$—CH_2

$C_{17}H_{35}COO$—CH +   3KOH $\longrightarrow$

$C_{17}H_{35}COO$—CH_2

$C_{17}H_{35}COOK$
+
$C_{17}H_{35}COOK$ +
+
$C_{17}H_{35}COOK$

Potassium stearate

CH_2OH

$CHOH$

CH_2OH

Glycerol

Potassium stearate is the soap formed in this particular case. The soap is a long-chain hydrocarbon with an ionic group at the end. The non-polar part dissolves grease, while the ionic end dissolves in water. This combination of properties gives it its cleansing action.

Experiment

Mandatory Experiment 16.1: Preparation of soap

Procedure 1 Add 3 cm³ of vegetable oil, 2.5 g of potassium hydroxide and 20 cm³ of ethanol, along with a few anti-bumping granules, to a flask. Swirl to mix.

2 Assemble the apparatus for reflux (Fig. 16.12), greasing all joints in the process.

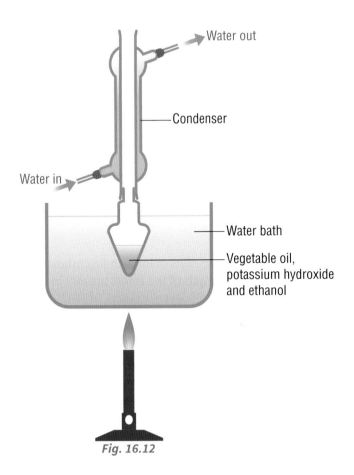

Water out

Condenser

Water in

Water bath

Vegetable oil, potassium hydroxide and ethanol

Fig. 16.12

Procedure
3 Reflux the mixture for 20 minutes, using a water bath.

4 When cool, reassemble for distillation. Remove the ethanol by distillation (Fig. 16.13).

5 Add about 15 cm³ of hot water to dissolve the residue.

6 Pour this solution into a beaker of brine. The soap will precipitate out. Filter the soap.

7 Test the soap for its lathering qualities by shaking a small sample of it with water. It should form a lather readily.

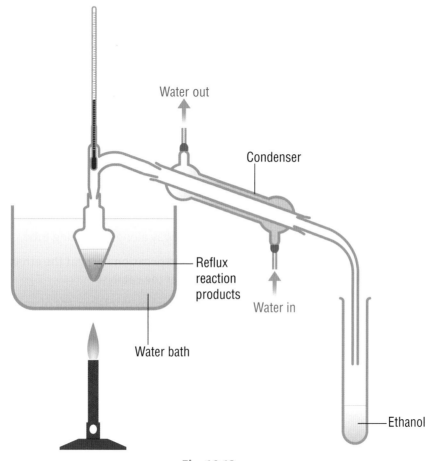

Fig. 16.13

Elimination reactions

Key definition

An **elimination reaction** is one in which an unsaturated compound is formed from a saturated compound by the removal of a small molecule such as water.

Alcohols may be converted into alkenes in a **dehydration** reaction, which involves the elimination of a molecule of water. The change in structure in elimination reactions is from **tetrahedral carbon to planar carbon**, the opposite of addition reactions.

$$\underset{\substack{| \quad | \\ H \quad H}}{\overset{\substack{H \quad H \\ | \quad |}}{H-C-C-OH}} \quad \xrightarrow[Al_2O_3]{heat} \quad \underset{\substack{H \qquad\qquad H}}{\overset{\substack{H \qquad\qquad H}}{C=C}} \quad + \quad H_2O$$

Ethene

Fig. 16.14 Dehydration of ethanol

Experiment

Mandatory Experiment 16.2: Preparation and properties of ethene

Procedure
1 Pour ethanol into a boiling tube to a depth of about 2 cm.

2 Push in enough glass wool to soak up all of the ethanol.

3 Set up the apparatus as shown in Fig. 16.15, with about 2 g of aluminium oxide heaped halfway along the boiling tube.

4 Heat the catalyst strongly, and occasionally heat the ethanol gently to drive the vapour over the catalyst.

5 Collect a few test tubes of ethene by displacement of water, stoppering the test tubes when they are filled. The first test tube filled can be discarded, as it contains a mixture of air and ethene.

6 When the reaction has concluded, remove the tube from the water, and then turn off the Bunsen burner.

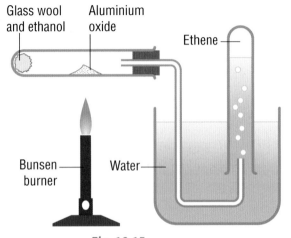

Fig. 16.15

Investigation of properties

Procedure

1 Ignite the ethene gas in one of the test tubes. Record whether the flame is coloured or clear, smoky or clean. Pour a few drops of limewater into the test tube. Stopper and shake well. The limewater will have turned milky.

2 Add a few drops of diluted bromine water to another test tube of ethene gas. Stopper and shake well. The bromine water will have decolourised.

3 Add a few drops of acidified potassium manganate(VII) solution to a third test tube of the ethene gas. Stopper and shake well. The manganate(VII) solution will have decolourised.

Redox reactions

Oxidation of organic compounds may take place by the process of combustion (burning) in oxygen, or by chemical reaction with other oxidising agents.

Combustion

Most organic compounds burn in air to form carbon dioxide and water. An example is the combustion of ethanol:

$$C_2H_5OH_{(l)} + 3O_{2(g)} \rightarrow 2CO_{2(g)} + 3H_2O_{(g)}$$

This reaction is exothermic, and ethanol is used as a fuel in countries where it can be produced cheaply.

Alkanes with all of their hydrogen atoms replaced by halogen atoms are non-flammable and some are used as fire extinguishers. Unfortunately, these compounds cause the same environmental problems as chlorofluorocarbons (CFCs), which are responsible for damaging the ozone layer in the upper atmosphere. Consequently, they are being replaced in fire extinguishers by carbon dioxide and other substances.

Reaction with other oxidising agents

Two oxidising agents commonly used for this purpose are potassium manganate(VII), $KMnO_4$, and sodium dichromate(VI), $Na_2Cr_2O_7$.

Potassium manganate(VII) is purple in colour and contains the MnO_4^- ion. The oxidation number of manganese in this compound is +7. The oxidation number changes to +4 (brown colour) or +2 (colourless), depending on the extent of the reduction of the manganese.

Sodium dichromate(VI) is orange in colour and contains the $Cr_2O_7^{2-}$ ion. The oxidation number of chromium in this compound is +6. The oxidation number changes to +3 (dark green colour) when the chromium is reduced.

(i) Oxidation of alcohols to aldehydes

Primary alcohols undergo oxidation to aldehydes:

[O]

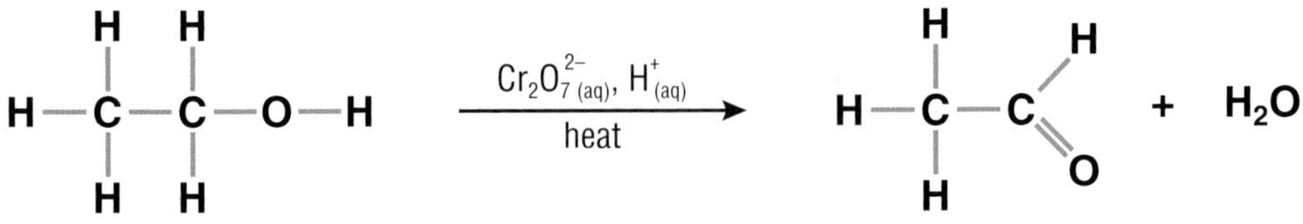

Ethanal

$$RCH_2OH \rightarrow RCHO$$

For example, ethanol (C_2H_5OH) is converted to ethanal (CH_3CHO):

In terms of structure, **tetrahedral carbon has changed to planar carbon.**

(ii) Oxidation of aldehydes to carboxylic acids

The ease of oxidation in forming carboxylic acids is one of the most notable characteristics of aldehydes.

[O]

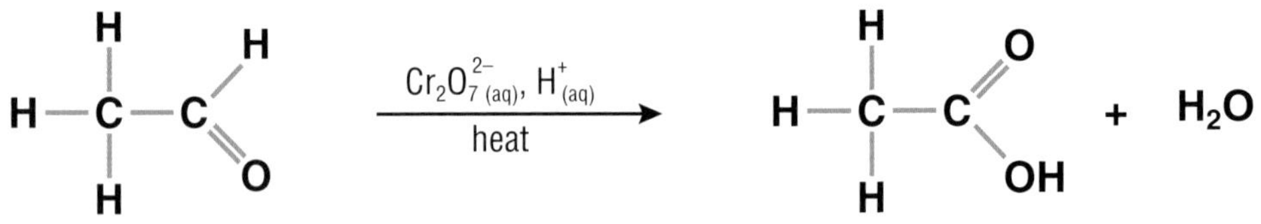

Ethanoic acid

$$RCHO \rightarrow RCOOH$$

For example, ethanal (CH_3CHO) is converted to ethanoic acid (CH_3COOH):

Since the planar carbonyl group, $C = O$, is part of both the aldehyde and carboxylic acid functional groups, there is **no change in structure** of the affected carbon.

The ease of oxidation of aldehydes is illustrated by three different reactions that can be used to identify the presence of the aldehyde functional group.

- When an aldehyde reacts on heating with acidified potassium manganate(VII) solution, the purple colour disappears. The aldehyde is oxidised to a carboxylic acid. For example, ethanal is oxidised to ethanoic acid:

CH_3CHO	$\rightarrow$	CH_3COOH
Mn^{+7}	$\rightarrow$	Mn^{+2}
purple		colourless

- Fehling's reagent contains copper(II) ions, which are blue in colour. On heating, aldehydes reduce the copper(II) ions to copper(I) ions, and a brick-red precipitate of copper(I) oxide is formed:

$$Cu^{2+} \xrightarrow{+ \ e^-} Cu^+$$

blue red

- Ammoniacal silver nitrate, referred to as Tollens' reagent, contains silver(I) ions (Ag^+). Aldehydes reduce the silver(I) ions on heating to metallic silver (Ag).

$$Ag^{+1} \xrightarrow{+ \ e^-} Ag\downarrow$$

colourless silver

If a very clean or new test tube is used, the silver will be deposited on its walls as a silver mirror.

If the three reactions above are attempted with a ketone such as propanone, no colour changes are seen because the ketone is not capable of reducing the reagents in question.

 Experiment

Mandatory Experiment 16.3(a): Properties of ethanal

Procedure

(i) Oxidation by acidified potassium manganate(VII) solution

1 Add 1 cm³ of potassium manganate(VII) solution and 4 cm³ of dilute sulfuric acid to about 2 cm³ of ethanal in a test tube.

2 Warm the test tube in a water bath and shake gently. The manganate(VII) solution decolourises.

(ii) Oxidation by Fehling's solution

1 Mix about 1 cm³ each of Fehling's solution No. 1 and Fehling's solution No. 2 in a test tube.

2 Swirl the contents so that the blue precipitate initially formed dissolves.

3 Add 1 cm³ of ethanal, heat gently and shake.

4 A brick-red precipitate is formed.

(iii) Silver mirror test (oxidation by ammoniacal silver nitrate)

1 Place 3 cm³ of silver nitrate solution and 1 cm³ of sodium hydroxide solution in a **clean** test tube.

2 Add aqueous ammonia solution dropwise, with shaking, until the precipitate formed in step 1 is just dissolved.

3 Add two or three drops of ethanal, shake and warm in a water bath.

4 A silver mirror forms on the inside wall of the test tube.

Ethanal is formed in the human body when ethanol from alcoholic drink is metabolised. Since the change is from alcohol to aldehyde, the process involves oxidation. The ethanal formed in the body is a cause of some of the unpleasant effects of an alcohol-induced hangover.

(iii) Oxidation of alcohols to carboxylic acids

Experiment

Mandatory Experiment 16.3(b): The oxidation of phenylmethanol to benzoic acid with potassium manganate(VII) solution in alkaline conditions

The primary alcohol phenylmethanol can be oxidised to the corresponding carboxylic acid benzoic acid using alkaline potassium manganate(VII) solution.

Phenylmethanol   Benzoic acid

The balanced equation for the reaction is:

$$3C_6H_5CH_2OH + 4KMnO_4 \rightarrow 3C_6H_5COOH + 4MnO_2 + H_2O + 4KOH$$

The oxidation state of Mn changes over the course of the reaction. The initial colour of the solution of manganate(VII) is dark purple. As it oxidises the phenylmethanol, the Mn^{7+} will be reduced to Mn^{4+}, precipitating out as MnO_2 – the brown solid is visible as the reaction progresses. The Mn^{4+} is further reduced to soluble Mn^{2+}, using sodium sulfite, which allows for all solid product to be easily isolated by filtration. Benzoic acid is sparingly soluble in water, and as the reaction cools, it will precipitate out.

Procedure

1 Place 1 cm³ of phenylmethanol in a 100 cm³ conical flask and add 0.5 g of anhydrous sodium carbonate.

2 Add 25 cm³ of 0.2M solution of potassium manganate(VII) and swirl.

3 Heat the solution at about 60°C for 20 minutes in a water bath. The solution turns brown on heating.

4 After cooling, add concentrated hydrochloric acid a few drops at a time, swirling well after each addition. Continue until fizzing ceases and the solution clears, leaving a brown residue of manganese(IV) oxide.

5 Add saturated sodium sulfite solution dropwise with swirling until the solution is completely clear.

Procedure 6 A precipitate of benzoic acid is formed as the solution cools. The process may be accelerated by standing the conical flask in ice water. The crystals are isolated by vacuum filtration and allowed to dry. The product is weighed so that a percentage yield may be calculated.

Reduction of carbonyl compounds

The oxidation of primary alcohols to aldehydes can be reversed by catalytic hydrogenation, using hydrogen passed over the surface of a heated catalyst such as nickel. For example, ethanal is reduced to ethanol:

Ethanal

Ethanol

Reactions as acids

Some organic compounds can act as acids, losing a proton in certain situations. The hydroxyl hydrogen is involved, not the carbon chain, so there is **no change in structure**. Organic acids are weak acids, with small K_a values, and do not have a strong tendency to donate a proton.

Acidic properties of alcohols

Alcohols are extremely weak acids, with very little tendency to donate protons. Forcing conditions are necessary to enable them to do so. Alcohols will react with very active metals such as sodium. For example, ethanol will react with sodium, releasing hydrogen gas and forming a salt, sodium ethoxide:

Sodium ethoxide

Reactions of carboxylic acids

Ethanoic acid (CH_3COOH) is a far stronger acid than ethanol, about 5×10^{12} times stronger.

The more reactive an acid is, the more stable its anion or conjugate base. When ethanoic acid loses a proton, its conjugate base, the ethanoate ion (CH_3COO^-), is formed. Two structures are possible for this ion.

Each has a carbon–oxygen single and a carbon–oxygen double bond. However, the actual carbon–oxygen bond lengths in the ion are equal, suggesting that the structure is in between the two structures shown. The effect is that the negative charge on the ion is spread out over three atoms, the carbon and both of the oxygens. This spreading out or **delocalisation** of charge is a stable arrangement, making the ion less reactive, and this is consistent with the acid itself being relatively reactive.

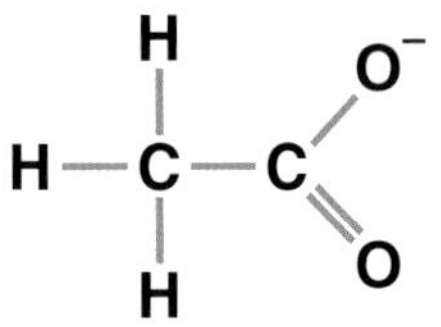

(i) Reaction with magnesium metal

Carboxylic acids react with magnesium metal, forming magnesium salt and releasing hydrogen gas.

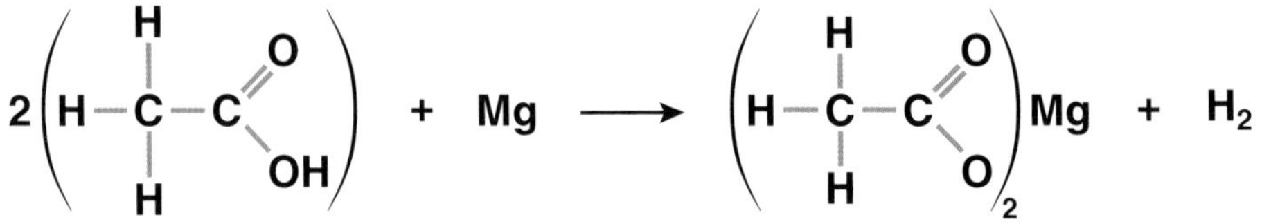

(ii) Reaction with sodium hydroxide

Carboxylic acids react with sodium hydroxide, forming the sodium salt and water.

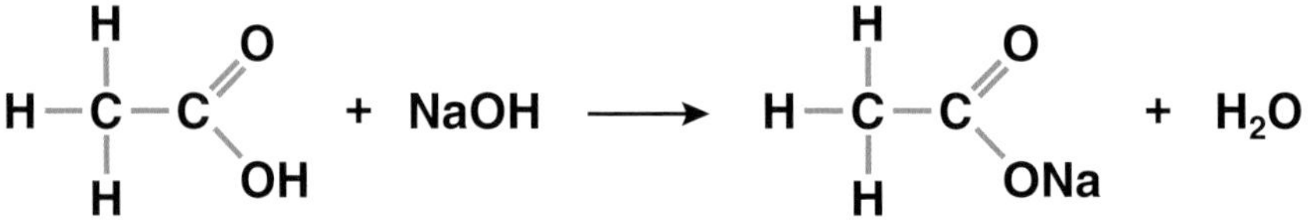

Sodium ethanoate

(iii) Reaction with sodium carbonate

Carboxylic acids react with sodium carbonate forming the sodium salt, water and releasing carbon dioxide gas.

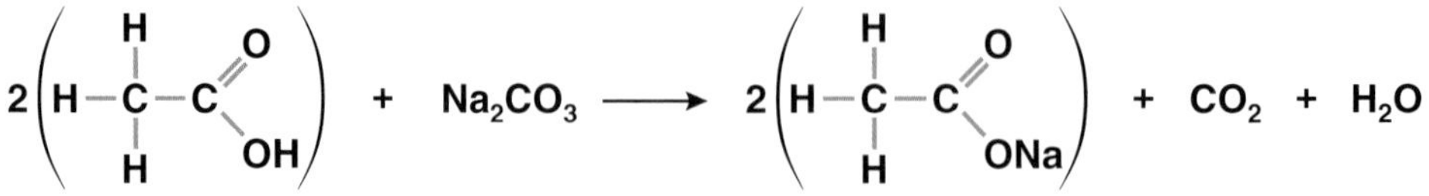

Sodium ethanoate

Mandatory Experiment 16.3(c): Properties of ethanoic acid

Procedure
1 **Test with magnesium:** Drop a 5 cm clean strip of magnesium into some distillate in a test tube and swirl. Bubbles of hydrogen gas will be given off, which will burn with a pop.

2 **Test with sodium carbonate:** Add 1 g of anhydrous sodium carbonate powder to some distillate in a test tube and swirl. Bubbles of carbon dioxide will be produced.

3 **Esterification:** Carefully add 2 drops of concentrated sulfuric acid to some distillate in a test tube. Add 1 cm³ of ethanol and warm gently. An oily layer with a sweet smell will be produced.

Organic synthesis

Synthesis is the formation of chemical compounds from simpler compounds. For example, salicylic acid – aspirin – is available from the bark of the willow tree, but is usually synthesised in the laboratory. Organic synthesis involves bond breaking and bond making.

Points to note

The synthesis of PVC from ethene

The first step is the chlorination of ethene to form 1,2-dichloroethane:

$$CH_2{=}CH_2 + Cl_2 \rightarrow CH_2Cl{-}CH_2Cl$$

The 1,2-dichloroethane is vaporised and heated to form chloroethene and hydrogen chloride:

$$CH_2Cl{-}CH_2Cl \rightarrow CH_2{=}CHCl + HCl$$

The chloroethene is polymerised by heating in the presence of a catalyst at high pressure. The product poly(chloroethene) is usually referred to as PVC. Two repeating units are shown:

$$
\begin{array}{cccc}
H & Cl & H & Cl \\
| & | & | & | \\
{-}C{-} & C{-} & C{-} & C{-} \\
| & | & | & | \\
H & H & H & H
\end{array}
$$

Questions

16.1 Outline the synthesis of ethane from ethanal.

Answer

The first step is the reduction of ethanal to ethanol by catalytic hydrogenation:

$$CH_3CHO + H_2 \rightarrow C_2H_5OH$$

The ethanol is then dehydrated to ethene, by passing its vapour over a hot aluminium oxide catalyst:

$$C_2H_5OH \rightarrow C_2H_4$$

Ethane is formed by the catalytic hydrogenation of ethene:

$$C_2H_4 + H_2 \rightarrow C_2H_6$$
Ethane

Key-points!

- An addition reaction is a reaction in which two molecules add together to form one larger molecule.

- A reaction mechanism is a detailed step-by-step account of how an overall reaction occurs.

- A polymer is a large molecule made up of many repeating units called monomers.

- A substitution reaction is a reaction in which an atom or group of atoms in a molecule is replaced by another atom or group of atoms.

Chromatography and Instrumentation in Organic Chemistry

17

Introduction to chromatography

Key definition

Chromatography is a type of separation technique that involves the use of a mobile phase and a stationary phase to separate the components of a mixture from each other.

Table 17.1 Simple chromatography methods

Method	Stationary phase	Mobile phase
Paper chromatography	Water on paper	Liquid
Thin layer chromatography	Solid	Liquid
Column chromatography	Solid	Liquid

Paper chromatography

Chromatography paper contains adsorbed water. When the chromatogram is being run, the solvent moves through the adsorbed water. Substances that are more soluble in the moving solvent tend to be carried on, while substances that are more soluble in water are held back.

 Experiment

Mandatory Experiment 17.1: Separation of a mixture of indicators using paper chromatography

Procedure

1 Add the solvent to the bottom of a tank to a depth of about 10 mm (Fig. 17.1).Cover the tank and allow to stand for a few hours. This will allow the tank to become saturated with solvent vapour.

2 Make a line with a pencil about 3 cm from the bottom of a rectangular sheet of chromatography paper and another line near the top.

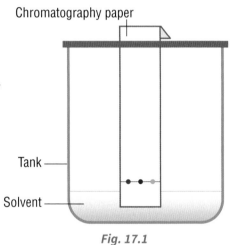

Fig. 17.1

3 Using a capillary tube, place a small spot of each indicator and of the mixture of indicators at different points on the line near the bottom of the paper. Dry using a hair dryer and repeat.

4 Place the chromatogram in the tank, taking care that the solvent level in the tank is below the line on which the indicator samples are spotted.

5 Run the chromatogram until the solvent reaches the line near the top of the paper.

6 Remove and dry.

7 Identify the indicators present in the mixture.

Thin layer chromatography

For thin layer chromatography (Fig. 17.2), thin layer chromatography plates and a glass tank are needed. The thin layer chromatography tank contains a suitable solvent and should be saturated with solvent vapour before use.

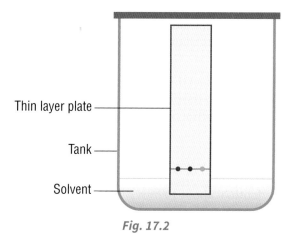

Fig. 17.2

Uses of thin layer chromatography

Thin layer chromatography is particularly useful in forensic work. It can be used, for example, to separate dyes taken from fabrics at the scene of a crime.

Column chromatography

In column chromatography, a small amount of the mixture to be separated is placed on a suitable column, and a suitable solvent is used to carry the mixture through the column. A particularly useful type of column is a solid-phase extraction column (Fig. 17.3).

Solid-phase extraction columns can be used to separate the components of a mixture of indicators.

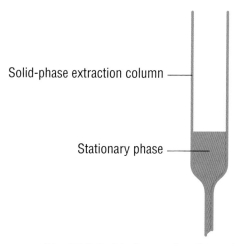

Fig. 17.3 Solid-phase extraction column

Gas chromatography (GC)

A gas chromatograph is an instrument particularly suited to separating the components of a volatile mixture. In gas chromatography, the mobile phase is a gas and the stationary phase is a non-volatile liquid (which is coated on fine particles of an inert solid).

A sample of the mixture to be separated is injected into the instrument and is carried through the column by the flow of gas. The components are separated and detected.

The separation is based on the fact that more volatile components of the mixture tend to be swept along faster by the gas than less volatile components, and also that different components are attracted to different extents by the non-volatile liquid in the column.

Table 17.2 Gas chromatography

Principle	Processes
Different components of a mixture have different interactions with the stationary and mobile phases	• Injection • Transport of the sample along the column • Separation in the column • Detection

In analytical work, a gas chromatograph is sometimes used in conjunction with a mass spectrometer. The gas chromatograph separates the different components of the mixture being analysed, and each component is then separately analysed by the mass spectrometer.

Uses of gas chromatography

These include drug tests on athletes and blood alcohol tests.

High-performance liquid chromatography (HPLC)

A high-performance liquid chromatograph is an instrument particularly suited to separating the components of a non-volatile mixture. In high-performance liquid chromatography, the mobile phase is a solvent and the stationary phase consists of very fine particles of silica.

High pressure has to be applied to the solvent to force it through the column. A sample of the mixture to be separated is injected into the instrument and is carried through the column by the solvent. The components are separated and detected.

The separation is based on the different tendencies of the different components of the mixture to be adsorbed onto the silica in the column.

Table 17.3 High-performance liquid chromatography (HPLC)

Principle	Processes
Different components of a mixture have different tendencies to adsorb onto very fine particles of a solid in the HPLC column	• Injection • Transport of the sample along the column • Separation in the column • Detection

Uses of high-performance liquid chromatography

These include analysis of growth promoters in meat and of vitamins in foods.

Table 17.4 Comparison of GC and HPLC

Method	Stationary phase	Mobile phase
Gas chromatography	Non-volatile liquid coated on an inert solid	Gas
High-performance liquid chromatography	Fine particles of silica	Solvent

Mass spectrometry

Table 17.5 Mass spectrometry

Principle	Processes
Positively charged ions are separated on the basis of their relative masses in a magnetic field	• Vaporisation • Ionisation • Acceleration • Separation • Detection

Table 17.6

Uses of mass spectrometry
Measurement of the relative atomic mass of an element
Measurement of the relative molecular mass of a substance
Identification of organic substances

In a mass spectrometer, molecules are ionised and broken into positively charged fragments with different masses. These are separated and the relative amounts recorded, giving the mass spectrum of the molecule. Different molecules have different mass spectra. The mass spectrum can be used to identify the substance.

Uses of mass spectrometry

Mass spectrometry is used to analyse gases from a waste dump. It is also used to analyse organic pollutants in water.

Ultraviolet absorption spectrometry

Ultraviolet absorption spectrometry is a technique involving the absorption of ultraviolet (UV) radiation. It is a **quantitative technique**, that is, it can be used to measure the amount of a substance in a sample.

In ultraviolet absorption spectrometry, a solution of the substance under investigation is placed between a source of ultraviolet light and a detector. The detector analyses the intensity of the light that reaches the detector relative to the intensity of the light passing into the solution. In this way, an absorption spectrum is obtained.

Table 17.7 Ultraviolet absorption spectrometry

Principle	Processes
Absorption of ultraviolet radiation by molecules results in the promotion of electrons from their ground state energy levels to higher energy states. Absorbance is directly proportional to concentration	• Ultraviolet light is passed through the sample and a blank • An absorption spectrum is obtained

Uses of ultraviolet absorption spectrometry

Ultraviolet absorption spectrometry is used in the analysis of drug metabolites and of plant pigments.

Infrared absorption spectrometry

Infrared absorption spectrometry is a **qualitative** technique involving the absorption of infrared (IR) radiation. It is a particularly useful technique for identifying organic compounds, as each compound has its own almost unique infrared spectrum.

In infrared absorption spectrometry, a sample of the substance under investigation is placed between a source of infrared light and a detector. The detector analyses the intensity of the light that reaches the detector relative to the intensity of the light going into the sample. In this way, an absorption spectrum is obtained.

Chemical Equilibrium 18

Reversible reactions

Ammonia is manufactured by reacting nitrogen with hydrogen:

$$N_2 + 3H_2 \rightleftharpoons 2NH_3$$

The symbol $\rightleftharpoons$ indicates that the reaction is **reversible**. The conversion of reactants to products is never complete no matter how long the reaction is allowed to continue.

> **Key definition**
>
> A **reversible reaction** is a reaction that can take place in either direction.

Chemical equilibrium

In a mixture of nitrogen gas and hydrogen gas in a closed container at 700 K, nitrogen molecules and hydrogen molecules only are present initially. As they react, forming ammonia molecules, the concentrations of both nitrogen and hydrogen decrease, while the concentration of ammonia increases. Eventually, however, they level off and become constant.

When the concentrations of reactants (N_2 and H_2) and product (NH_3) have become constant, a state of chemical equilibrium is said to have been reached.

At equilibrium, the rate of the forward reaction equals the rate of the reverse reaction.

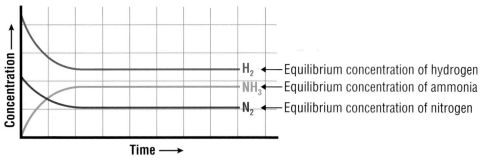

Fig. 18.1 *Concentrations of nitrogen, hydrogen and ammonia level off to equilibrium values*

Equilibrium constants

In the reaction

$$H_2 + I_2 \rightleftharpoons 2HI$$

as much hydrogen iodide is decomposing at equilibrium as is being formed, and so the concentrations of all three substances remain constant. There is a constant relationship that holds here, namely

$$\frac{[HI]^2}{[H_2] \times [I_2]} = \text{constant}$$

where the square brackets denote concentrations in mol l^{-1}. In general, if m moles of A react with n moles of B forming p moles of C and q moles of D:

$$mA + nB \rightleftharpoons pC + qD$$

$$\frac{[C]^p[D]^q}{[A]^m[B]^n} = K_c$$

where K_c is a constant, called the **equilibrium constant** in terms of molar concentration. This relationship is known as the **equilibrium law**.

The value of the equilibrium constant depends on the temperature. If the forward reaction is exothermic, the equilibrium constant decreases as the temperature rises; if it is endothermic, it increases.

Questions

18.1 Write an expression for the equilibrium constant (K_c) for the following reversible reaction:

$$2NO + O_2 \rightleftharpoons 2NO_2$$

Answer

$$K_c = \frac{[NO_2]^2}{[NO]^2[O_2]}$$

Points to note

Important points about equilibrium constants

- The value of K_c only applies at equilibrium.
- K_c is constant only if the temperature remains constant.
- The value of K_c is not affected by changes in concentrations of reactants or products.
- The units of K_c depend on the relative numbers of moles on each side of the equation for the reaction. In a reaction in which there are equal numbers of moles on each side of the equation, such as

$$H_2 + I_2 \rightleftharpoons 2HI$$

K_c has no units, as all units cancel in the K_c expression. Otherwise, K_c has units. For example, the unit of K_c for the reaction

$$2NO + O_2 \rightleftharpoons 2NO_2$$

is mol^{-1} l.

Calculations of equilibrium constant values

If the equilibrium concentrations of all species in a given reaction are known, as in Question 18.2, the equilibrium constant value may readily be calculated.

Question

18.2 In a reaction at a particular temperature between nitrogen and hydrogen forming ammonia

$$N_2 + 3H_2 \rightleftharpoons 2NH_3$$

it was found that at equilibrium the concentrations of N_2, H_2 and NH_3 were 0.06 mol l^{-1}, 0.07 mol l^{-1} and 0.02 mol l^{-1}, respectively. Calculate the value of the equilibrium constant (K_c) for this reaction at this temperature.

Answer

$$K_c = \frac{[NH_3]^2}{[N_2]^2[H_2]^3} = \frac{(0.02)^2}{(0.06)(0.07)^3} = 19.44 \ mol^{-2} \ l^2$$

To find the equilibrium constant for a reaction, it is usually necessary to calculate the equilibrium concentrations of all the species first.

Question

18.3 Four moles of $COCl_2$ are placed in a 4-litre flask at 668 K. The following reaction occurs:

$$COCl_2 \rightleftharpoons CO + Cl_2$$

and, at equilibrium, 1.6 moles of $COCl_2$ remain. Calculate K_c for the reaction.

Answer

The equation for the reaction is:

$$COCl_2 \rightleftharpoons CO + Cl_2$$

	$COCl_2$	CO	Cl_2
Initial amount	4 moles	0 moles	0 moles
Change	$-(4-1.6)$ moles	$+4-1.6$ moles	$+4-1.6$ moles
Equilibrium amount	1.6 moles	2.4 moles	2.4 moles
Equilibrium concentration	$1.6/4 = 0.4$ mol l^{-1}	$2.4/4 = 0.6$ mol l^{-1}	$2.4/4 = 0.6$ mol l^{-1}

$$K_c = \frac{[CO][Cl_2]}{[COCl_2]} = \frac{0.6 \times 0.6}{0.4} = 0.9$$

In reversible reactions where neither the forward nor the reverse reactions causes a change in the number of molecules present, it is possible to calculate the equilibrium constant **even if the volume of the equilibrium mixture is unknown**, using the method shown in Question 18.4.

18.4 In the reaction

$$C_4H_9COOH + C_2H_5OH \rightleftharpoons C_4H_9COOC_2H_5 + H_2O$$

at 473 K, it is found that if an initial mixture containing 2 moles of C_4H_9COOH and 2 moles of C_2H_5OH is allowed to come to equilibrium, 1 mole of C_4H_9COOH remains. Calculate the equilibrium constant for the reaction at 473 K.

Answer

The equation for the reaction is:

$$C_4H_9COOH + C_2H_5OH \rightleftharpoons C_4H_9COOC_2H_5 + H_2O$$

	C_4H_9COOH	C_2H_5OH	$C_4H_9COOC_2H_5$	H_2O
Initial amount	2 moles	2 moles	0 moles	0 moles
Change	2 – 1 moles	2 – 1 moles	+ 1 mole	+ 1 mole
Equilibrium amount	1 mole	1 mole	1 mole	1 mole
Equilibrium concentration	$1/V$ mol l^{-1}	$1/V$ mol l^{-1}	$1/V$ mol l^{-1}	$1/V$ mol l^{-1}

$$K_c = \frac{[C_4H_9COOC_2H_5][H_2O]}{[C_4H_9COOH][C_2H_5OH]} = \frac{(1/V)(1/V)}{(1/V)(1/V)} = 1$$

Calculations of equilibrium concentrations

In examples of this type, a quadratic equation in terms of x will usually be arrived at during the calculation. For a quadratic equation $ax^2 + bx + c = 0$, the value of x is found using the formula:

$$x = \frac{-b \pm \sqrt{(b^2 - 4ac)}}{2a}$$

Two different values of x will usually be obtained, one of which (often either a negative value or a value which is too large to be possible) will have to be rejected.

Question

18.5 At 760 K, the value of K_c for the reaction

$$PCl_5 \rightleftharpoons PCl_3 + Cl_2$$

is 33 mol l^{-1}. Calculate the equilibrium concentrations of all species if 10 moles of PCl_5 are placed in a 1-litre flask at 760 K and allowed to reach equilibrium.

Answer

The balanced equation for the reaction is:

$$PCl_5 \rightleftharpoons PCl_3 + Cl_2$$

	PCl_5	PCl_3	Cl_2
Initial amount	10 moles	0 moles	0 moles
Change	$-x$ moles	$+x$ moles	$+x$ moles
Equilibrium amount	$10 - x$ moles	x moles	x moles
Equilibrium concentration	$(10 - x) / 1$	$x / 1$	$x / 1$

$$K_c = 33 \text{ mol } l^{-1} = \frac{[PCl_3] \times [Cl_2]}{[PCl_5]}$$

$$33 \text{ mol } l^{-1} = \frac{[PCl_3] \times [Cl_2] \text{ mol } l^{-1}}{[PCl_5]} = \frac{(x) \times (x) \text{ mol } l^{-1}}{10 - x}$$

$$x^2 = 33(10 - x)$$

$$= 330 - 33x$$

$$x^2 + 33x - 330 = 0$$

Using the formula $x = (-b \pm \sqrt{[b^2 - 4ac]}) / 2a$, we obtain:

$$x = (-33 \pm \sqrt{[1089 + 1320]}) / 2a$$

$$= (-33 \pm \sqrt{[2409]}) / 2$$

$$= (-33 \pm 49.081565) / 2$$

$$= 16.081565 / 2 \text{ or } -82.081565 / 2$$

$$= 8.04 \text{ or } -41.04$$

The negative value of x can be disregarded.

Concentrations at equilibrium:

$[PCl_5]$	$[PCl_3]$	$[Cl_2]$
$10 - x / 1$ moles l^{-1}	$x / 1$ moles l^{-1}	$x / 1$ moles l^{-1}
$= 1.96$ moles l^{-1}	$= 8.04$ moles l^{-1}	$= 8.04$ moles l^{-1}

In reversible reactions where neither the forward nor the reverse reactions causes a change in the number of moles present, it is possible to calculate the **equilibrium amounts** of all species, **even if the volume is unknown**, using the method shown in Question 18.6.

Question

18.6 Ethanoic acid reacts with propan-1-ol at 373 K, according to the equation:

$$CH_3COOH + C_3H_7OH \rightleftharpoons CH_3COOC_3H_7 + H_2O$$

If the equilibrium constant for the reaction at this temperature is 6.25, calculate the equilibrium amounts in moles of all species when 210 g of CH_3COOH and 210 g of C_3H_7OH are placed in a flask at 373 K.

Answer

$$210 \text{ g } CH_3COOH = 210/60 = 3.5 \text{ moles}$$
$$210 \text{ g } C_3H_7OH = 210/60 = 3.5 \text{ moles}$$

Let V litres be the total volume of the mixture at equilibrium. Assume that x moles of propyl ethanoate and water, respectively, are formed at equilibrium.

	CH_3COOH	C_3H_7OH	$CH_3COOC_3H_7$	H_2O
Initial amount	3.5 moles	3.5 moles	0 moles	0 moles
Change	$-x$ moles	$-x$ moles	$+x$ moles	$+x$ moles
Equilibrium amount	$3.5 - x$ moles	$3.5 - x$ moles	$+x$ moles	$+x$ moles
Equilibrium concentration	$(3.5 - x)/V$	$(3.5 - x)/V$	x/V	x/V

$$K_c = \frac{[CH_3COOC_3H_7][H_2O]}{[CH_3COOH][C_3H_7OH]} = \frac{(x/V)(x/V)}{((3.5-x)/V)((3.5-x)/V)} = 6.25$$

From this is got the following quadratic equation:

$$5.25x^2 - 43.75x + 76.5625 = 0$$

Using the formula $x = (-b \pm \sqrt{[b^2 - 4ac]})/2a$, we obtain

$$x = (-43.75 \pm \sqrt{[1914.0625 - 1607.8125]})/10.5$$
$$= (-43.75 \pm \sqrt{[306.25]})/10.5$$
$$= (-43.75 \pm 17.5)/10.5$$
$$= 26.25/10.5 \text{ or } +61.25/10.5$$
$$= 2.5 \text{ or } 5.83333$$

Since x is the number of moles of propyl ethanoate or water formed, $x = 5.8333$ is impossible, because the initial amounts (3.5 moles each) of ethanoic acid and propanol are not capable of producing 5.83333 moles of propyl ethanoate and water, respectively.

Amounts at equilibrium:

CH_3COOH	C_3H_7OH	$CH_3COOC_3H_7$	H_2O
1 mole	1 mole	2.5 moles	2.5 moles

Le Chatelier's principle

comes up EVERY YEAR as a definition.

Henry Louis Le Chatelier

Key definition

Le Chatelier's principle: When a system at equilibrium is subjected to a stress, the equilibrium shifts in such a way as to minimise the effect of the stress.

Table 18.1 summarises the changes at equilibrium predicted by Le Chatelier's principle (X refers to one of the components of the equilibrium mixture).

Table 18.1

Type of stress	Resultant change
Increase in concentration of X	Reaction that removes X is favoured
Decrease in concentration of X	Reaction that forms X is favoured
Increase in temperature	Endothermic reaction is favoured
Decrease in temperature	Exothermic reaction is favoured
Increase in pressure	Reaction that produces less molecules is favoured
Decrease in pressure	Reaction that produces more molecules is favoured
Adding a catalyst	No change

Question

18.7 In the reversible reaction

$$H_2 + Cl_2 \rightleftharpoons 2HCl$$

in which the forward reaction is exothermic, what is the effect at equilibrium of:

(i) Lowering the temperature

(ii) Lowering the pressure

(iii) Making the reaction container smaller

(iv) Decreasing the amount of catalyst

(v) Decreasing the amount of HCl

(vi) Decreasing the amount of H_2

(vii) Decreasing the amount of Cl_2?

Answer

(i) **Lowering the temperature:** This favours the exothermic reaction, forming hydrogen chloride.

(ii) **Lowering the pressure:** This has no effect, since there is the same number of molecules on the left-hand side of the equation as on the right-hand side.

(iii) **Making the reaction container smaller:** This has no effect, since there is the same number of molecules on the left-hand side of the equation as on the right-hand side.

(iv) **Decreasing the amount of catalyst:** This has no effect, since the reaction mixture is already at equilibrium. (Using a catalyst lessens the time needed to reach equilibrium, if equilibrium has not been reached already.)

(v) **Decreasing the amount of HCl:** This favours the reaction forming hydrogen chloride.

(vi) **Decreasing the amount of H_2:** This favours the reaction forming hydrogen and chlorine.

(vii) **Decreasing the amount of Cl_2:** This favours the reaction forming hydrogen and chlorine.

 Experiment

Mandatory Experiment 18.1: Simple experiments to illustrate Le Chatelier's principle

A solution of iron(III) chloride reacts with a solution of thiocyanate ions as follows:

$$Fe^{3+} + CNS^- \rightleftharpoons Fe(CNS)^{2+}$$

  yellow   red

This reaction is suitable for illustrating Le Chatelier's principle because it involves very definite colour changes. The effect of concentration changes and of temperature changes can be shown.

The effects of (i) concentration changes and (ii) temperature changes on the equilibrium between Fe^{3+} and $Fe(CNS)^{2+}$

(i) Concentration changes

A solution of iron(III) chloride reacts with a solution of thiocyanate ions as follows:

$$Fe^{3+} + CNS^- \rightleftharpoons Fe(CNS)^{2+}$$

  yellow   red

Adding hydrochloric acid reduces the concentration of Fe^{3+} by forming a complex ion containing iron and chlorine. This causes a shift of equilibrium to the left. The equilibrium can be shifted to the right-hand side by adding some potassium thiocyanate solution.

Procedure

1 Mix together about 5 cm³, respectively, of solutions of iron(III) chloride and potassium thiocyanate in a beaker. Note the formation of the red complex. Divide the mixture into three portions in separate boiling tubes. Keep one of these as a control.

2 Using a fume cupboard, add some concentrated hydrochloric acid to the second tube until the red colour disappears. This happens because the equilibrium shifts to the left.

3 Add an equivalent amount of water to the third tube and compare. This comparison should indicate that the extent of lightening the colour is not due to a diluting effect.

4 To the second tube, add some potassium thiocyanate solution. The mixture goes red. This happens because the equilibrium shifts to the right.

(ii) Temperature changes

In the equilibrium

$$Fe^{3+} + CNS^- \rightleftharpoons Fe(CNS)^{2+}$$

yellow   red

the forward reaction is exothermic. If the temperature is lowered the equilibrium moves in the exothermic direction, increasing the amount of $Fe(CNS)^{2+}$ present and the red colour darkens. If the temperature is raised the equilibrium moves in the endothermic direction, increasing the amount of Fe^{3+} present and the red colour lightens.

Procedure

1 Mix together about 5 cm³, respectively, of solutions of iron(III) chloride and potassium thiocyanate in a beaker. Note the formation of the red complex. Divide the mixture into three portions in separate boiling tubes. Keep one of these as a control.

2 Stand one tube into a beaker of very hot water. The red colour lightens and then turns yellow because the equilibrium moves to the left.

3 Stand a second tube into a beaker of ice water. The red colour becomes more intense because the equilibrium moves to the right.

Industrial applications of Le Chatelier's principle

(i) Application of Le Chatelier's principle to the industrial synthesis of ammonia

Fritz Haber

The synthesis of ammonia from its elements

$$N_2 + 3H_2 \rightleftharpoons 2NH_3 \quad \Delta H = -92 \text{ kJ mol}^{-1}$$

is an important process in the fertiliser industry. The process used to make ammonia is called the Haber process.

In the industrial synthesis of ammonia, the objective is to produce the maximum possible amount of ammonia at the lowest cost and in the shortest possible time. A balance has to be struck between factors that favour a reasonable rate of reaction and those that favour a reasonable yield.

1 Temperature

$$N_2 + 3H_2 \rightleftharpoons 2NH_3 \quad \Delta H = -92 \text{ kJ mol}^{-1}$$

Since the forward reaction is exothermic, it is favoured by a lowering of the reaction temperature at equilibrium. The extent to which this can be done is limited by the fact that the temperature must be high enough to allow the reaction to proceed at a reasonable rate. In practice, temperatures of about 673 K are used. This results in a low yield, but unreacted nitrogen and hydrogen can be collected and sent back into the reaction vessel again and again.

2 Pressure

$$N_2 + 3H_2 \rightleftharpoons 2NH_3$$
4 moles   2 moles

An increase in pressure at equilibrium favours the formation of ammonia. For this reason, the reaction is carried out under pressure. The Haber process uses high pressures (about 200 atmospheres) to increase the yield of ammonia.

3 Catalyst

In the absence of a catalyst, the reaction has a high activation energy. A catalyst is used both because it brings the system to equilibrium faster and because, by lowering the activation energy, it keeps fuel costs down by allowing the reaction to be carried out at a lower temperature.

(ii) Application of Le Chatelier's principle to the catalytic oxidation of sulfur dioxide to sulfur trioxide

In the industrial manufacture of sulfuric acid, the slowest step is the following reaction:

$$SO_2 + \tfrac{1}{2}O_2 \rightleftharpoons SO_3 \quad \Delta H = -98 \text{ kJ mol}^{-1}$$

The process used to make sulfur trioxide is called the **contact process**. The sulfur trioxide is the desired product, as it reacts readily with water forming sulfuric acid:

$$SO_3 + H_2O \rightarrow H_2SO_4$$

1 Temperature

$$SO_2 + \tfrac{1}{2}O_2 \rightleftharpoons SO_3 \quad \Delta H = -98 \text{ kJ mol}^{-1}$$

Since the forward reaction is exothermic, this reaction is favoured at equilibrium by a lowering of the reaction temperature. In practice, a temperature of about 713 K is chosen, as this is the lowest temperature that can be used without reducing the rate to too low a level.

2 Pressure

$$SO_2 + \tfrac{1}{2}O_2 \rightleftharpoons SO_3$$

1½ moles   1 mole

The forward reaction brings about a reduction in the number of molecules present, and so is favoured by high pressures. In practice, a high yield is obtained using atmospheric pressure or a pressure slightly higher than that, and so higher pressures are not economically justified.

3 Concentration

The forward reaction is favoured if the sulfur trioxide is removed as it is formed. Sulfuric acid synthesis plants therefore incorporate a method for removal of the sulfur trioxide formed, allowing unreacted oxygen and sulfur dioxide to react further.

4 Catalyst

A catalyst is used as it brings the reactants to equilibrium faster by lowering the activation energy.

Key-points!

- A reversible reaction is a reaction that can take place in either direction.
- Chemical equilibrium is said to be dynamic because, at equilibrium, there are reactions continually occurring, and the rate of the forward reaction equals the rate of the reverse reaction.
- Le Chatelier's principle: When a system at equilibrium is subjected to a stress, the equilibrium shifts in such a way as to minimise the effect of the stress.

Acids and Bases 2 **19**

Self-ionisation of water

Water undergoes reaction with itself to a slight extent as follows:

$$H_2O + H_2O \rightleftharpoons H_3O^+ + OH^-$$

This is called the self-ionisation of water, as one of the water molecules dissociates into a H^+ and an OH^- ion.

- It is found that at 298 K

$$K_w = [H_3O^+][OH^-] = 1 \times 10^{-14}$$

  where the square brackets denote concentrations in moles per litre. K_w is called the dissociation constant of water.

- The value of K_w, like any equilibrium constant, is temperature-dependent. The value of K_w increases as the temperature increases, and decreases as the temperature decreases.

The pH scale

Since the concentrations of species in aqueous solution are often very small – for example, $[H_3O^+] = 1 \times 10^{-7}$ M in pure water at 298 K, and is even less in basic solutions – a logarithmic scale is found to be useful in dealing with such concentrations.

Such a scale, called the pH scale, was developed by Søren Sørensen, a Danish chemist, in 1909.

- Since H^+ exists as H_3O^+ in solution:

$$pH = -\log_{10} [H_3O^+]$$

- The square brackets denote concentration in mol l^{-1}.
- At 298 K, the pH of pure water $= -\log_{10} [H_3O^+]$
$$= -\log_{10} (10^{-7})$$
$$= -(-7) = 7$$

- Since K_w varies with temperature, the pH of pure water varies also. The pH of pure water decreases as the temperature increases.

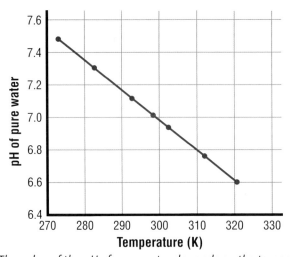

Fig. 19.1 *The value of the pH of pure water depends on the temperature*

Question

19.1 Calculate the pH of a solution with a H_3O^+ concentration of 0.001 M.

Answer

$$pH = -\log_{10} [H_3O^+]$$
$$= -\log_{10} (0.001)$$
$$= 3$$

Question

19.2 Calculate the H_3O^+ concentration of a solution with a pH of 2.

Answer

$$pH = -\log_{10}[H_3O^+] = 2$$
$$-pH = \log_{10}[H_3O^+] = -2$$
$$[H_3O^+] = \text{antilog}\,(-2)$$
$$= 0.01\ M$$

Limitations of the pH scale

- The pH scale is not useful outside the 0 to 14 range.

- This is because in more concentrated solutions of strong acids and bases, the acid or base does not dissociate fully in solution, making a pH calculation difficult.

- The pH scale is limited to aqueous solutions.

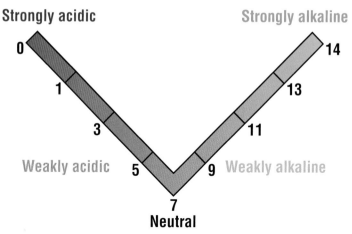

Strongly acidic 0

1

3

Weakly acidic 5

7
Neutral

9 **Weakly alkaline**

11

13

Strongly alkaline 14

Fig. 19.2 The pH scale

Measuring pH

- **Universal indicator** solution, or universal indicator paper, can be used to find the pH of a solution. Universal indicator is a mixture of indicators that changes colour as the pH is changed. The pH of a solution is measured after adding universal indicator by comparing the colour of the solution with a colour chart.

- The pH of a solution can also be measured using a **pH meter**. This instrument gives a numerical reading for the pH directly.

Calculation of pH of solutions of strong acids

Question

19.3 Find the pH of a 0.00004 M solution of hydrochloric acid.

Answer

$$pH = -\log_{10}[H_3O^+]$$
$$= -\log_{10}(0.00004)$$
$$= 4.40$$

Question

19.4 What is the pH of a solution containing 3.15 g of HNO_3 in 500 cm^3 of solution?

Answer

The nitric acid solution contains 3.15 g of nitric acid in 500 cm^3.

$$= \frac{3.15 \times 1000 \text{ g l}^{-1}}{500}$$
$$= 6.3 \text{ g l}^{-1}$$

The molar mass of HNO_3 is 63 g mol^{-1}.

Therefore, $[HNO_3]$ $= 6.3 / 63$ mol l^{-1} = 0.1 mol l^{-1}

Since HNO_3 is a strong acid, $[H_3O^+] = [HNO_3]$ = 0.1 mol l^{-1}

pH $= -\log_{10}[H_3O^+]$
$= -\log_{10}(0.1)$
$= 1$

Calculation of the pH of solutions of strong bases

In calculating the pH of a strong base, the idea of pOH is used. pOH is defined as $-\log_{10}[OH^-]$.

Point to note

$$pH = 14 - pOH$$

Question

19.5 Find the pH of a 0.001 M NaOH solution.

Answer

$$[NaOH] = 0.001 \text{ mol l}^{-1}$$
$$[OH^-] = [NaOH]$$
$$pOH = -log_{10}[OH^-]$$
$$= -log_{10}(0.001)$$
$$= 3$$
$$pH = 14 - pOH$$
$$= 14 - 3$$
$$= 11$$

Question

19.6 What is the pH of a solution containing 0.8 g of NaOH per litre?

Answer

The NaOH solution contains 0.8 g of NaOH in 1 litre.

The molar mass of NaOH is 40 g mol^{-1}.

Therefore: $[NaOH]$ $= 0.8 / 40 \text{ mol l}^{-1}$

$= 0.02 \text{ mol l}^{-1}$

Since NaOH is a strong base, $[OH^-] = [NaOH] = 0.02 \text{ mol l}^{-1}$

$$pOH = -log_{10}[OH^-]$$
$$= -log_{10}(0.02)$$
$$= 1.6990$$
$$pH = 14 - pOH$$
$$= 14 - 1.6990$$
$$= 12.30$$

Solutions of weak acids

Weak acids when dissolved in water transfer a relatively small number of their protons to the water, unlike strong acids, for which total proton transfer occurs. A weak acid such as ethanoic acid (CH_3COOH) will react as follows:

$$CH_3COOH + H_2O \rightleftharpoons CH_3COO^- + H_3O^+$$

At equilibrium,

$$K_a = [CH_3COO^-][H_3O^+] / [CH_3COOH]$$

where K_a is called the **dissociation constant** of the acid. (The term **ionisation constant** is also used for K_a.)

In general, a weak acid, HX, has a **dissociation constant** K_a, where $K_a = [X^-][H_3O^+] / [HX]$. The weaker the acid, the smaller the value of K_a.

Question

19.7 Write an expression for the dissociation constant, K_a, for the following weak acid: HNO_2.

Answer

HNO_2 dissociates in water as follows:

$$HNO_2 + H_2O \rightleftharpoons NO_2^- + H_3O^+$$

$$K_a = \frac{[NO_2^-][H_3O^+]}{HNO_2}$$

Question

19.8 A weak acid, HX, is 3.5% dissociated in a 0.1 M aqueous solution. Find the value of the acid dissociation constant, K_a.

Answer

The reaction is:

$$HX + H_2O \rightleftharpoons X^- + H_3O^+$$

Ignoring the concentration of water, which is present in excess, the initial concentrations of each of the other species are:

[HX]	[X⁻]	[H₃O⁺]
0.1	0	0

The equilibrium concentrations are:

[HX]	[X⁻]	[H₃O⁺]
0.1 – 0.0035	0.0035	0.0035
= 0.0965	0.0035	0.0035

Substituting these values into the equilibrium constant expression:

$$K_a = [X^-][H_3O^+] / [HX] = (0.0035)^2 / 0.0965 = 1.27 \times 10^{-4}$$

Calculation of pH of solutions of weak acids

It is possible to work out the pH value of a solution of a weak acid whose concentration is known using the formula $pH -log_{10}\left[\sqrt{(K_a \times M_a)}\right]$, where M_a is the concentration of the weak acid in moles per litre. This formula is based on the simplifying assumption that the concentration of the acid does not change. This approximation is justified because the extent of dissociation of a weak acid is small.

Question

19.9 Calculate the pH of a 0.1 M solution of ethanoic acid, given that the K_a value for this acid is 1.8×10^{-5}.

Answer

$$pH = -\log_{10}\left[\sqrt{(K_a \times M_a)}\right]$$

$$= -\log_{10}\left[\sqrt{(1.8 \times 10^{-5} \times 0.1)}\right]$$

$$= -\log_{10}\left[\sqrt{(0.0000018)}\right]$$

$$= -\log_{10}(0.001342)$$

$$= 2.87$$

Question

19.10 Find the pH of a solution containing 30 g of CH_3COOH per litre of solution.

Answer

The ethanoic acid solution contains 30 g of ethanoic acid in 1 litre.

The molar mass of CH_3COOH is 60 g mol^{-1}.

Therefore:

$$[CH_3COOH] = 30/60 \text{ mol l}^{-1}$$

$$= 0.5 \text{ mol l}^{-1}$$

$$pH = \log_{10}\left[\sqrt{(K_a \times M_a)}\right]$$

$$= -\log_{10}\left[\sqrt{(1.8 \times 10^{-5} \times 0.5)}\right]$$

$$= -\log_{10}\left[\sqrt{(0.000009)}\right]$$

$$= -\log_{10}(0.003)$$

$$= 2.52$$

Solutions of weak bases

Weak bases, like weak acids, only dissociate to a slight extent in water. Ammonia when placed in water reacts as follows:

$$NH_3 + H_2O \rightleftharpoons NH_4^+ + OH^-$$

At equilibrium:

$$K_b = [NH_4^+][OH^-] / [NH_3]$$

K_b is called the **dissociation constant** of the base. (The term **ionisation constant** is also used for K_b.) The weaker the base, the smaller the value of K_b.

Question

19.11 Write an expression for the dissociation constant, K_b, for the following weak base: $C_2H_5NH_2$.

Answer

$C_2H_5NH_2$ reacts with water as follows:

$$C_2H_5NH_2 + H_2O \rightleftharpoons C_2H_5NH_3^+ + OH^-$$

$$K_b = \frac{[C_2H_5NH_3^+][OH^-]}{[C_2H_5NH_2]}$$

Calculation of pH of solutions of weak bases

The K_b value for a weak base can be used to work out the pH of a solution of the base, provided that the concentration of the solution is known. The formula $pOH = -\log_{10}\left[\sqrt{(K_b \times M_b)}\right]$, where M_b is the concentration of the weak base in moles per litre, can be used. This formula is based on the simplifying assumption that the concentration of the base is constant.

Question

19.12 Find the pH of a 0.001 M solution of ammonia, given that the K_b value for this base is 1.8×10^{-5}.

Answer

$$pOH = -\log_{10}\left[\sqrt{(K_b \times M_b)}\right]$$
$$= -\log_{10}\left[\sqrt{(1.8 \times 10^{-5} \times 0.001)}\right]$$
$$= -\log_{10}\left[\sqrt{(0.0000018)}\right]$$
$$= -\log_{10}(0.000134)$$
$$= 3.872$$

$$pH = 14 - pOH$$
$$= 14 - 3.872$$
$$= 10.13$$

19.13 Find the pH of a solution containing 6.8 g of NH_3 per litre of solution.

Answer

The ammonia solution contains 6.8 g of ammonia in 1 l.

The molar mass of NH_3 is 17 g mol^{-1}.

Therefore:

$$[NH_3] = 6.8 / 17 \text{ mol l}^{-1}$$
$$= 0.4 \text{ mol l}^{-1}$$
$$pOH = -\log_{10}\left[\sqrt{(K_b \times M_b)}\right]$$
$$= -\log_{10}\left[\sqrt{(1.8 \times 10^{-5} \times 0.4)}\right]$$
$$= -\log_{10}\left[\sqrt{(0.0000072)}\right]$$
$$= -\log_{10}(0.00268)$$
$$= 2.572$$
$$pH = 14 - pOH$$
$$= 14 - 2.572$$
$$= 11.43$$

Choice of indicator and titration curves

An acid–base indicator is a weak acid or base that has a different colour when it is dissociated into its ions than when it is undissociated.

In an acid–base titration, a base is added to an acid (or vice versa).

The pH changes slowly at first, then as neutralisation is nearly complete, a rapid change in pH occurs, followed by a levelling off of the pH.

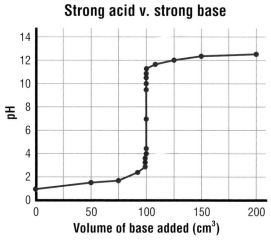

Strong acid v. strong base

Fig. 19.3 pH changes during titration of 0.1 M HCl with 0.1 M NaOH

- For a **strong acid–strong base** titration (where both solutions have a concentration of 0.1 M), the graph of pH v. cm³ of base added shows a rapid change in pH between 3.5 and 10.5 (Fig. 19.3). Any indicator changing colour in this pH range will be useful for detecting the end point of the titration. Therefore, indicators such as **methyl orange**, **methyl red** and **phenolphthalein** are suitable in this type of titration.

Weak acid v. strong base

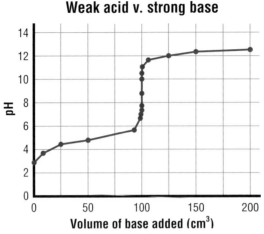

Fig. 19.4 pH changes during titration of 0.1 M CH₃COOH with 0.1 M NaOH

In the titration of a **weak acid** with a **strong base**, there is a rapid change in pH between 6.5 and 10.5 (Fig. 19.4). **Phenolphthalein** is the most suitable indicator for this type of titration.

Strong acid v. weak base

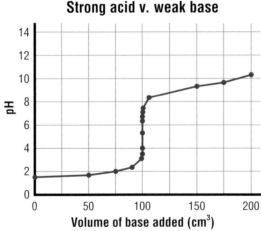

Fig. 19.5 pH changes during titration of 0.1 M HCl with 0.1 M NH₃

- In the titration of a **strong acid** with a **weak base**, the graph of pH v. cm³ of base added shows a rapid change in pH between 3 and 7 (Fig. 19.5). Therefore, **methyl orange** and **methyl red** are the most suitable indicators for this type of titration.

- The titration curve for a **weak acid–weak base** titration shows a very gradual change in pH near and at the end point. There is no sharp end point and no **suitable indicator**, so this type of reaction is not used to determine the concentration of a solution of a weak acid or a weak base.

Theory of acid–base indicators

Indicators are weak acids and bases that change colour when the pH of a solution in which they are present is changed. Consider a weak acid indicator, HIn. In water, this dissociates as follows:

$$HIn + H_2O \rightleftharpoons In^- + H_3O^+$$

The undissociated acid (HIn) has a different colour to that of its conjugate base In⁻.

The dissociation constant for the acid is: $K_a = [In^-] [H_3O^+] / [HIn]$

Addition of acid shifts the equilibrium in the reaction

$$HIn + H_2O \rightleftharpoons In^- + H_3O^+$$

to the left, resulting in the formation of more HIn. If this occurs to a sufficient extent, the colour of HIn predominates. Addition of base, on the other hand, shifts the equilibrium right, forming more In⁻. If this occurs to a sufficient extent, the colour of In⁻ predominates.

If the indicator is a weak base, XOH, its behaviour can be explained as follows. In water, XOH dissociates:

$$XOH \rightleftharpoons X^+ + OH^-$$

The undissociated base, XOH, has a different colour to that of the dissociated form, X⁺. Addition of acid shifts the equilibrium in the reaction

$$XOH \rightleftharpoons X^+ + OH^-$$

to the right, resulting in the formation of more X⁺. If this occurs to a sufficient extent, the colour of X⁺ predominates. Addition of base to a solution of the indicator shifts the equilibrium to the left, forming more XOH. If enough base is added, the colour of XOH predominates.

Key definition

An **acid–base indicator** is a weak acid or base that has a different colour when it is dissociated into its ions than when it is undissociated.

Key-points!

- $K_w = [H_3O^+] [OH^-] = 1 \times 10^{-14}$
- The pH of a solution is the negative logarithm to the base 10 of the hydrogen ion concentration.
- An acid–base indicator is a weak acid or base that has a different colour when it is dissociated into its ions than when it is undissociated.

20 Water

Hardness in water

> **Key definition**
>
> **Hard water** is water that will not easily form a lather with soap.

Hardness is caused by dissolved calcium and magnesium salts, e.g. calcium sulfate ($CaSO_4$) and magnesium chloride ($MgCl_2$). In effect, hardness in water is caused by calcium and magnesium ions, $Ca^{++}_{(aq)}$ and $Mg^{++}_{(aq)}$.

Soap molecules are the sodium or potassium salts of long-chain carboxylic acids such as stearic acid, e.g. sodium stearate ($C_{17}H_{35}COONa$).

$$C_{17}H_{35}COONa + water \rightarrow C_{17}H_{35}COO^-_{(aq)} + Na^+_{(aq)}$$

This process releases the stearate ion, which is the active part of soap. If the water is hard, i.e. containing calcium or magnesium ions, these ions will immediately precipitate with the dissolved stearate ions forming insoluble calcium stearate or magnesium stearate. For example, with calcium ions:

$$Ca^{++}_{(aq)} + 2C_{17}H_{35}COO^-_{(aq)} \rightarrow (C_{17}H_{35}COO^-)_2Ca_{(s)}$$

These precipitates appear as an unsightly scum in the water. Furthermore, the effect is to remove the stearate ions from the solution so that they are no longer available to produce lather and act as soap.

Hardness caused by dissolved calcium hydrogencarbonate, $Ca(HCO_3)_2$, can be removed **by boiling** the water. Such hardness is said to be **temporary**. Hardness caused by salts other than calcium hydrogencarbonate cannot be removed by boiling and is said to be **permanent**.

Key definition

Temporary hardness is hardness in water that can be removed by boiling.

Causes of temporary hardness

Temporary hardness is found in parts of the country where limestone, i.e. calcium carbonate ($CaCO_3$), is found in the earth. As rain falls, the water comes in contact with carbon dioxide in the atmosphere.

As a result, a dilute solution of carbonic acid falls on the ground and seeps into the earth. In limestone regions, the insoluble calcium carbonate on or in the earth reacts with the carbonic acid, forming soluble calcium hydrogencarbonate:

$$H_2CO_{3(aq)} + CaCO_{3(s)} \rightarrow Ca(HCO_3)_{2(aq)}$$

The presence of dissolved calcium ions now means that the water is hard, with consequent problems such as soap wastage.

Removing temporary hardness

If water containing temporary hardness, i.e. containing dissolved calcium hydrogencarbonate, is heated or boiled, the following reaction occurs:

$$Ca(HCO_3)_{2(aq)} + heat \rightarrow CaCO_{3(s)} + CO_{2(g)} + H_2O_{(l)}$$

This means that a precipitate of calcium carbonate is formed. Since the calcium ions

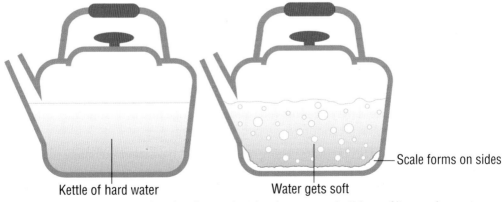

Kettle of hard water   Water gets soft   Scale forms on sides

Fig. 20.1 Boiling hard water in a kettle causes a build-up of limescale on the inside of the kettle

are now combined in an insoluble substance they are no longer available to react with soap anions. Consequently, the hardness is removed.

An undesirable side-effect of this is that the calcium carbonate precipitate can stick to the inside surfaces of the vessel involved, perhaps a kettle or central heating pipes or boiler. The build-up of this substance, called limescale, can cause problems such as wasting heat or even explosions due to pipes becoming completely clogged.

Experiment

Specified Demonstration: Tests on scale deposits in a kettle

Procedure

1 Place a small quantity of limescale in a test tube.

2 Add 5 cm^3 of dilute hydrochloric acid.

3 Quickly connect the test tube to a test tube containing 2 cm^3 of limewater to test any gas evolved.

4 Repeat the experiment using methanoic acid, vinegar and water in turn, instead of hydrochloric acid.

5 The limewater will turn milky when the limescale reacts with the acidic solutions, showing that carbon dioxide has been released.

Causes of permanent hardness

Permanent hardness is caused by any source of calcium ions other than calcium hydrogencarbonate as well as by sources of magnesium ions other than magnesium hydrogencarbonate. Normally, the chlorides and sulfates of calcium and magnesium cause permanent hardness. For example, water acquires permanent hardness by flowing through rocks such as gypsum, which is mainly calcium sulfate.

Key definition

Permanent hardness is hardness in water that can be removed by methods other than boiling (such as ion exchange).

Removing permanent hardness

Permanent hardness may be removed by ion exchange and by distillation. Unlike temporary hardness, it cannot be removed by boiling.

Ion exchange involves the water being passed through a cation exchange resin. The resins used are usually complex sodium compounds, represented here as Na_2R. The calcium and magnesium ions in the hard water swap places with the sodium ions in the resin.

$$Na_2R_{(s)} + Ca^{++}_{(aq)} \rightarrow CaR_{(s)} + 2Na^+_{(aq)}$$

In this way, the hardness-causing calcium and magnesium ions are removed from the water and replaced by sodium ions, which do not cause hardness.

Deionisation

More advanced ion exchange resins remove all ions from the water. The resin is a mixture of a cation exchanger, which replaces metal ions in water by hydrogen ions (H^+), and an anion exchanger, which replaces anions in water by hydroxide ions (OH^-). The H^+ and OH^- ions then react with each other as follows:

$$H^+ + OH^- \rightarrow H_2O$$

The effect of the resin is that dissolved salts are replaced with the water molecules formed by the combination of hydrogen and hydroxide ions. The water is said to have been **deionised**.

Deionised water is not quite as pure as distilled water, as the ion exchange resin merely removes dissolved ions from the water. Distilling the water removes all dissolved and suspended solids and dissolved gases from the water.

Points to note

Temporary hardness may be removed by ion exchange and by distillation as well as boiling.

Permanent hardness may be removed by ion exchange and by distillation but not by boiling.

Water treatment

Water treatment plants receive the raw untreated water from a range of sources such as rivers and lakes. As the water flows into the treatment plant, it passes through a metal grid or screen that removes floating matter such as branches, twigs or litter. The water is stored in large tanks where suspended particles settle to the bottom, before the following procedures are carried out.

1 Flocculation

A flocculating agent (coagulant) is added to and mixed with the water. This causes the small, suspended particles to stick together to form larger heavier particles called flocs. Aluminium sulfate is used for this purpose, although it is used in conjunction with synthetic polyelectrolytes.

2 Sedimentation

The flocculated water is pumped into the bottom of sedimentation tanks, so as not to disturb the clearer water at the top. The suspended particles settle to the bottom.

3 Filtration

Remaining suspended particles are now removed by filtration. The water is allowed to fall through beds of graded sand and gravel. The sand in the filter bed acts as a filter and removes the tiny particles from the water.

4 Chlorination

As water is likely to contain disease-causing bacteria, it must be sterilised in the treatment plant to get the bacteria down to safe levels. This is done by chlorination – the addition of chlorine or chlorine compounds to kill microorganisms by oxidation. Both chlorine and sodium hypochlorite react with water to form chloric(I) acid, HOCl, which is the active disinfecting agent.

5 Fluoridation

In Ireland and in some other countries, fluoridation of drinking water is carried out to prevent tooth decay. The fluoride ion F^- is added, usually using sodium fluorosilicate (Na_2SiF_6) as its source.

6 pH adjustment

It may be necessary to adjust the pH of the water before it leaves the treatment plant. Tap water should have a pH in the range of 6–8. If the water is too acidic, i.e. the pH is too low, lime is added to raise the pH. On the other hand, if the pH is too high, sulfuric acid is added.

Table 20.1 Stages in water treatment

Stage	Action	Result
Flocculation	Flocculating agent added	Small particles clump together to facilitate settlement
Sedimentation	Water allowed to stand in tanks	Suspended particles sink to bottom
Filtration	Water passes through beds of sand and gravel	Suspended particles are filtered out
Chlorination	Chlorine or sodium hypochlorite added to water	Microorganisms are killed
Fluoridation	Fluoride ions added	Tooth decay is prevented
pH adjustment	Lime added to acidic water, or sulfuric acid added to alkaline water	pH is adjusted to the range 6–8

Sewage treatment

1 Primary treatment

The sewage is forced through metal screens that remove large solids and physically break up the sewage. The effluent flows into a settling tank and rises slowly, allowing the sludge to settle.

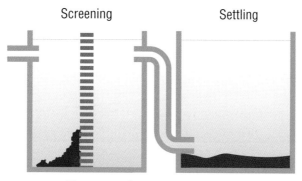

Fig. 20.2 *Primary sewage treatment*

2 Secondary treatment

The waste is oxidised by microorganisms in a **trickling filter** or in an **activated sludge unit**. In a trickling filter, the effluent flows through a bed of stones where microorganisms digest the nutrients in the presence of air, i.e. aerobically. An activated sludge unit also operates aerobically. The effluent is fed continuously into an aerated tank that is kept oxygenated by mechanical agitators. Once again, microorganisms decompose most of the organic matter.

After the biological stage, the effluent is subjected to further **settlement** in tanks.

3 Tertiary treatment

Tertiary treatment is a very costly process. Phosphates are removed by precipitation. They are reacted with a compound such as aluminium sulfate, $Al_2(SO_4)_3$, producing an insoluble salt – in this case aluminium phosphate ($AlPO_4$) – which can be removed by filtration.

The most common method of removing nitrates is biological denitrification. The effluent containing the nitrates is placed in a tank that has no free oxygen. Bacteria in the tank require oxygen and they take it from the only available source – oxygen bonded to nitrogen in nitrate ions, i.e. $NO_3^- \rightarrow N_2$. In other words, the bacteria reduce nitrates to nitrogen gas.

Table 20.2 Stages in sewage treatment

Stage	Type	Action	Result
Primary	Physical	Screening and settlement	Solids are removed
Secondary	Biological	Exposure to micro-organisms	Nutrients are oxidised
Tertiary	Chemical and biological	Phosphates precipitated; nitrates denitrified	Phosphates and nitrates are removed

Eutrophication

Eutrophication is caused by the over-enrichment of water by nutrients such as phosphates and nitrates. In effect, the nutrients behave as fertilisers that increase the growth of plants such as algae in lakes and rivers.

The algae are short lived. As they decay, much of the dissolved oxygen in the water is used up, leading to the death of many forms of animal life.

Waterways can also be polluted by the run-off of excess fertiliser from farmland. If the quantity used is not carefully controlled, excess nitrate may be washed into rivers or lakes by rainwater. Once again, eutrophication may result.

Heavy metal pollution

Metals with high relative atomic masses such as mercury, cadmium and lead are known as heavy metals. When recycling is inadequate, quantities of these elements are dumped, e.g. car batteries containing lead or dry batteries containing cadmium. Dipositive ions of these metals, i.e. Hg^{2+}, Cd^{2+} and Pb^{2+}, sometimes get into waterways from industrial effluent and consequently into drinking water. These elements are cumulative poisons in that frequent exposure causes a build-up in the body, resulting in serious health damage.

Before the effluent is run into a waterway, the metal ions can be removed by means of precipitation. For example, lead(II) hydroxide, $Pb(OH)_2$, is insoluble in water, so that if effluent containing Pb^{2+} ions is treated with calcium hydroxide solution, the lead will precipitate as $Pb(OH)_2$:

$$Pb^{2+}_{(aq)} + 2OH^-_{(aq)} \rightarrow Pb(OH)_{2(s)}$$

Hydroxide precipitation is ineffective for mercury removal, but alternatives such as carbonate or sulfide precipitation are available.

Water quality

Water quality is controlled by EU legislation. Heavy metal limits have to be set in waterways because of the toxic effects of metals like mercury, cadmium and lead. Limits on phosphates and nitrates help to reduce the occurrence of eutrophication in waterways. Limits are also set for chemical species dissolved in drinking water.

Key-points!

- Hard water is water that will not easily form a lather with soap.
- Temporary hardness is hardness in water that can be removed by boiling.
- Permanent hardness is hardness in water that can be removed by methods other than boiling (such as ion exchange).
- Temporary hardness may be removed by ion exchange and by distillation as well as boiling.
- Permanent hardness may be removed by ion exchange and by distillation but not boiling.
- Primary sewage treatment involves screening and settlement and is a physical process.
- Secondary sewage treatment involves the breakdown by bacteria of organic matter to less harmful materials.
- Tertiary sewage treatment involves the removal of phosphates and nitrates from the effluent resulting from secondary treatment.

21 Water Analysis

Atomic absorption spectrometry (AAS)

The concentration of a heavy metal in water can be measured using an atomic absorption spectrometer. In this instrument, the sample to be analysed is dissolved and introduced into the instrument as a fine spray. It is heated to a high temperature in a flame, with the result that it is converted into atoms of the element to be analysed.

A special lamp, whose cathode contains the element whose concentration is being measured, generates light characteristic of the element. This light is passed through the atomised sample and a certain amount of the light is absorbed by the sample. The amount of light at one particular wavelength that passes through the sample is measured by the instrument. The amount of light absorbed depends on the amount of the element present.

Table 21.1 Principle and processes of atomic absorption spectrometry

Principle	Processes
Atoms in the ground state absorb light of a particular wavelength characteristic of the element Absorbance is directly proportional to concentration	• Sample solution is sprayed into a flame; the sample element is converted into atoms of the element • Ground state atoms absorb radiation from a source made from the element • Absorbance is measured

Uses of atomic absorption spectrometry

Atomic absorption spectrometry can be used to detect and measure the concentration of heavy metals, such as lead and cadmium, that may be present in water.

Colorimetry

The intensity of the colour of a coloured solution is proportional to the concentration of the coloured substance present. A colorimeter passes light of a particular wavelength through a sample of the coloured solution and measures the amount of light absorbed by the solution.

If the absorbance is measured for a range of solutions of known concentration of the coloured substance being studied, a calibration curve may be drawn. This is a graph of absorbance against concentration. The concentration of an unknown solution of the same substance may then be obtained. A sample is placed in the colorimeter, the absorbance noted and the concentration is read off from the graph.

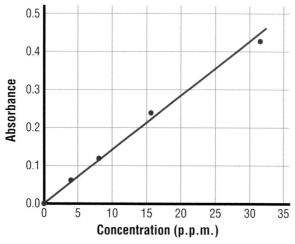

Fig. 21.1 A calibration curve

> ## Point to note
>
> The general principle underlying **colorimetry** is that the absorbance is proportional to the concentration of the solution.

A colorimeter may be used to estimate the free chlorine in swimming-pool water or bleach. When chlorine compounds are added to swimming-pool water, the active agent is usually chloric(I) acid, HOCl. Chloric(I) acid and its conjugate base, the chlorate(I) ion ClO^-, together make up what is called 'free chlorine'. These species react with iodide ions in solution in the same way as chlorine itself does, oxidising them to iodine:

$$Cl_{2(aq)} + 2KI_{(aq)} \rightarrow I_{2(aq)} + 2KCl_{(aq)}$$

The more concentrated the chlorine in water, the more intense the colour of the iodine solution formed.

Mandatory Experiment 21.1: Determination of free chlorine in swimming-pool water or bleach using a colorimeter or comparator

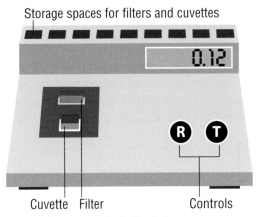

Storage spaces for filters and cuvettes

0.12

Cuvette Filter   Controls

Fig. 21.2 A digital colorimeter

Procedure **(i) Determination of chlorine using a colorimeter**

1 Using a 250 cm³ volumetric flask, dilute 2.5 cm³ of Milton sterilising fluid to 250 cm³ with deionised water.

2 Using the diluted Milton solution, 5% ethanoic acid solution and 2% potassium iodide solution, prepare solutions in labelled volumetric flasks, as summarised in the table.

Table 21.2

Chemical	Flask A	Flask B	Flask C	Flask D	Flask E
5% Ethanoic acid	5 cm³	5 cm³	5 cm³	5 cm³	5 cm³
2% Potassium iodide	5 cm³	5 cm³	5 cm³	5 cm³	5 cm³
Diluted Milton	0 cm³	1 cm³	2 cm³	4 cm³	8 cm³
Concentration of NaOCl in ppm	0	4	8	16	32
Total volume in flask	50 cm³	50 cm³	50 cm³	50 cm³	50 cm³

3 Switch on the colorimeter and place a 440 nm wavelength filter in the filter slot. Pour each of the five standard solutions into a cuvette, rinsing each cuvette first with the solution it is to contain.

4 Zero the colorimeter in accordance with the manufacturer's instructions.

5 Measure and record the absorbance of each solution.

6 Plot a graph of absorbance versus concentration (in terms of chlorine) for the five standard solutions.

7 Add 5 cm^3 of 5% ethanoic acid solution and then 5.0 cm^3 of 2% potassium iodide solution to a 50 cm^3 volumetric flask, labelled F. Fill the flask up to the mark with the swimming-pool water or diluted bleach. Allow about 5 minutes for the colour to develop.

8 Measure and record the absorbance for the solution in Flask F.

9 Using the graph, find the concentration of NaOCl in the sample.

10 Multiply by 71 / 74.5 to calculate the concentration of free chlorine in the sample.

(ii) Determination of chlorine using a comparator

Free chlorine oxidises DPD No. 1 tablets to a water-soluble red product. The more concentrated the chlorine in the water, the more intense the red colour produced.

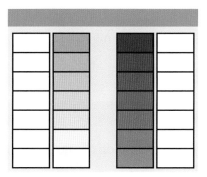

Fig. 21.3 A comparator

Procedure

1 Use some of the water being tested to rinse the compartments of the comparator.

2 Fill each compartment with fresh portions of the sample.

3 Add a DPD No. 1 tablet to each compartment, and crush each tablet with a stirring rod.

4 With the lid fitted, shake the comparator until the tablets have dissolved completely.

5 Compare the colour produced in the sample with the pre-calibrated standards built into the comparator.

6 Choose the best colour match, and read the free chlorine concentration of the selected standard in ppm (mg l^{-1}).

Uses of colorimetry

Colorimetry can be used in the analysis of lead in water and of fertilisers. In each case, suitable reagents have to be added in order to produce a coloured solution.

Suspended solids

Turbidity in water is a cloudiness or lack of clarity caused by suspended particles. These are insoluble substances that are too finely divided to settle to the bottom but are dispersed throughout the water sample. The cloudiness may reduce light penetration in surface water and interfere with photosynthesis in aquatic plants.

Question

21.1 500 cm^3 of water was filtered and it was found that the mass of the filter paper had increased by 0.33 g after drying. Calculate the total suspended solids in the water.

Answer

Total suspended solids = 0.33 g in 500 cm^3

$$= \frac{0.33 \times 1000}{500} \text{ g l}^{-1}$$

$$= 0.66 \times 1000 \text{ mg l}^{-1}$$

$$= 660 \text{ ppm}$$

Experiment

Mandatory Experiment 21.2(a): Determination of total suspended solids (expressed as ppm) in a water sample by filtration

Procedure
1 Find the mass of a dry filter paper.
2 Filter 1 litre of the water sample.
3 Dry the filter paper in an oven.
4 Find the mass of the dried filter paper.
5 By subtraction find the mass of suspended solids.
6 Calculate the mass of total suspended solids in mg l^{-1} (ppm).

Dissolved solids

Dissolved solids can affect the colour or taste of water. If the amount of dissolved solids is very high, it may be an indication that the sample is of salt water.

21.2 100 cm^3 of a filtered water sample in a beaker was evaporated to dryness and it was found that the mass of the beaker had increased by 0.055 g after drying. Calculate the total dissolved solids in the water.

Answer

Total dissolved solids $= 0.055$ g in 100 cm^3

$$= \frac{0.055 \times 1000}{100} \text{ g l}^{-1}$$

$$= 0.55 \times 1000 \text{ mg l}^{-1}$$

$$= 550 \text{ ppm}$$

Experiment

Mandatory Experiment 21.2(b): Determination of total dissolved solids (expressed as ppm) in a water sample by evaporation

Procedure

1 Find the mass of a clean dry 250 cm^3 beaker.

2 Add 100 cm^3 of a filtered water sample to the beaker.

3 Evaporate to dryness in an oven.

4 Find the mass of the dry beaker when cool.

5 Calculate the increase in mass of the beaker, which equals the mass of total dissolved solids in the water sample. Express the result in mg/l (ppm).

Measurement of pH

The pH of a solution can be measured accurately using a pH meter. A pH meter consists of three main parts: a pair of electrodes that dip into the solution being measured, an electronic circuit, and a readout device.

- The pair of electrodes, usually combined in a single probe, develops a voltage between them. The size of the voltage depends on the hydrogen ion concentration and consequently on the pH.

- The electronic circuit amplifies this voltage sufficiently so that it can register on a readout device.

- Most readout devices are digital and the pH is displayed directly.

- As pH meters are very sensitive instruments, they are easily disturbed in use or storage. They must be calibrated periodically using buffer solutions, which are resistant to changes in pH.

Uses of pH meters

Uses of pH meters include:

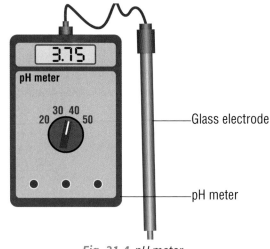

Fig. 21.4 pH meter

- Analysis of river and lake water to determine the existence of pollutants.

- Measurement of the pH of collected rainwater to test for the occurrence of acid rain.

- Measurement of the pH of water in water treatment plants to determine if pH adjustment is necessary to make the water suitable for use by consumers.

- Measurement of pH at regular stages in the course of an acid–base titration in order to plot a titration curve.

 Experiment

Mandatory Experiment 21.2(c): Determination of the pH of a water sample

Procedure

1 Calibrate the pH meter and dip the electrode or probe into the water sample. Record the steady reading.

2 Alternatively, add a few drops of universal indicator or dip a strip of pH paper into the water sample. Compare the colour obtained with the appropriate colour charts. Record the pH of the matching colours.

3 Repeat for each water sample.

Total hardness

The total hardness of a water sample is estimated by titrating the sample with a standard solution of the disodium salt of ethylenediaminetetraacetic acid (edta).

- This reagent forms stable complexes with calcium and magnesium ions when the pH is >9.

- This pH level is achieved by adding a buffer solution, i.e. a solution that resists changes in pH, of pH = 10.

- Edta reagent is used to measure the total quantity of dissolved Ca^{2+} and Mg^{2+} ions in a water sample; in other words, the total hardness.

- Since edta cannot distinguish between Ca^{2+} and Mg^{2+} ions, the total hardness is conveniently expressed as ppm of calcium carbonate, $CaCO_3$.

- This is merely a convention. Calcium carbonate is insoluble in water and does not directly cause hardness itself.

The disodium salt of edta is a primary standard, more soluble in water than edta itself, and is consequently more commonly used as the reagent than edta. If Na_2H_2Y represents this salt, it ionises in aqueous solution to H_2Y^{2-}, which complexes in a 1:1 ratio with either Ca^{2+} or Mg^{2+} ions (which are represented as M^{2+}). The equation for the reaction is as follows:

$$H_2Y^{2-} + M^{2+} \rightarrow MY^{2-} + 2H^+$$

Solutions of edta should be stored in plastic containers rather than glass bottles. If the solution is stored in glass bottles, its concentration will decrease appreciably with time as metal ions are extracted out of the glass.

The indicator Eriochrome Black T is used to detect the end point.

- This indicator is dark blue in colour, but changes to wine-red when complexed to calcium or magnesium ions. Thus, when the indicator is added to the water sample, a wine-red colour appears if these ions are present.

- However, edta forms a more stable complex with the metal ions, so as the titration proceeds the metal ions break away from the indicator and complex with the edta. When this occurs to a sufficient extent, the dark blue colour of the indicator is restored.

- The end point is detected when the wine-red colour just changes to blue. The reaction between the red indicator–metal complex and the edta reagent at the end point can be represented as follows:

$$MIn^- + H_2Y^{2-} \rightarrow HIn^{2-} + MY^{2-} + H^+$$
$$\text{wine-red} \qquad\qquad \text{blue}$$

Question

21.3 50 cm^3 of a hard water sample required 23.85 cm^3 of a 0.01 M edta solution for complete complexing of the metal ions. Calculate the total hardness of the water in ppm of calcium carbonate.

Answer

$$H_2Y^{2-} + M^{2+} \rightarrow MY^{2-} + 2H^+$$

(The ratio of edta ion : metal ion = 1:1)

$V_1 \times M_1 \times n_2 = V_2 \times M_2 \times n_1$

$50.0 \times M_1 \times 1 = 23.85 \times 0.01 \times 1$

M_1
$= 23.85 \times 0.01 \times 1 / (50.0 \times 1)$

$= 0.00477$ moles/litre of Ca^{2+} and Mg^{2+}

$= 0.00477 \times 100$ g/l $CaCO_3$

$= 0.477$ g/l $CaCO_3$

$= 0.477 \times 1000$ ppm $CaCO_3$

$= 477$ ppm $CaCO_3$

= total hardness of water sample

Experiment

Mandatory Experiment 21.3: Estimation of the total hardness of a water sample using edta

Procedure
1. Rinse the burette with the edta solution, the pipette with the hard water, and the conical flask with deionised water.

2. Fill the burette to the mark with the edta solution, making sure that the part below the tap is filled.

3. Pipette 50 cm³ of the hard water sample into the conical flask and add 2–3 cm³ of the buffer (pH 10) solution.

4. Using the spatula, add the solid indicator to the flask in minimal quantities, with swirling, until a deep wine-red colour is obtained.

5. Carry out one 'rough' titration and a number of accurate titrations until two titres agree to within 0.1 cm³. The end point is reached when the colour just changes from wine-red to dark blue.

6. Use the data to calculate the total hardness of the water sample.

Measurement of dissolved oxygen

The dissolved oxygen present in a water sample can be measured by an iodine–thiosulfate titration, using the Winkler method.

- Under alkaline conditions, manganese(II) sulfate produces a white precipitate of manganese(II) hydroxide:

$$Mn^{2+}_{(aq)} + 2OH^-_{(aq)} \rightarrow Mn(OH)_{2(s)}$$

- This is then oxidised by the dissolved oxygen in the water, forming a brown precipitate:

$$2Mn(OH)_{2(s)} + O_{2(aq)} \rightarrow 2MnO(OH)_{2(s)}$$

- The mixture is then acidified with concentrated sulfuric acid. Under these conditions, the Mn(IV) oxidises the iodide ions to free iodine:

$$MnO(OH)_{2(s)} + 4H^+_{(aq)} + 2I^-_{(aq)} \rightarrow Mn^{2+}_{(aq)} + I_{2(aq)} + 3H_2O_{(l)}$$

The free iodine is then titrated with standard sodium thiosulfate solution in the usual way.

$$I_{2(aq)} + 2S_2O_3^{2-}_{(aq)} \rightarrow 2I^-_{(aq)} + S_4O_6^{2-}_{(aq)}$$

Overall:

1 mole O_2 = 2 moles $MnO(OH)_2$ = $2I_2$ = 4 moles $S_2O_3^{2-}$, i.e. the ratio of dissolved oxygen to thiosulfate is 1:4.

21.4 50 cm^3 of water was analysed for dissolved oxygen using the Winkler method. The iodine liberated required 15.6 cm^3 of a 0.004 M sodium thiosulfate solution for complete reaction. Calculate the dissolved oxygen content of the water.

Answer

$$V_1 \times M_1 \times n_2 = V_2 \times M_2 \times n_1$$

$$50.0 \times M_1 \times 4 = 15.6 \times 0.004 \times 1$$

$$M_1 = 15.6 \times 0.004 \times 1 / (50.0 \times 4)$$

$$= 0.000312$$

Concentration of dissolved oxygen $= 0.000312 \times 32$ g/l

$$= 0.009984 \text{ g/l}$$

$$= 9.984 \text{ ppm}$$

 **Experiment**

Mandatory Experiment 21.4: Estimation of dissolved oxygen by redox titration

Procedure

1 Rinse a 250 cm^3 reagent bottle with deionised water, shaking vigorously to wet the inside and so avoid trapped air bubbles.

2 Immerse the bottle in a basin of the water sample in order to fill the bottle, making sure that there are no trapped air bubbles.

3 Add about 1 cm^3 each of manganese(II) sulfate solution and of alkaline potassium iodide solution to the bottle, using a dropper placed well below the surface of the water. This allows the two solutions to sink to the bottom of the bottle.

4 Stopper the bottle so that no air is trapped – some water will overflow at this point.

5 Invert the bottle repeatedly for about a minute, and then allow the brown precipitate to settle out.

6 Carefully add 1 cm^3 of concentrated sulfuric acid to the bottle, by running the acid down the side of the bottle.

7 Restopper the bottle, being careful not to trap any air. Redissolve the precipitate by inverting repeatedly. If not all the precipitate has dissolved at this point, add a little more acid and repeat the mixing process. The brown colour of iodine should now be visible.

8 Rinse the pipette, burette and conical flask with deionised water.

9 Rinse the pipette with the iodine solution and the burette with the sodium thiosulfate solution.

10 Pipette 50 cm³ of the iodine solution into a conical flask and titrate with 0.005 molar sodium thiosulfate solution.

11 Add about 1 cm³ of starch indicator when a pale yellow colour is present. A dark blue colour is produced and the titration is continued until this colour just disappears.

12 Carry out a number of accurate titrations until two titres agree to within 0.1 cm³.

13 Calculate the results in (i) moles of oxygen per litre, (ii) grams of oxygen per litre, and (iii) dissolved oxygen in ppm.

Biochemical oxygen demand (BOD)

The oxygen content of water can be assessed by measuring the **biochemical oxygen demand (BOD)**. This is a measure of the amount of oxygen required by bacteria to change all of the organic material present in a water sample to carbon dioxide and water by aerobic oxidation.

Key definition

The **biochemical oxygen demand** of a water sample is the amount of dissolved oxygen in ppm used up by the sample over a period of five days at 20°C in the dark.

To measure the BOD, an experiment is set up in which a water sample that is saturated in oxygen is allowed to stand at 20°C for 5 days.

- The sample is kept in the dark to prevent the production of oxygen by photosynthesis by plant life.

- The experiment is carried out at a fixed temperature to allow a valid comparison of the BOD values of different samples.

- The Winkler method of measuring dissolved oxygen is carried out on the sample of water at the beginning and end of a 5-day period.

- The difference between the two results is the BOD.

- If the sample is polluted, it must be diluted by a known factor by clean well-oxygenated water. This ensures that the dissolved oxygen does not run out before the end of the 5-day period.

- The result of the BOD calculation is multiplied by the dilution factor to get the true BOD value.

21.5 A sample of water from a polluted river was tested to measure the BOD. A 50 cm^3 sample was measured by pipette into a 500 cm^3 volumetric flask, which was made up to the mark with well-oxygenated clean water. The flask was inverted a number of times.

(i) 50 cm^3 of the diluted sample was analysed for dissolved oxygen by the Winkler method. The iodine liberated required 77.0 cm^3 of a 0.005 M sodium thiosulfate solution for complete reaction. Calculate the dissolved oxygen in the sample.

(ii) A second 50 cm^3 sample required 23.0 cm^3 of a 0.005 M sodium thiosulfate solution, having been left in the dark for 5 days at 20°C. Calculate the dissolved oxygen in this sample after 5 days.

(iii) Calculate the BOD of the water in the stream.

Answer

(i) $V_1 \times M_1 \times n_2$ $= V_2 \times M_2 \times n_1$

$50.0 \times M_1 \times 4$ $= 77.0 \times 0.005 \times 1$

M_1 $= 77.0 \times 0.005 \times 1 / (50.0 \times 4)$

$= 0.001925$

Concentration of dissolved oxygen $= 0.001925$ M

$= 0.001925 \times 32$ g/l

$= 0.0616$ g/l

$= 61.6$ ppm

(ii) $V_1 \times M_1 \times n_2$ $= V_2 \times M_2 \times n_1$

$50.0 \times M_1 \times 4$ $= 23.0 \times 0.005 \times 1$

M_1 $= 23.0 \times 0.005 \times 1 / (50.0 \times 4)$

$= 0.000575$

Concentration of dissolved oxygen $= 0.000575$ M

$= 0.000575 \times 32$ g/l

$= 0.0184$ g/l

$= 18.4$ ppm

(iii)   BOD of diluted sample $= 61.6 - 18.4$

$$= 43.2 \text{ ppm}$$

BOD of original sample $= 43.2 \times 10$ (original sample was diluted by a factor of 10)

$$= 432 \text{ ppm}$$

Key-points!

- The principle underlying atomic absorption spectrometry is that atoms in the ground state absorb light of a particular wavelength characteristic of the element. Absorbance is directly proportional to concentration.

- The processes involved in atomic absorption spectrometry are: (1) the sample solution is sprayed into a flame and the sample element is converted into atoms of the element, (2) ground state atoms absorb radiation from a source made from the element and (3) absorbance is measured.

- The general principle underlying colorimetry is that the absorbance is proportional to the concentration of the solution.

- The biochemical oxygen demand of a water sample is the amount of dissolved oxygen in ppm used up by the sample over a period of 5 days at 20°C in the dark.

Option 1

22

Option 1A: Industrial chemistry

Contributions of chemistry to society

Useful materials that are being continually produced by the chemical industry include:

- In the area of health, medicines and the chemicals needed to make water safe to drink.

- In agriculture, crop yields are improved by the use of fertilisers, herbicides and pesticides.

- A wide variety of metals, plastics, synthetic fibres, fuels, detergents, enzymes, dyes, paints, semiconductors, liquid crystals, and chemicals used in food processing.

Industrial chemical processes

> **Key definition**
>
> A **batch process** is an industrial process in which an amount of the product is made in a reaction vessel during a definite time interval, and is then removed from the vessel.

Batch processes are widely used in the manufacture of pharmaceuticals.

> **Key definition**
>
> A **continuous process** is an industrial process in which the reactants are continuously fed into the reaction vessel, and the products are continuously removed.

The manufacture of magnesium oxide from seawater is an example of a continuous process.

> **Key definition**
>
> A **semi-continuous process** is an industrial process in which part of the process is a continuous process and part is a batch process.

For example, the brewing of beer is a batch process, but the process of adding carbon dioxide and of bottling the beer is continuous.

Characteristics of industrial chemical processes

1 Feedstock

The reactants in an industrial process are called the **feedstock**. In the industrial synthesis of ammonia, the reactants are nitrogen gas and hydrogen gas. Feedstock is produced from the raw materials.

> **Key definition**
>
> The **feedstock** is the reactants in an industrial process.

2 Reaction rate

The temperature, pressure and catalyst for an industrial chemical reaction all affect the reaction rate, so the best conditions have to be selected for the process to occur at the optimum rate.

3 Product yield

The reaction conditions chosen for a chemical reaction in industry must result in a satisfactory yield. However, as in the industrial synthesis of ammonia, there may need to be a compromise found between the conditions for a good yield and the conditions for a satisfactory rate.

4 Co-products

Co-products have to be separated from the main products and either disposed of or, if they are useful, sold or used onsite.

> **Key definition**
>
> **Co-products** are the other products formed along with the main product being manufactured.

5 Waste disposal and effluent treatment

Satisfactory methods of controlling air emissions, of disposing of waste and in particular of effluent treatment have to be used.

6 Quality control

Instrumentation is invaluable in monitoring the quality of materials at various stages of an industrial process. In the industrial synthesis of ammonia, analyses of the gas mixtures at all stages of ammonia production can be carried out using gas chromatography and infrared spectroscopy. The performance of the catalyst can be monitored using these methods.

7 Safety

Safety considerations include monitoring of hazards, onsite training of the staff in first aid and in fire fighting, and safety features incorporated in the plant.

The location of the site is also important. The site should be designed to allow access by fire engines to central parts of the plant.

8 Costs

Fixed costs include labour costs, plant depreciation, land rental and repayments on loans.

> **Key definition**
>
> **Fixed costs** in an industrial process are those costs that have to be paid regardless of the rate of production.

Variable costs include the cost of heat, electricity and raw materials as well as the costs of waste disposal.

> **Key definition**
>
> **Variable costs** in an industrial process are those costs that depend directly on the level of plant output.

Methods that are used to reduce costs include the following: use of heat exchangers, use of catalysts, recycling of feedstock and the sale of useful co-products.

9 Site location

Site location should take into account the source of raw materials, the proximity of a market for the product, the availability of water and of transport for raw materials and products, and the availability of a suitable workforce.

10 Construction materials

Plant construction materials must not react with the feedstocks, solvents, catalysts or products involved in the process. The construction materials therefore need to be unreactive and resistant to corrosion by the chemicals with which they come in contact.

Industrial Case Study: Manufacture of magnesium oxide from seawater

The manufacture of magnesium oxide from seawater is an industrial process carried out by Premier Periclase in Drogheda, Co. Louth. The process involves formation of magnesium hydroxide from the reaction of dissolved magnesium salts in seawater with calcium hydroxide, followed by further reactions.

Type of process

The process is continuous, with the raw materials being fed in continuously and the magnesium oxide being continuously produced.

Feedstock (raw materials, preparation)

The feedstock consists of calcium hydroxide (slaked lime) and purified seawater. Limestone and freshwater are the raw materials for the calcium hydroxide. Seawater is, of course, the raw material for the purified seawater.

Treatment of raw materials

The limestone is very pure calcium carbonate and is crushed and washed before being heated in a limekiln to form calcium oxide (quicklime):

$$CaCO_{3(s)} \rightarrow CaO_{(s)} + CO_{2(g)}$$

Freshwater is then added to the quicklime to produce calcium hydroxide:

$$CaO_{(s)} + H_2O_{(l)} \rightarrow Ca(OH)_{2(aq)}$$

The seawater is taken from the Boyne estuary and stored in a large reservoir, where sand and other solid impurities settle out. It is then pumped to the Premier Periclase plant.

The seawater is acidified with sulfuric acid and passed downwards through a tower against a rising current of air, which removes carbon dioxide. Excess sand and other particles are then removed from the seawater by a settling process.

Reaction rate and product yield

In the reaction of seawater with calcium hydroxide, soluble magnesium ions (Mg^{2+}) form a precipitate with hydroxide ions from the calcium hydroxide:

$$MgCl_{2(aq)} + Ca(OH)_{2(aq)} \rightarrow CaCl_{2(aq)} + Mg(OH)_{2(s)}$$

The reaction, which is very rapid, is carried out in large circular tanks. The reaction in which magnesium hydroxide is converted into magnesium oxide

$$Mg(OH)_{2(s)} \rightarrow MgO_{(s)} + H_2O_{(l)}$$

is carried out in a multiple hearth furnace. A high temperature (900°C) is used. This increases the rate of reaction. In the furnace, there are three stages:

- Removal of the remaining water from the wet magnesium hydroxide
- Reaction to form magnesium oxide at 900°C
- Cooling

The fine powder that leaves the furnace is converted into pellets under pressure. The pellets are fed into kilns where at a very high temperature the magnesium oxide changes into larger crystals. The kilns transform low-density magnesium oxide into high-density sinter magnesium oxide (periclase). This product has a buff-brown colour and is chemically unreactive.

The yield of magnesium oxide is approximately 2 g from each litre of seawater.

Co-products (separation, disposal or sale)

The main co-product is calcium chloride, which is in solution in the used seawater. There are at present no commercially profitable co-products from the Premier Periclase process.

Waste disposal and effluent control

Dust is removed from combustion gases using electrostatic precipitators. Following this, the gases are scrubbed with water. This process removes sulfur oxides and some grit. Used seawater contains some calcium hydroxide, which is neutralised using fresh acidified seawater. The water is then filtered and pumped out to sea.

Extensive environmental monitoring is carried out in the plant; for example, monitoring of waste gases for dust and sulfur oxides, and monitoring of effluent for pH and suspended solids.

Quality control

Analyses of samples are carried out at various stages of the process, using, for example, automated acid–base titrations.

Safety

There is a safety training programme for staff onsite. Hazards are regularly monitored and engineering work is carried out to make dangerous or moving machinery safe. Personal protective equipment is used when required.

Costs

The fixed costs include labour costs, plant maintenance and plant depreciation. The variable costs include the cost of electricity, fuel and materials, and the costs of waste disposal.

Cost reduction can be achieved in a number of ways. For example, heat from waste gases can be reclaimed and used to preheat the intake air to the limekiln.

Site location

The location of the Premier Periclase site is suitable for a number of reasons.

- There is a highly skilled workforce available.
- The site is close to a plentiful supply of limestone.
- The site is close to a supply of seawater.
- The site is convenient for rail, road and sea transport.
- The site already had suitable equipment (e.g. large rotary kilns), which was previously used for cement making.

Suitable materials for the construction of the plant

The lime rotary kiln has a steel outer tube, with internal refractory bricks (i.e. bricks with a very high melting point). The sintering kiln is made of higher-quality refractory bricks because of the higher temperatures used. Acid-handling equipment in the plant is made of stainless steel. The reactors, in which calcium hydroxide and magnesium hydroxide respectively are formed, are made of concrete.

Uses of product

Pure periclase has a very high melting point (2800°C). Heat-treated periclase is chemically unreactive. It is therefore suitable for use as a heat-resistant material in the walls of furnaces, for example in steelmaking.

The Irish chemical industry

The chemical industry is one of the major industries in this country. Materials produced by the industry include pharmaceuticals, adhesives and alumina (which is exported for conversion into aluminium). Apart from alumina, another specific product of the Irish chemical industry is aspirin.

Option 1B: Atmospheric chemistry

The atmosphere

The lowest part of the atmosphere is the troposphere, which is the layer within 15 kilometres of the Earth's surface. The troposphere contains about 90% of the air in the atmosphere. The stratosphere is the layer of the atmosphere immediately above the troposphere.

Dry air contains approximately 78% nitrogen (N_2), 21% (O_2) and 1% argon (Ar). It contains about 0.03% carbon dioxide (CO_2), although this amount is known to be increasing. Air usually contains a significant but varying quantity of water vapour.

Fractional distillation of oxygen and nitrogen

The process of fractional distillation is used to obtain oxygen gas and nitrogen gas from air. Air must be liquefied before it can be fractionally distilled. This liquefaction occurs by a combination of increasing the pressure and lowering the temperature.

The air is first filtered to remove dust. It is then compressed and carbon dioxide and water vapour are removed. Next, the air is cooled to about 103 K. It is then cooled further by allowing it to expand suddenly. This cools the air to a sufficient extent to liquefy it.

Liquid air is mainly a mixture of liquid nitrogen, which boils at 77 K, and liquid oxygen, which boils at 90 K. The liquid air is allowed to boil off through a fractionating column. The nitrogen, having a lower boiling point, boils off first. The oxygen then boils off when the temperature reaches 90 K.

Uses of oxygen

The most important industrial use of oxygen is in steelmaking, where it is used to burn impurities out of molten iron. Pure oxygen is used with ethyne in oxyacetylene torches, which are used for cutting and welding metals. Oxygen is given in hospitals to patients who suffer from lung conditions to make it easier for them to breathe.

Nitrogen

Nitrogen, at 78%, is by far the most abundant substance in the atmosphere. It occurs freely in nature as the diatomic gas, N_2, with the two nitrogen atoms joined by a covalent triple bond. The bond energy of the $N \equiv N$ bond is very large, which means that a lot of energy is needed to break the bond. Consequently, nitrogen is very stable and chemically unreactive.

Uses of nitrogen

When oil tankers empty their cargoes, nitrogen gas, being inert, is used to flush out the explosive vapours from their tanks. The tanks remain full of nitrogen until they are refilled with their next cargo of oil.

Food is kept fresh by storing it in nitrogen. In the consequent absence of oxygen, the microorganisms that cause food to go off are unable to survive. Thus, the food remains fresh for a longer period.

Nitrogen fixation

Nitrogen fixation is the conversion of atmospheric nitrogen to compounds that are used by plants.

The nitrogen cycle

The nitrogen cycle indicates why the level of nitrogen in the atmosphere does not change. Some nitrogen is removed from the atmosphere by bacterial nitrogen fixation. More is removed by the action of lightning followed by rain. Some atmospheric nitrogen is used in the manufacture of artificial fertilisers. However, certain bacteria convert nitrates in soil into nitrogen gas, which is released back into the atmosphere to begin the nitrogen cycle again.

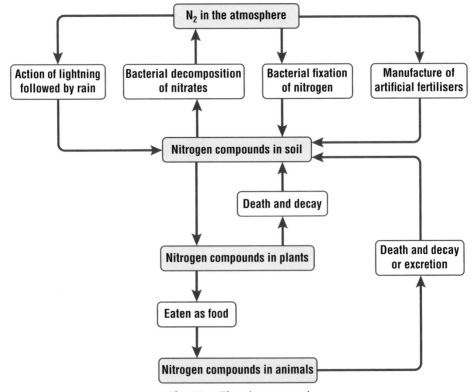

Fig. 22.1 The nitrogen cycle

Oxides of carbon

When carbon is burned in a limited supply of oxygen, incomplete combustion occurs and carbon monoxide is formed:

$$C_{(s)} + \tfrac{1}{2}O_{2(g)} \rightarrow CO_{(g)}$$

Carbon monoxide is a neutral gas that is also formed when the incomplete combustion of hydrocarbons occurs. It is a deadly poison, which prevents the uptake of oxygen by the haemoglobin in blood.

Carbon monoxide has no smell or colour, does not irritate the lungs or the eyes, so it can easily be breathed in without being noticed. Carbon monoxide is emitted through vehicle exhausts, particularly in the absence of catalytic converters, and is also found in cigarette smoke.

When carbon is burned in excess oxygen, complete combustion occurs and carbon dioxide is formed:

$$C_{(s)} + O_{2(g)} \rightarrow CO_{2(g)}$$

Carbon dioxide is also formed when complete combustion of hydrocarbons occurs. In brewing, carbon dioxide is a co-product in the production of ethanol by fermentation:

$$C_6H_{12}O_{6(aq)} \rightarrow 2C_2H_5OH_{(aq)} + 2CO_{2(g)}$$

Carbon dioxide is an acidic gas, which is used to make fizzy drinks. It is dissolved in water under pressure, with the result that bubbles of gas are produced when the container is opened.

 Experiment

Specified Demonstration: The effect of carbon dioxide on universal indicator solution

Procedure

1 Place about 25 cm³ of universal indicator into a 100 cm³ beaker and dilute with an equal volume of water. Place the beaker on a magnetic stirrer, add a pellet and start the stirrer at a slow speed.

2 Place a few marble chips in a test tube. The test tube has a two-holed stopper, with a delivery tube dipping into the beaker, and a teat pipette containing dilute HCl. The end of the delivery tube should be well below the surface of the universal indicator.

3 Add dilute HCl from the teat pipette, a few drops at a time.

4 As the carbon dioxide bubbles through the indicator, a series of colour changes can be observed.

Carbon dioxide in water

Carbon dioxide is an **acidic oxide**.

> **Key definition**
>
> An **acidic oxide** is an oxide that increases the hydrogen ion concentration in water.

Carbon dioxide is fairly soluble in water:

$$CO_{2(g)} + \text{excess } H_2O \rightleftharpoons CO_{2(aq)}$$

A small proportion of dissolved carbon dioxide reacts with the water to form carbonic acid, H_2CO_3:

$$CO_{2(aq)} + H_2O_{(l)} \rightleftharpoons H_2CO_{3(aq)}$$
$$\text{Carbonic acid}$$

As this is a weak acid, it dissociates to a small extent in aqueous solution:

$$H_2CO_{3(aq)} \rightleftharpoons H^+_{(aq)} + HCO_3^-{}_{(aq)}$$
$$\text{Carbonic acid} \qquad \text{Hydrogencarbonate ion}$$

The hydrogencarbonate ion, HCO_3^-, is itself a weak acid so further dissociation can occur, but to a lesser extent:

$$HCO_3^-{}_{(aq)} \rightleftharpoons H^+_{(aq)} + CO_3^{2-}{}_{(aq)}$$
$$\text{Hydrogencarbonate ion} \qquad \text{Carbonate ion}$$

This is more likely to occur under alkaline conditions.

The carbon cycle

The carbon cycle indicates why the level of carbon dioxide in the atmosphere does not change greatly over short periods of time. Some carbon dioxide is removed from the atmosphere by dissolving in rain or in ocean water.

The major process by which atmospheric carbon dioxide levels are reduced is photosynthesis. Atmospheric carbon dioxide is used by green plants in photosynthesis to make more complex carbon compounds. These may be eaten by animals, which digest them and use them for energy in respiration.

Alternatively, they may be used by the plants themselves in respiration. In both cases, carbon dioxide is formed and returned to the atmosphere. Another way that carbon dioxide is returned to the atmosphere is when fossil fuels are burned.

Greenhouse effect and global warming

The sun emits energy, some of which is absorbed by the Earth. This absorbed energy heats the Earth, and the Earth in turn radiates energy, mostly infrared, back into space. Some gases found in the atmosphere absorb infrared radiation, thus preventing it from escaping into space. The effect of this is to make the Earth warmer.

This trapping of heat in the atmosphere is referred to as the greenhouse effect. It keeps the Earth at a comfortable temperature and makes life, as we know it, possible.

Problems arise when growing amounts of certain gases in the troposphere enhance the greenhouse effect. There is now a great deal of evidence that the Earth is getting hotter, i.e. that global warming is taking place, and that emissions of greenhouse gases caused by human activities are responsible.

It is widely accepted that the enhanced greenhouse effect will change weather patterns. Among the effects predicted are: warmer weather, particularly in high latitudes; changes in prevailing winds and in rainfall distribution; rising sea levels with consequent flooding and loss of land.

Greenhouse gases

Water vapour, carbon dioxide, methane and chlorofluorocarbons are the most significant greenhouse gases. Water vapour is so abundant in the atmosphere that it makes the largest contribution to the greenhouse effect.

Global warming causes the amount of water vapour in the troposphere to increase by evaporation of the oceans. However, the precise effects of this on climate are not clear.

The amount of carbon dioxide in the troposphere has been increasing for the past 150 years, largely as a result of the widespread combustion of fossil fuels such as coal and oil. The destruction of the world's forests makes the problem worse because it reduces the amount of photosynthesis taking place, which would otherwise use up some of the carbon dioxide.

Methane gas (CH_4) is produced in marshes, compost heaps, rubbish dumps, rice paddy fields, biogas digesters and in the digestive tracts of animals such as cattle. The concentration of methane in the troposphere is rising. However, if the methane passes through the troposphere into the stratosphere, it helps to solve the problem of damage to the ozone layer by chlorine atoms.

Chlorofluorocarbons (CFCs) have a large greenhouse factor but concentrations are small and decreasing. Apart from their contribution to the increased greenhouse effect, CFCs are notorious for damaging the ozone layer.

Acid rain

Unpolluted rainwater is slightly acidic. It has a pH of approximately 5.7 due to the acidic gas, carbon dioxide, in the atmosphere. Emissions of acidic gases into the atmosphere lead to a lowering of pH, with the formation of what is referred to as acid rain. This acid rain damages soil, poisons fish, attacks trees and erodes buildings. The main causes of acid rain are oxides of nitrogen and oxides of sulfur.

Oxides of nitrogen

Oxides of nitrogen are released from car exhausts and power plants where the high temperatures bring about the oxidation of atmospheric nitrogen. They are also formed in some biological processes and by lightning discharges.

Nitrogen monoxide (NO) is quickly oxidised in air to nitrogen dioxide (NO_2). Nitrogen dioxide dissolves in water and reacts to form a mixture of nitrous acid (HNO_2) and nitric acid (HNO_3):

$$2NO_{2(g)} + H_2O_{(l)} \rightarrow HNO_{2(aq)} + HNO_{3(aq)}$$

When this occurs in the atmosphere, the result is acid rain.

Oxides of sulfur

Oxides of sulfur are mainly formed by the combustion of fossil fuels, particularly coal. They can also be released by volcanoes and by the decay of organic matter.

Sulfur in fossil fuels forms sulfur dioxide (SO_2), which is a dangerous pollutant. Sulfur dioxide dissolves in water to form sulfurous acid (H_2SO_3):

$$SO_{2(g)} + H_2O_{(l)} \rightarrow H_2SO_{3(aq)}$$

In the atmosphere, sulfur dioxide is oxidised to sulfur trioxide (SO_3). Sulfur trioxide dissolves in rainwater to form sulfuric acid (H_2SO_4).

$$SO_{3(g)} + H_2O_{(l)} \rightarrow H_2SO_{4(aq)}$$

Thus, the release of SO_2 into the atmosphere is likely to result in rain containing H_2SO_3 and H_2SO_4.

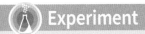 Experiment

Specified Demonstration: The effect of sulfur dioxide on universal indicator solution

Procedure
1. Place about 25 cm³ of universal indicator into a 100 cm³ beaker and add an equal volume of water. Place the beaker on a magnetic stirrer, add a pellet and start the stirrer at a slow speed.

2. Place a spatula full of sodium sulfite in a test tube. The test tube has a two-holed stopper, with a delivery tube dipping into the beaker, and a teat pipette containing dilute HCl. The end of the delivery tube should be well below the surface of the universal indicator.

3 Add dilute HCl from the teat pipette, a few drops at a time.

4 As the sulfur dioxide bubbles through the indicator, a series of colour changes can be observed as the pH drops.

Scrubbing waste gases

Limestone is used to reduce sulfur dioxide emissions from coal-fired power stations. Coal is mixed with finely ground limestone. The high temperatures in the furnace cause the limestone to decompose:

$$CaCO_{3(s)} \rightarrow CaO_{(s)} + CO_{2(g)}$$

The calcium oxide reacts with much of the sulfur dioxide forming calcium sulfite:

$$CaO_{(s)} + SO_{2(g)} \rightarrow CaSO_{3(s)}$$

This prevents the release of sulfur dioxide into the atmosphere. The process is called scrubbing.

The ozone layer

Ozone (O_3) is a form of oxygen with three oxygen atoms. It is formed in the stratosphere by the following photochemical reactions (reactions caused by light energy):

$$O_{2(g)} + energy \rightarrow O^{\bullet}{}_{(g)} + O^{\bullet}{}_{(g)}$$

$$O_{2(g)} + O^{\bullet}{}_{(g)} \rightarrow O_{3(g)}$$

• In the first of the two reactions, radiation from the sun splits oxygen molecules into high-energy oxygen atoms. In the second reaction, oxygen atoms ($O^{\bullet}$) combine with oxygen molecules, O_2, to form ozone molecules, O_3.

• The ozone produced absorbs ultraviolet radiation from the sun to re-form diatomic oxygen, O_2. This reaction is the photodissociation of ozone:

$$O_{3(g)} + uv \rightarrow O_{2(g)} + O^{\bullet}{}_{(g)}$$

In this way, ozone acts as a sunscreen by absorbing the ultraviolet radiation, which is damaging to plants and animals when it reaches Earth. Ultraviolet radiation causes sunburn and ultimately skin cancer in humans.

• Ozone is also removed from the stratosphere by nitrogen monoxide (NO). Oxides of nitrogen enter the atmosphere as a result of biological activity, and also during the combustion of fossil fuels. Ozone is also removed by reaction with atoms of oxygen, where an oxygen atom and an ozone molecule produce two molecules of oxygen.

• Ozone is being made and destroyed all the time and a balance exists to maintain the ozone concentration. This balance is upset when certain substances get into the stratosphere.

Damage to the ozone layer

Chlorofluorocarbons or CFCs are substituted hydrocarbons such as CCl_2F_2 and CCl_3F.

Because of their unreactive nature, CFCs are extremely useful compounds. Apart from their original use as refrigerants, they are also useful as air-conditioning gases, as aerosol propellants and as fire extinguishers.

- The stability of CFCs and their insolubility in water means that they remain a long time (i.e. have a long residence time) in the troposphere, where they have a large greenhouse effect.

- Having spent a long time in the troposphere, CFCs eventually reach the stratosphere, where they are broken down by the sun's ultraviolet radiation.

  The reaction results in the release of chlorine atoms from the CFC molecule. The chlorine atoms produced remove ozone:

  $$Cl^{\bullet}_{(g)} + O_{3(g)} \rightarrow ClO^{\bullet}_{(g)} + O_{2(g)}$$

  The chlorine oxide radicals ($ClO^{\bullet}$) formed in the reaction then react with oxygen atoms to regenerate chlorine atoms:

  $$ClO^{\bullet}_{(g)} + O^{\bullet}_{(g)} \rightarrow Cl^{\bullet}_{(g)} + O_{2(g)}$$

  The net effect is that a chain reaction occurs. Consequently, one CFC molecule may destroy 100,000 ozone molecules. Chlorofluorocarbons are the main cause of damage to the ozone layer.

- When methane molecules reach the stratosphere, they react with chlorine atoms:

  $$CH_{4(g)} + Cl^{\bullet}_{(g)} \rightarrow CH_3^{\bullet}_{(g)} + HCl_{(g)}$$

  This reaction has the effect of removing individual chlorine atoms from the stratosphere by changing them into hydrogen chloride gas (HCl). Since hydrogen chloride does not destroy ozone, the overall result of the reaction is protective of the ozone layer.

- Winter conditions over the Antarctic bring about a situation where HCl changes into chlorine molecules. These remain in the stratosphere until ultraviolet light splits them into atoms, with subsequent serious depletion of the ozone layer over the Antarctic.

Replacements for CFCs

Concern about the effect of CFCs on the ozone in the stratosphere has led to a severe reduction in their use. Replacements include hydrochlorofluorocarbons (HCFCs) such as dichlorofluoroethane ($C_2H_3Cl_2F$). These molecules contain C – H bonds, which are broken down in the troposphere. This initiates the breakdown of the entire molecule, with the result that the chlorine in HCFCs is unable to reach the stratosphere. Work is continuing to find substitute compounds and to develop technology aimed at the recovery and recycling of CFCs.

Other compounds being used to replace CFCs are alkanes and hydrofluorocarbons (HFCs). Like HCFCs, these compounds are broken down in the troposphere. One example of an HFC is tetrafluoroethane (CH_2FCF_3).

Key-points!

- A batch process is an industrial process in which an amount of the product is made in a reaction vessel during a definite time interval, and is then removed from the vessel.

- A continuous process is an industrial process in which the reactants are continuously fed into the reaction vessel, and the products are continuously removed.

- A semi-continuous process is an industrial process in which part of the process is a continuous process and part is a batch process.

- The feedstock is the reactants in an industrial process.

- Co-products are the other products formed along with the main product being manufactured.

- Fixed costs in an industrial process are those costs that have to be paid regardless of the rate of production.

- Variable costs in an industrial process are those costs that depend directly on the level of plant output.

- Nitrogen fixation is the conversion of atmospheric nitrogen to compounds that are used by plants.

23 Option 2

Option 2A: Materials

Crystals

Key definition

A **crystal** is a solid in which the atoms, ions or molecules of which it is composed are arranged in a regular three-dimensional structure.

Different types of crystal are summarised in Table 23.1.

Table 23.1

Crystal type	Species occupying lattice points	Binding forces	Examples
Ionic	Positive and negative ions	Ionic bonds	Sodium chloride
Molecular (non-polar)	Molecules	van der Waals forces	Iodine
Molecular (polar)	Molecules	van der Waals forces and dipole–dipole attractions	Ice
Metallic	Positive ions	Metallic bond	Sodium
Covalent macromolecular	Atoms	Covalent bonds (sometimes with van der Waals forces)	Diamond, graphite

The properties of different types of crystal are summarised in Table 23.2.

Table 23.2

Type of crystal	Strength	Melting points	Electrical conductivity	Solubility
Ionic	Hard, but brittle	High	Conducts when molten or in solution	Usually dissolves in polar solvents
Molecular	Relatively weak	Low	Non-conductor	Depends on the type of molecule
Metallic	Most are hard, though malleable and ductile	Variable	Good conductors	Insoluble except in mercury
Covalent macromolecular	Usually hard	High	Non-conductor (except graphite)	Insoluble

Buckminsterfullerene

Until the discovery of fullerenes, scientists believed that only two allotropes of carbon, namely diamond and graphite, existed. In the mid-1980s, English chemist Harold Kroto and his American colleagues Robert Curl and Richard Smalley used a laser to vaporise atoms from a solid graphite disc. The atoms were allowed to cool and condense in the vapour phase and were then studied using mass spectrometry. By this means they discovered a different allotrope of carbon consisting of 60 atoms bonded together in a structure like a football. This C_{60} structure was given the name buckminsterfullerene.

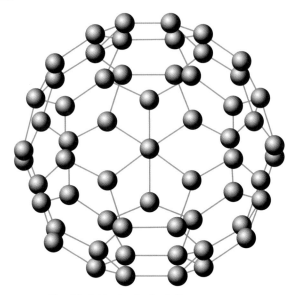

Fig. 23.1 Buckminsterfullerene

X-ray determination of structure

When X-rays are directed at the surface of a crystal, they are scattered from the surface. The pattern that is detected from the scattering – a diffraction pattern – can be used to work out the structure of the crystal.

The British father and son team of **William and Lawrence Bragg** developed the use of diffraction patterns to work out the structure of crystals. They received a Nobel Prize for working out the structure of sodium chloride.

Another Nobel Prize winner who used X-ray crystallography was **Dorothy Hodgkin**. She determined the crystal structure of the complex organic molecule, penicillin, using an electronic computer to carry out the complex calculations involved. Hodgkin later worked out the structure of vitamin B_{12}.

Addition polymers

Alkenes are the raw materials in the industrial manufacture of plastics. In the polymerisation of ethene, the molecule **adds to itself** to produce a saturated hydrocarbon chain that consists of repeating $-CH_2CH_2-$ units.

The resulting solid substance is called poly(ethene) or polythene and has many uses. Polythene is an example of a **polymer**, a large molecule made up of many identical repeating units called **monomers**.

Depending on the conditions used, two forms of polythene can be produced: low-density polythene and high-density polythene.

Low-density polythene

This type of polythene has a significant degree of branching. This prevents the molecules from packing closely together. Because the molecules take up more space, the density of the polymer is reduced. Low-density polythene is very flexible and melts at about 360 K.

High-density polythene

There are few side branches in this form of polythene and this allows the molecules to pack more tightly. Because the molecules take up less space, the density of the polymer is increased. High-density polythene has a higher melting point: about 400 K. It is more rigid than low-density polythene.

Polymers of substituted alkenes

1 Poly(chloroethene)

Chloroethene ($CH_2=CHCl$) polymerises to form poly(chloroethene). This polymer also resembles poly(ethene), but this time every second carbon in the chain has a chlorine atom attached. The polymer is commonly known as PVC.

2 Poly(phenylethene)

Phenylethene, in which one of the carbon atoms has a phenyl group (C_6H_5) attached, polymerises to form poly(phenylethene). In this polymer, every second carbon in the chain has a phenyl group attached. The polymer is commonly known as polystyrene.

3 Poly(tetrafluoroethene)

Tetrafluoroethene, in which all four hydrogen atoms in the parent ethane molecule have been replaced by fluorine atoms, polymerises to form poly(tetrafluoroethene). In this polymer, each carbon in the chain has two fluorine atoms attached. The polymer is commonly known as Teflon or PTFE.

4 Poly(propene)

Propene, $CH_2=CHCH_3$, polymerises to form poly(propene). This product differs from polythene in that every second carbon in the chain has a methyl group attached.

Table 23.3 Uses of polymers

Monomer	Polymer	Common name	Uses
Ethene	Poly(ethene)	Polythene	**Low density:** plastic bags, squeezy bottles; **High density:** buckets, lunch boxes
Chloroethene	Poly(chloroethene)	Polyvinylchloride (PVC)	Garden hoses, window frames, gutters
Phenylethene	Poly(phenylethene)	Polystyrene	Insulation, packaging
Tetrafluoro-ethene	Poly(tetrafluoroethene)	Teflon (PTFE)	Non-stick coating, artificial arteries and veins, plumbing tape
Propene	Poly(propene)	Polypropylene	Ropes, stacking chairs

Discovery of polythene

Polythene was discovered by accident in 1933. The British chemists **Eric Fawcett** and **Reginald Gibson** were studying the effect of high pressure on chemical reactions. At the end of one experiment involving ethene, carried out at high temperature and pressure, the walls of the reaction vessel were found to be coated with a white, waxy solid. This solid was recognised to be a polymer of ethene.

High-density polythene was discovered as a result of the work of the German chemist **Karl Ziegler** in the early 1950s. He discovered that certain organic catalysts, which had metal atoms in their molecules, allowed polythene to be manufactured at lower pressures and therefore more economically.

Discovery of poly(tetrafluoroethene) – Teflon

In 1938, the American chemist **Roy Plunkett** opened a cylinder of the gas tetrafluoroethene and found a waxy white powder inside. He realised that the tetrafluoroethene gas molecules had combined in a polymerisation reaction.

Poly(tetrafluoroethene), later called Teflon, was found to have some remarkable properties, which were not affected by extreme temperatures. It was inert and also had a slippery feel.

Recycling of plastics

Polystyrene is a completely recyclable plastic. After collection, it is sorted from other plastics to allow separate recycling.

After sorting, the polystyrene is shredded and then washed and dried. Finally, it is re-extruded, that is, melted and forced under pressure through a moulding device.

Metals

The properties of metals differ from those of non-metals.

Table 23.4

Physical properties of metals	Physical properties of non-metals
Most metals are hard	Some solid non-metals are hard but brittle and have relatively low melting points
Most metals have lustre	Non-metals do not have lustre
Metals are malleable and ductile	Non-metals are neither malleable nor ductile
Metals are good conductors of heat and electricity	Non-metals are good insulators

Alloys

Key definition

An **alloy** is a mixture of two or more elements, at least one of which is a metal.

The elements are usually mixed by melting them, mixing the molten elements, and then allowing the mixture to solidify.

Table 23.5

Alloy	Constituent elements
Brass	Copper and zinc
Bronze	Copper and tin
Stainless steel	Iron, chromium, nickel and carbon

Steel contains mainly iron with, typically, about 0.3% of carbon and small, carefully measured amounts of transition metals such as chromium, nickel, tungsten, titanium, vanadium and manganese. These elements are chosen to give the steel particular properties to suit its use, such as hardness, rigidity, flexibility and resistance to corrosion. Steel is much harder than iron and can be used in making cutting tools, girders for bridges and steel-framed buildings, and reinforcements for building foundations, amongst many other uses.

Option 2B: Electrochemistry and extraction of metals

The beginnings of electrochemistry

- In Italy in 1786, **Luigi Galvani** noticed that a dissected frog's leg twitched when it came into contact with two different metals.

- **Alessandro Volta** stated in 1794 in Italy that the frog leg twitched because of the difference in potential between two dissimilar metals connected by the animal tissue. He found by experiment that electricity flowed when two different metals were used without any animal tissue present. By 1800, he had gone on to invent the first practical battery – the Voltaic pile. Volta's battery used cells composed of two different metals, for example, silver and zinc. These batteries produced a useful electric current.

- **Humphry Davy** in London in the early 1800s improved the design of the Voltaic pile, and developed more powerful batteries. In the years 1807–1808, he discovered several elements, including potassium and sodium, using electrochemical methods.

- In London during the years 1833–1836, **Michael Faraday** discovered the laws of electrolysis, including the proportionality between the mass of product deposited during electrolysis and the current passed.

The electrochemical series

In most cases, the higher a metal is in the electrochemical series, the more reactive it is. To establish the relative positions of zinc and copper, a piece of zinc is immersed in a 1 M solution of a water-soluble zinc compound, such as zinc sulfate.

The piece of zinc is then connected by means of a wire through an ammeter to a piece of copper immersed in a 1 M solution of a water-soluble copper compound, such as copper sulfate. The two solutions are connected by means of a salt bridge that contains a solution of an electrolyte. The voltage can then be measured.

Electrolysis of molten salts

The electrolysis of molten lead(II) bromide is carried out using carbon or platinum electrodes. The electrolyte is composed of Pb^{2+} ions and Br^- ions. The Pb^{2+} ions move to the cathode, where they are reduced:

$$Pb^{2+}_{(l)} + 2e^- \rightarrow Pb_{(l)}$$

The Br^- ions move to the anode, where they are oxidised:

$$2Br^-_{(l)} - 2e^- \rightarrow Br_{2(g)}$$

Bromine is reactive and would react with an anode that was not inert. Bromine does not react with either carbon or platinum.

The overall reaction for the electrolysis is:

$$Pb^{2+}_{(l)} + 2Br^-_{(l)} \rightarrow Pb_{(l)} + Br_{2(g)}$$

Corrosion

Key definition

Corrosion of a metal is the surface chemical reaction on the metal by the action of air, water or other chemicals.

Corrosion of metals is caused by the action of air, water and other chemicals, such as acids, on the metal surface. The very reactive alkali metals have to be stored under paraffin to prevent corrosion occurring. The paraffin excludes the corroding agents.

Some metals form oxide coatings when exposed to air. The oxide coatings formed by aluminium, nickel, chromium and magnesium do not flake off easily, and so these metals are protected from further corrosion.

Corrosion of iron or steel

The corrosion of iron or steel results in the formation of hydrated iron(III) oxide (rust), which does not protect the metal from further corrosion. If a drop of water is placed on a piece of clean steel, an electrochemical cell is formed with a cathode and an anode. The cathode and anode regions differ in composition.

- The anode gets eaten away as the iron is oxidised:

$$Fe_{(s)} \rightarrow Fe^{2+}_{(aq)} + 2e^-$$

- At the cathode, the dissolved oxygen in the water reacts as follows:

$$H_2O_{(l)} + \tfrac{1}{2}O_{2(aq)} + 2e^- \rightarrow 2OH^-_{(aq)}$$

- The Fe^{2+} and OH^- ions diffuse away from the electrodes and form a precipitate of iron(II) hydroxide:

$$Fe^{2+}_{(aq)} + 2OH^-_{(aq)} \rightarrow Fe(OH)_{2(s)}$$

- This is then oxidised by dissolved oxygen to form rust, $Fe_2O_3.xH_2O$, where x is variable.

Acceleration of corrosion

The presence of salt in water, which is likely near the sea, or in winter when de-icing salts are used on roads, accelerates corrosion of iron and steel. This is because it increases the conductivity of the electrochemical cell solution. If iron is in contact with a metal such as lead, which is below it in the electrochemical series, as for example when lead piping is joined to an iron storage tank, the rate of corrosion is accelerated greatly.

Prevention of corrosion

Corrosion of iron and steel may be prevented or retarded by painting to exclude air or by coating with tin, plastic, grease or oil. The protection against rust afforded by these methods lasts only until the coating is scratched. Galvanising, which involves coating the metal with zinc, affords protection even after scratching. Since zinc is above iron in the electrochemical series, it rather than the iron reacts, forming ions which go into solution:

$$Zn_{(s)} \rightarrow Zn^{2+}_{(aq)}$$

The zinc corrodes and the iron is protected. This is a type of cathodic protection, where the cathode is protected and the anode is eaten away.

If a sacrificial anode made from a more reactive metal such as magnesium or zinc is connected to steel, the steel is protected. This method is widely used to protect the steel of ships and underground or submerged oil pipelines and water pipes. The anode is eaten away and the steel, which is the cathode, is protected.

Other ways of preventing corrosion include alloying steel with a metal such as chromium, which forms a more stable oxide coating.

Extraction of sodium – the Downs cell

- The electrolyte is a molten mixture of sodium chloride and calcium chloride. The calcium chloride is added to reduce the melting point of the mixture – this reduces the amount of electricity needed.

- Steel cathodes are used.

- The anodes are made of inert carbon, so that the chlorine gas formed at the anode during the electrolysis will not react with them.

- The steel gauze, which separates the two electrode compartments, prevents the sodium formed at the cathode from reaction with this chlorine.

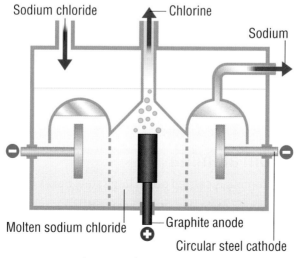

Fig. 23.2 The Downs cell

At the cathode, the reaction is:

$$Na^+_{(l)} + e^- \rightarrow Na_{(l)}$$

The molten sodium formed floats on the electrolyte and is removed using the collecting pipe.

The anode reaction is:

$$Cl^-_{(l)} - e^- \rightarrow \tfrac{1}{2}Cl_{2(g)}$$

i.e. producing chlorine gas, which is removed through the hood.

The overall reaction in the Downs cell is:

$$NaCl_{(l)} \rightarrow Na_{(l)} + \tfrac{1}{2}Cl_{2(g)}$$

Uses of sodium

Sodium is the most widely used of the alkali metals. Sodium vapour is used in street lighting. Sodium, alloyed with potassium, is used as a coolant in some nuclear reactors.

Extraction of alumina from bauxite

- Crushed bauxite is added, with mixing, to a hot solution of sodium hydroxide. The following reaction occurs, in which soluble sodium aluminate is formed:

$$2NaOH_{(aq)} + Al_2O_3.3H_2O_{(s)} \rightarrow 2NaAlO_{2(aq)} + 4H_2O_{(l)}$$

- The impurities in the ore, which are mainly oxides of iron, silicon and titanium, do not dissolve, and are allowed to settle before being removed by filtration.

- The clear sodium aluminate solution is next pumped to precipitator tanks. Here the solution is seeded with very pure, small crystals of aluminium oxide-3-water. On cooling, the following reaction occurs:

$$2NaAlO_{2(aq)} + 4H_2O_{(l)} \rightarrow 2NaOH_{(aq)} + Al_2O_3.3H_2O_{(s)}$$

- The precipitate of hydrated aluminium oxide is removed by vacuum filtration, while the sodium hydroxide solution is recycled to the start of the process.

- The hydrated aluminium oxide is then heated at about 1373 K to remove the water of crystallisation:

$$Al_2O_3.3H_2O_{(s)} \rightarrow Al_2O_{3(s)} + 3H_2O_{(l)}$$

The alumina formed is a white powder.

Aluminium from alumina

The electrolysis of alumina is carried out in large steel boxes lined with carbon.

- Carbon anodes and a carbon cathode are used.

- The electrolyte used is a mixture of molten cryolite (Na_3AlF_6) and aluminium fluoride (AlF_3). The aluminium oxide dissolves in the electrolyte.

- Cryolite is used as a solvent in the electrolysis to save energy, because it has a much lower melting point than alumina itself.

- A low voltage is used in the electrolysis to avoid decomposing the electrolyte.

- During the electrolysis, the following reactions occur:

$$\text{Cathode: } 2Al^{3+}_{(l)} + 6e^- \rightarrow 2Al_{(l)}$$

$$\text{Anode: } 3O^{2-}_{(l)} - 6e^- \rightarrow 1\tfrac{1}{2}O_{2(g)}$$

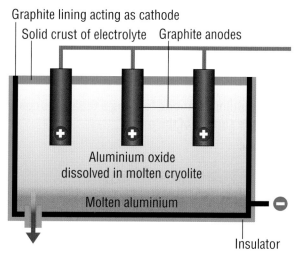

Fig. 23.3 The electrolysis of alumina

- The molten aluminium formed settles at the bottom of the tank, and is siphoned from there.

- The electrolysis is carried out at a high temperature, at which the large carbon anodes are steadily burned away by the oxygen liberated there and have to be replaced at regular intervals.

- The electrolysis of alumina consumes enormous amounts of electricity and is therefore normally carried out where electricity is relatively cheap.

Environmental aspects of aluminium production

The extraction of aluminium oxide from bauxite results in the formation of very large amounts of red mud, which is unsightly.

Uses of aluminium

- Aluminium is used to make strong, light, corrosion-resistant alloys, which are used in the construction of aeroplanes and ships.

- Aluminium is a good conductor of heat and so is used to make saucepans and as cooking foil.

- It is an excellent electrical conductor and so is used in electricity wires.

Anodising

The natural coating of aluminium oxide, which forms on the surface of aluminium as soon as the metal is exposed to the air, can be thickened by an electrolytic process called **anodising**. The purpose of anodising is to produce a very hard coating or one that is very resistant to corrosion.

- In anodising, the aluminium is used as an anode in the electrolysis of dilute sulfuric acid.

- Graphite, platinum or another inert cathode can be used.

- The electrolysis of the dilute acid results in the formation of oxygen at the anode:

$$H_2O_{(l)} \rightarrow 2H^+_{(aq)} + \frac{1}{2}O_{2(g)} + 2e^-$$

  This reacts with the aluminium anode forming a tenacious coating of aluminium oxide on the surface of the metal.

- The cathode reaction is:

$$2H^+_{(aq)} + 2e^- \rightarrow H_{2(g)}$$

- The anodised aluminium is porous. This allows it to be dyed easily. The anodised aluminium used in aluminium windows and doors is often dyed.

Recycling of aluminium

The recycling of aluminium is an economically viable process. It is also desirable from an environmental point of view. When aluminium is being recycled, the aluminium waste is melted. The impurities are either burned off or separated from the aluminium.

Transition metals

> **Point to note**
>
> **Transition metals** have variable valencies, form coloured compounds and they and their compounds have catalytic properties.

Iron and copper are transition elements:

- They form **coloured compounds**, such as iron(II) sulfate-7-water, which is green, and copper(II) sulfate-5-water, which is blue.

- They have a number of **different oxidation states (variable valencies)** – iron in its compounds usually has an oxidation state of +2 or +3, while copper in its compounds usually has an oxidation state of +2 or +1.

- They have **catalytic activity** – for example, an iron catalyst is used in the Haber process for the synthesis of ammonia, while finely divided copper is used in the industrial synthesis of methanal.

Manufacture of iron and steel

Iron occurs naturally in ores such as haematite (impure Fe_2O_3), magnetite (impure Fe_3O_4) and iron pyrites (impure FeS).

Manufacture of iron

The raw materials for the blast furnace process for the extraction of iron from ores such as haematite are: coke, limestone and the ore itself. In the blast furnace process, the ore, coke and limestone are fed regularly into the furnace from the top. Hot air is added from the bottom.

- Coke is mainly composed of carbon, and the ore is reduced by reaction with carbon:

$$Fe_2O_{3(s)} + 3C_{(s)} \rightarrow 2Fe_{(s)} + 3CO_{(g)}$$

- The carbon monoxide causes further reduction in the upper, cooler regions of the furnace:

$$Fe_2O_{3(s)} + 3CO_{(g)} \rightarrow 2Fe_{(s)} + 3CO_{2(g)}$$

Most of the reduction of the iron ore is caused by carbon monoxide. The gases formed (CO, CO_2) are drawn off through ducts.

- The limestone decomposes into calcium oxide and carbon dioxide. The calcium oxide reacts with impurities in the iron ore, forming slag:

$$CaO + SiO_2 \rightarrow CaSiO_3$$

$$CaO + Al_2O_3 \rightarrow CaAl_2O_4$$

The molten iron and slag trickle down into the hearth, where the less dense slag floats on the iron. The slag and iron are separately tapped off into large tanks.

- At this stage, the iron is not very pure and, if allowed to solidify, forms pig iron.

The slag is used in road making.

Manufacture of steel

To make steel from iron, the iron must first be purified.

- Oxygen is blown onto the surface of the liquid iron at the base of the furnace. This oxidises silicon, manganese and some iron, and the products are removed as slag. Carbon is also oxidised and the gaseous products escape to the atmosphere.

- The molten iron, which is now sufficiently pure, is poured into a ladle and carefully measured amounts of carbon and other elements are added. This process is called the **basic oxygen process**.

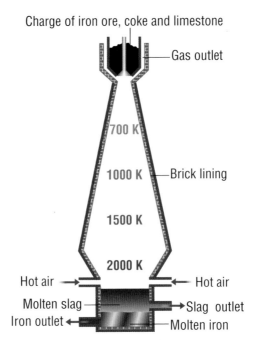

Charge of iron ore, coke and limestone

Gas outlet

700 K

1000 K — Brick lining

1500 K

2000 K

Hot air → ← Hot air

Molten slag → Slag outlet

Iron outlet ← Molten iron

Fig. 23.4 The blast furnace

Properties of different steels

Alloying carbon with iron to make steel increases the hardness and strength of the metal. Other metals may be added in controlled amounts as well. By a correct choice of metal, and proportion of this metal added to iron, steels can be made which are very hard or very resistant to corrosion or of great strength. Metals such as tungsten are used to harden steel. Corrosion-resistant steels are made using chromium and nickel. Manganese is used to make very tough steel.

Uses of iron and steel

Steel is used in the manufacture of car bodies and in the construction of bridges and buildings. The uses of iron are more limited. It is used, for example, in manhole covers, chains and gates.

Electric arc process for steel manufacture

Steel is made from recycled steel, which is melted in an electric arc furnace before it is refined and cast and rolled into steel products.

1 Charging

An overhead crane is used to add the scrap to the furnace. Lime (calcium oxide) is added to absorb the acidic impurities during the melting and refining stages and to form slag.

2 Melting

An electric arc is struck between carbon electrodes and the scrap. This generates very high temperatures, melting the steel quickly.

3 Refining

Oxygen is blown onto the molten steel to oxidise non-acidic impurities to their oxides. Excess carbon burns to form carbon monoxide and carbon dioxide:

$$2C_{(s)} + O_{2(g)} \rightarrow 2CO_{(g)}$$

$$2CO_{(g)} + O_{2(g)} \rightarrow 2CO_{2(g)}$$

Non-metals present, such as silicon, will form oxides which then react with lime to form calcium silicate, a component of slag:

$$Si + O_2 \rightarrow SiO_2$$

$$CaO + SiO_2 \rightarrow CaSiO_3$$

Phosphorus and aluminium oxides are removed in a similar manner.

Slag is less dense than liquid steel and floats on top, which means that it can be easily removed. Tilting the furnace pours off the liquid slag.

4 Tapping

The liquid steel is next released from the furnace into an insulated ladle. The composition of the steel is adjusted by adding the required amounts of alloying elements.

5 Casting

The molten steel is then poured into a casting machine where a slab of solid steel is formed.

Environmental aspects of iron and steel production

If iron is being extracted from a sulfide ore, some sulfur dioxide will be formed in the blast furnace. When coke is being produced from coal, for use in the blast furnace, smoke and sulfur dioxide are formed. Emissions of these must be kept to a minimum. Fumes from a blast furnace must also be cleared of dust particles before being released into the atmosphere.

All emissions from the steelmaking plant have to be carefully monitored. Fumes are filtered to remove dust particles and water used for cooling purposes is recycled. The use of natural gas for heating eliminates emissions of sulfur dioxide, which can be a problem if oil or coal is used instead.

Key-points!

- A crystal is a solid in which the atoms, ions or molecules of which it is composed are arranged in a regular three-dimensional structure.

- See Table 23.1 for a summary of different types of crystal.

- See Table 23.2 for a summary of the properties of different types of crystal.

- A polymer is a large molecule made up of many identical repeating units called monomers.

- See Table 23.4 for the physical properties of metals and non-metals.

- An alloy is a mixture of two or more elements, at least one of which is a metal.

- Corrosion of a metal is the surface chemical reaction on the metal by the action of air, water or other chemicals.

- Transition metals have variable valencies, form coloured compounds, and they and their compounds have catalytic properties.

STUDY GUIDE

Date:

Time:

Section to
be revised:

Date:

Time:

Section to
be revised:

Date:

Time:

Section to
be revised:

Date:

Time:

Section to
be revised:

Date:

Time:

Section to
be revised:

Date:

Time:

Section to
be revised:

Night before exam:

Sections to be revised:

STUDY GUIDE

Date: | | | | |

Time: | | | | |

Section to be revised: | | | | |

Date: | | | | |

Time: | | | | |

Section to be revised: | | | | |

Date: | | | | |

Time: | | | | |

Section to be revised: | | | | |

Date: | | | | |

Time: | | | | |

Section to be revised: | | | | |

Date: | | | | |

Time: | | | | |

Section to be revised: | | | | |

Date: | | | | |

Time: | | | | |

Section to be revised: | | | | |

Night before exam:

Sections to be revised:

STUDY GUIDE

Date:				
Time:				
Section to be revised:				

Date:				
Time:				
Section to be revised:				

Date:				
Time:				
Section to be revised:				

Date:				
Time:				
Section to be revised:				

Date:				
Time:				
Section to be revised:				

Date:				
Time:				
Section to be revised:				

Night before exam:

Sections to be revised:

STUDY GUIDE

Date:				
Time:				
Section to be revised:				

Date:				
Time:				
Section to be revised:				

Date:				
Time:				
Section to be revised:				

Date:				
Time:				
Section to be revised:				

Date:				
Time:				
Section to be revised:				

Date:				
Time:				
Section to be revised:				

Night before exam:

Sections to be revised: